Individual Differences:
Traits and Factors

Individual Differences:
Traits and Factors

ALLAN R. BUSS AND WAYNE POLEY
University of Alberta

GARDNER PRESS., INC.,
NEW YORK

Distributed by Halsted Press
Division of John Wiley & Sons, Inc.

NEW YORK • TORONTO • LONDON • SYDNEY

GARDNER PRESS, INC.
32 Washington Square West
New York, New York 10011

Distributed solely by the Halsted Press Division
of John Wiley & Sons, Inc., New York

Library of Congress Cataloging in Publication Data

Buss, Allan R
  Individual differences.

  Bibliography: p.
  Includes indexes.
  1. Individuality. I. Poley, Wayne, joint
author. II. Title.
BF697.B87 1976   155.2   76–8909
ISBN 0–470–15099–8

PRINTED IN THE UNITED STATES OF AMERICA
 2 3 4 5 6 7 8 9

To our parents

PREFACE

The post World War II era has witnessed rapid growth in the study of individual differences, that is, the question of "how" and "why" people differ in behavior. The recent advances that have been made in studying human individual differences have been parallelled by such developments as the widespread use of computers, which has facilitated the analysis of the measurement of individual differences, and an incresing interest in regard to such socially important issues as the study of race, sex, and social class differences. It would be difficult to determine whether the latter developments were a by-product of the study of individual differences or served as an impetus to further research in this area. In any case, the study of individual differences, which is one of the oldest traditions in psychology (Chapter 1), is currently undergoing a renewed interest—partly because of the social importance of questions concerning individual differences and partly because of the advances in related areas that have permitted the rersearcher to deal with this topic in a much more sophisticated manner. Concerning the latter, advances in measurement and scaling theory, factor analysis, behavior genetic analysis, learning theory, and personality theory have all provided an extensive "knowledge base" from which the study of individual differences may draw.

One of the major goals of this book is to provide an introduction to the study of individual differences that considers both "how" and "why" individuals differ. The important strides that have been made in the above-mentioned related areas provide a means of supplementing the purely descriptive task of documenting "how" individuals differ by attempting to explain "why" they differ. Chapters 3 to 6 attempt to answer "how" individuals differ, and Chapters 7 to 10 are more concerned with explaining "why" individuals differ.

This book is written from the perspective of using *traits* as the basic units of analysis for discussing individual differences. Because factor analysis is gaining increasing acceptance as a useful and relatively sound technical method for discovering and identifying traits, all of Chapter 2 has been devoted to developing the basic logic of this mathematical model. For the most part, the traits discussed in the entire text have been identified through the use of factor analysis.

This brings us to the major impetus for undertaking the writing of this book. It is our belief that there is a real need for a book that bridges the gap between introductory treatments of traits and individual differences and the more advanced original contributions to the area which typically are quite technically demanding. It is hoped that this book will introduce the student to both the technical and substantive findings concerning individual differences, and thereby serve as a stimulus for going on to master the methodological techniques that have been closely associated with this area. In other words, we have avoided writing an introductory technical and methodological book on individual differences, which would probably have the effect of the undergraduate student's failing to appreciate the exciting substantive and theoretical issues in the area. Being introduced to the latter, along with a working awareness of the factor analytic model, seemed to us the best compromise for a beginner's book on individual differences.

It is expected that this book will be most useful to upper-level undergraduate students as well as graduate students in the areas of differential psychology, psychological testing, and personality. It can also serve as useful supplemental reading for those psychologists in applied areas (e.g., industrial, educational, and clinical psychology) who are interested in applying factor-analytic contributions to their respective fields. Research psychologists working in applied settings are finding it increasingly necessary to employ sound measurement practices as an indispensable tool for evaluating both how and why individuals differ.

ALLAN R. BUSS
WAYNE POLEY

Edmonton, Alberta
February, 1976

CONTENTS

Chapter 1

INTRODUCTION

Defining Trait Psychology

A *trait* may be considered as a relatively broad and stable disposition to behave in certain ways that are relatively transitutional, that is, a given trait may be manifested in a variety of situations. Of course, there is no firm rule to determine exactly how broad and how stable a behavioral disposition should be in order to qualify as a trait. A given trait may characterize a number of individuals, but there may be individual differences in the amount or level of a trait. Hence the concept of trait implies a dimension along which people may be ordered. The study of traits is an integral part of the fields of personality, psychological assessment, and individual differences. Of these three areas, trait psychology probably contributes most to the field of individual differences, which is the description and explanation of differences between people. In undertaking the study of individual differences, one is immediately faced with the problem of the almost unlimited number of ways in which individual differences can be described. Grouping similar responses under a single construct such as a trait makes the study of individual differences more manageable by reducing the total number of possible constructs under investigation to a reasonable number. If the chosen traits are able to account for the various responses without a significant loss of information, they can be considered as more basic psychological dimensions or essentially as "elements" of individuality.

It is useful to contrast two major perspectives in the study of traits based on Allport's (1937) discussion of *nomothetic* and *idiographic* approaches. The nomothetic approach is more widely accepted and applied in contemporary psychology. It attempts to assess the individual in terms of traits shared by all other persons of a specified population but allowing for quantitative differences among individuals. Individuality by this definition, then, would consist of the values of a person on a number of traits. Presented graphically, this gives a person's trait *profile*. Because the probability of another individual obtaining an identical profile is remote, we can say that each person is unique, even though he shares his traits with other members of the population. The nomothetic approach to the study of individual differences is the one adopted throughout the text.

Proponents of the idiographic approach consider the nomothetic approach to be a poor approximation to the uniqueness of the person. The idiographic approach searches for qualitative rather than quantitative differences between individuals. A person is considered to be unique because the way in which he expresses his characteristic is unique. However, this approach is limited, because for each person it is difficult to study a phenomenon that changes or is different. If we adopt the principle that psychology is a social science that seeks to formulate general laws or principles characteristic of a large number of instances, then, clearly, the nomothetic approach is the only option. As we have seen, the uniqueness of each individual may still be accommodated within a nomothetic approach to individual differences.

Traits may be classified as falling into one of three major areas or domains: mental abilities, temperament, and motivation, although, as we see later, there are traits that straddle more than domain (e.g., cognitive style traits). If we translate the three basic kinds of traits into the dynamic functioning of the individual, we can say that behavior consists largely of free operants or voluntary responses in pursuit of various goal objects (motivation) guided by an information-processing system (mental abilities) and making periodic adjustments according to contingencies of reward and punishment (temperament). Of course, to complete the formulation we must also allow for the fact that there are some relatively broad behavioral dimensions that will fluctuate to some degree from day to day within the individual. In particular, motivation (needs) and temperament will exhibit these fluctuations, leading to the concept of *states* as distinguished from relatively stable traits.

The total number of traits within each of the three major areas is an issue of some controversy, and recommendations here depend largely on the criterion of breadth used for inclusion of a trait in the taxonomy. However, the consideration of 15 to 20 traits in each area is a reasonable compromise between parsimony and comprehensiveness. We then have a total of 45 to 60 dimensions on which to describe any given individual. This degree of relative complexity has two immediate implications. First, it allows for considerable power in representing the fore mentioned uniqueness; that is, each individual will tend to have a unique profile. This conclusion follows from the relatively large number of traits or dimensions of individual differences we can use in characterizing a given individual, as well as from the observation that for a given trait there is a wide range of possible values. The second implication is that there is a high probability that any given individual will have extreme scores on a small number of the traits—a principle that is sometimes referred to as the "normality of the abnormal."

A primary concern in the study of traits, then, is to identify the most important traits in mental abilities, temperament, and motivation, and to describe their relationships to one another. In addition to addressing the descriptive question, we are interested in explaining the origins of traits, particularly in terms of the broad contributions of genetic and environmental influences. A more refined breakdown of the genetic influences includes the physiological events that mediate between genes and behavior. Environmental influences, in turn, can be discussed in terms of the various experiential influences in the development of the individual in which processes such as learning play a crucial role.

Early Historical Antecedents

The historical origins of trait concepts go as far back as the beginnings of individual psychological assessment. Psychological assessment is not synonymous with the concept of trait, but the former is necessary to identify the latter. Psychological testing has been traced to the ancient Chinese (around 1115 B.C.) by DuBois (1965), where aptitude tests were used to screen applicants for higher positions in the civil service. Testing was implemented in terms of job samples of behavior to demonstrate proficiency in the five basic arts of music, archery, horsemanship, writing, and arithmetic. Although archery and horsemanship are quite specific skills, music, writing, and arithmetic aptitudes are more directly analogous to modern trait concepts (it should be recalled traits refer to relatively broad behavioral dispositions). The Greek philosophers also contributed to the development of trait concepts and psychological testing. Plato (in *The Republic*) proposed an aptitude test to select persons who would be suited to a military career. Plato also gave us the classification of the three major areas of psychological functioning: cognitive, conative, and affective, corresponding to our more modern distinctions of mental abilities, motivation, and temperament.

Aside from psychological assessment itself, another important historical antecedent for the study of traits is a focus on the individual rather than the group as an effective unit in society. Trait concepts are not incompatible with the study of groups—on the contrary, a considerable amount of research is conducted to describe and explain group differences in terms of various traits of the members of the groups. However, the initial identification of traits appears to have been facilitated by the study of the individual rather than of an entire group. It is worth noting, then, that the social context through the earlier centuries of European history did not favor the development of the study of the individual. Williams (1961) points out that in the Middle Ages "individual" meant "inseparable"; that is, the individual was described in terms of the group to which he belonged. In the words of Williams:

> The complexity of the term is at once apparent in this history, for it is the unit that is being defined, yet defined in terms of its membership of a class. The separable entity is being defined by a word that has meant 'inseparable' . . . The crucial history of the modern description is a change in emphasis which enabled us to think of 'the individual' as a kind of absolute without immediate reference . . . to the group of which he is a member (p. 73).

This inseparability of individual and group was cemented by the Church. Lewis Mumford (1961) has stated: "At no moment of his life was even the worst sinner outside the circle of fellowship, unless he had drawn upon himself the Church's most bitter punishment, excummunication: a living death" (p. 150).

In contrasting this era with contemporary life, Campbell (1956) wrote:

> The problem of mankind today is . . . the opposite to that of men in those great co-ordinating mythologies which now are known as lies. Then all meaning was in the group, in the great anonymous forms, none in the self-expressive individual; today no meaning is in the group—none in the world: all is in the individual (p. 338).

Sociologically, this shift may be seen as primarily due to the complementary forces of Protestantism and capitalism. Protestantism made the individual face God alone, without the support provided by the medieval church, whereas capitalism expressed its need for individuals, not groups. Engels wrote of industrialized London in 1844: "The dissolution of mankind into monads of which each one has a separate principle and a separate purpose, the world of atoms, is here carried out to its utmost extreme" (p. 58).

In considering further the social forces that were favorable for the development of the study of individual differences, the measurement and quantification of individual differences may be viewed in the context of reflecting capitalistic values, in which measurement and quantification play such an important role in determining salaries, prices, losses, profits, markets, and the like. Just as it is possible to measure and quantify man's products, it is possible to measure and quantify man himself. Thus the emphasis on measurement, quantification, and science and technology, which was intimately bound to the growth of capitalism, made nineteenth century Britain the natural birthplace for the scientific study of individual differences to take place.

The more complex the society, the greater the need for specialization of human talent. By the nineteenth century the forces of democracy and capitalism in Britain had created a specialization of occupations and a large governmental bureaucracy to oversee the administration of the British Empire and all its activities. Specialization and bureaucracy came to characterize all aspects of social life —including business, government, science, the arts, religion, and the like. Capitalism as an economic system was making Britain wealthy. The basic idea of efficiently producing a surplus of products and exchanging them on the open national and international market yielded good returns to both the private sector and government, and they permitted the growth of science, technology, additional markets, specialization, and so forth. In short, a capitalistic society *created* individual differences in the sense of providing opportunities for previously unheard-of specialization of human talent. Capitalism at this time had produced mainly two large classes—the bourgeoisie and proletariat. Within each of these separate classes, however, there was a high degree of occupational diversity. *Genotypic* (see Chapter 9) individual differences served as a necessary prerequisite for the development of the modern differentiated state, but once the latter process was well underway, the capitalistic structure fed back to the pool of human talent, thereby developing, encouraging, and promoting even greater *phenotypic* (see Chapter 9) individual differences than had previously been the case. Phenotypic individual differences became manifest in all aspects of social life. The days of the "universal man" were over.

In summary, then, democratic capitalism paved the way for the scientific study of individual differences in at least two important ways. First, the rise of the modern capitalistic state depended on and fostered the growth of the division of labor and occupational specialization of human talent. The spread of rationalism to all sectors of society (government, science, economics, art, religion, etc.) had produced a highly advanced and differentiated society requiring a professional bureaucratic machinery to maintain coordination. For the first time in the history of man, phenotypic individual differences ran rampant. Second, the measurement, quantification, and description of individual differences was closely associated with an economic society which depended on and encouraged the measurement and quantification of its material products. The rise of a capitalistic economy was producing a new image of man, which paved the way for the measurement and quantification of psychological characteristics. Science and technology had been highly successful in the material world—might not these principles and techniques be successfully applied to the realm of mental phenomena?

The systematic study of individual differences and psychometrics, with the complementary study of traits, did not begin until the early 1900s. However, a philosophical movement known as *faculty psychology* preceded this by over a century. Thomas Reid, a Scottish philosopher, came to be a major representative of this school. In *Essays on the Intellectual Powers of Man* (1785) he offered a list of intellectual powers (abilities) such as perception, memory and conception. In *Essays on the Active Powers of the Human Mind* (1788) he proposed a list of active powers such as self-preservation, hunger, and desire for power. These are analogous to more modern trait concepts in motivation and needs. Influenced partly by the work of Reid, Franz Joseph Gall founded the school of *phrenology,* which gained considerable popular support through the nineteenth century. Phrenology proposed that there was a relationship between contours of the skull (believed to reflect the state of the brain) and "powers of the mind." Although scientific support for this doctrine was not forthcoming, it may be seen as an antecedent of contemporary attempts to relate physiological properties to psychological traits.

The Beginning of the Modern Period

The modern period of trait psychology may be viewed as beginning with the work of Sir Francis Galton (1822–1911), a noted biologist, geographer, statistician, world traveler, and founder of the scientific study of individual differences. The importance of Galton to trait psychology is that he advocated *measuring* and *quantifying* both physical and mental traits on a large scale. It was toward this end that in 1884 at the International Health Exhibition he set up his anthropometric laboratory (which was afterward moved to the Kensington Museum in London) and subsequently in 1904 the Galton Laboratory, which was eventually made a part of the University of London.

Galton's contributions to the modern study of traits were numerous—probably the most important being the development of statistical procedures for describing variation in traits among individuals. Of special significance here is Galton's advancement of two related concepts: the correlation coefficient and the regression toward the mean. Working with scatter plots of data on the stature of sons as a function of the stature of their fathers, Galton noted that there is a regression toward the mean for extreme scores; that is, tall fathers tend to have tall but not quite so tall sons, whereas the reverse situation holds for short fathers. Galton developed an index of correlation to describe the strength of relationship between two variables, which later was polished by Karl Pearson (1857–1936), a devoted student and colleague of Galton. The resulting correlation coefficient has now become such a fundamental tool within the area of trait psychology that it is impossible to imagine this field without this useful descriptive statistic. Indeed, as we shall see in the following chapter, more advanced statistical procedures for identifying traits such as factor analysis are extensions of the basic idea of identifying relationships between variables, or in other words, determining what goes with what.

Besides the inroads made in the technical area with respect to measuring traits, Galton wrote extensively on the explanation or interpretation of why individuals differ. Of particular concern to Galton was the area of intelligence, and he took great pains to document the hereditary basis for individual differences in this global trait. Probably the most important thinker to affect Galton's views was his half-cousin Charles Darwin (1809–1882). Galton applied the idea of the inheritance of physical traits to the area of mental traits. He was able to make a smooth transition to mental structures and functions of the idea of specialization of physical structures and their functions. This notion was quite compatible with a capitalistic economy, which required specialized talent.

In 1869 Galton published *Hereditary Genius* which extensively documented the finding that there is a tendency for gifted people to run in certain families. From this beginning Galton developed his ideas concerning mental inheritance and the attendant social problem of improving the British race—the latter christened *eugenics* in 1883. In this year Galton's *Inquiries into Human Faculty and its Development* was published and is considered (Boring, 1950) as the beginning of a truly scientific study of individual differences. For Galton it became apparent that to measure and analyze individual differences, it was first necessary to invent *tests*, in particular, *mental tests*, to tap the various mental functions. Galton was a superb inventor of mental tests, some of which included the Galton whistle for measuring auditory functions, tests for the discrimination of depth of color, visual acuity, color-blindness, and the like, as well as reaction time tests and tests of kinesthetic discrimination.

These tests largely tap sensory functions rather than the more cognitive and ideational functions usually associated with intelligence. This observation brings out the underlying theoretical stance adopted by Galton—it was through the measurement of sensory capacities, that is, discrimination, that one could estimate the level of intellectual functioning. Although such a view seems a bit naive to us today, one can better understand such a position in light of the then-current ideas regarding the mind and its development. Galton was heavily influenced in his thinking here by the British empiricists such as Locke, Berkeley, and Hume. Especially noteworthy is Locke's concept of *tabula rasa* which embodied the belief that the newborn child is a "clean slate" and that sensory stimulation provides the building blocks for the mental processes. Galton fully capitulated to this view, as reflected by the following quotation: "The only information that reaches us concerning outward events appears to pass through the avenue of our senses; and the more perceptive the senses are of difference, the larger is the field upon which our judgement and intelligence can act" (Galton, 1883, p. 27).

Although the heredity-environment issue is discussed in later chapters, it is interesting to note in historical perspective an implicit contradiction in Galton's substantive interpretation of individual differences in intelligence. With respect to Galton's thinking, the lineage of which can be traced back to Locke, he subscribed to a view of the development of mental ability completely consistent with the position of environmental determination of individual differences. However, as noted previously, Galton adopted a completely hereditary interpretation of differences in mental functioning. We see here a paradox that apparently escaped Galton's attention: if mental functioning depends on sensory experiences, then is not one compelled to attribute individual differences in mental function to individual differences in environmental sensory experiences?

It is, perhaps, unfortunate that Galton took a wrong turn in subscribing to the ideas of the British empiricists, because this prevented him from measuring in a more direct way individual differences in intelligence. Unfortunately also, Galton's representative in North America, James McKeen Cattell (1860–1944), spread the "measurement of intelligence by measurement of sensory functions" approach and thereby led the field of trait psychology down a blind alley. Not surprisingly, there was little relationship between sensory measures and independent estimates of intelligence based on teachers' ratings. Part of the attraction that sensory tests had for Cattell was that such measures were very precise and exact—although, of course, such precision in no way altered the erroneous identity relation between sensory functioning and higher mental functioning. Fortunately for the development of trait psychology there were those psychologists who, just before the turn of the century, argued for a radically different approach in trying to measure mental ability.

As often happens in science, important conceptual breakthroughs have the appearance of being rather simple and obvious in retrospect. Such is the case with respect to the insights of the French psychologist Alfred Binet (1857–1911), who was the director of the psychological laboratory at the Sorbonne when he proposed to measure intelligence more directly by using more complex tests. Working initially with Victor Henri (1872–1940) and later with Theophile Simon, Binet proposed using tests for measuring memory, imagery, imagination, attention, comprehension, suggestibility, esthetic appreciation, moral sentiments, strength of will, and motor skills. It is apparent that Binet indeed had a multitrait view of higher mental functioning that was an early forerunner of the more modern multitrait views of the complexity of abilities.

Just as there were significant social forces that helped pave the way for the early beginnings of trait psychology, the development of the modern period was similarly influenced. Thus Binet's efforts were initially directed toward the pressing social problem of identifying those children whose intellectual capacity was such that they could not profit from the traditional Parisian school system. In North

America the development of the mental test movement, receiving its impetus from the outbreak of World War I, furthered the measurement and quantification of mental functioning, thereby indirectly advancing the trait approach. Rapid classification of the million and a half of new recruits for the war effort was urgently required if the diverse abilities and talents were to be maximally used. This social-historical event potentially could have led to the extension of the multitrait view of mental functioning implicit in Binet's earlier work, although the two major tests developed for screening new recruits (the army alpha for literates and beta for illiterates) yielded single scores. For that reason the development of the multitrait approach had to await the work of T. L. Kelley, K. J. Holzinger, and, especially L. L. Thurstone's on factor analysis during the 1930s. As illustrated in the following chapter, the importance of Thurstone was that he provided a statistical tool par excellence for the identification of multitraits. Beginning with Thurstone's multitrait or multifactor approach, there was no looking back—trait psychology moved ahead and gained significant ground in both theory and technical procedures for their identification.

The Historical Development of Two Approaches Within Psychology

Historically one may discern the development of two broad approaches within psychology which have traditionally had little contact. The *correlational approach* (as represented by the pioneering work of Galton, Spearman, and others) is concerned with measuring personality traits and determining "what goes with what," both in terms of arriving at a parsimonious taxonomy of dimensions along which people vary and in terms of relating traits to performance variables such as scholastic achievement. This tradition within psychology developed rather independently of the *experimental approach* (as represented by Wundt, Pavlov, and others) which was characterized by manipulating experimental variables in the laboratory for the purposes of explaining changes in basic psychological processes such as learning, perception, sensation, memory, motivation, and thinking. Whereas the correlational approach is primarily concerned with individual differences in various processes as revealed by traits, the experimental psychologist has ignored individual differences by treating such variance as "error" in his quest for seeking general laws of behavior.

Another important historical difference between the correlational and experimental approaches is that the correlational approach has tended to be multivariate, that is, simultaneously dealing with a large number of variables; whereas the experimental researcher has tended to focus his attention on one independent factor he has varied and one dependent factor he has observed (bivariate). The main disadvantage of the bivariate approach is that it is unable to deal simultaneously with the large number of relationships between several variables; hence the meaning of a particular variable is tied to an insufficient data base. The multivariate researcher recognizes the complexity of psychological phenomena and takes great pains to apply statistical techniques capable of arriving at a statement of organized complexity.

More recently there are signs of rapprochement between the traditional psychological approaches. Thus Cronbach (1957, 1975a) has argued that one should simultaneously consider the variance among organisms (individual differences) and the variance associated with various experimental treatments (treatment differences). In this way greater prediction is achieved. For example, it may turn out that certain kinds of individuals, as identified by traits, will differentially profit from different types of instructional method (treatment conditions). In this way individual differences variance is incorporated into the design of an experiment, thereby achieving greater understanding of the effects of the independent variables. A related strategy involves the implications individual differences in traits have in basic psychological processes such as learning, perception, and sensation. This line of attack is nicely represented by the work of Eysenck and Gray and is considered in detail in the chapter on temperament. Finally, it should be noted that with the advancement of multivariate statistical procedures the early bivariate experimental researcher has been largely superseded by the multivariate experimental researches. There are now several variations of analysis of variance designs that allow for the simultaneous treatment of several independent variables. However, it is only when one or more of the independent variables involves treatments based on individuals grouped according to organismic variables or traits (blocking or stratified sampling) that such designs deal simultaneously with individual differences variance and treatment variance.

Trait Psychology Today

If one were to justify a trait approach within psychology today, one would not necessarily have to develop esoteric arguments cloaked in technical, philosophic, and/or scientific jargon. In terms of sheer utility and practical importance to today's society, trait psychology is one of the more important subfields with a contribution to make to several different psychological areas. The assessment of a person's psychological traits plays a crucial role in such fields as educational psychology, clinical assessment, career counseling, and industrial psychology. To the extent that it is desirable to be able to measure individual differences in traits for various practical purposes, then the area of trait psychology will continue to be a subfield attracting considerable efforts toward theoretical and technological advancement.

With respect to technical advancements within the field of trait psychology, psychological measurement depends highly on statistical developments, including the widespread use of the computer in the post-World-War-II era which has permited the handling of large amounts of data. The demand for psychological testing from major social institutions also added impetus to the growth of the statistical-psychometric field. Expanding educational and industrial-business institutions also have felt that psychological testing would be useful in selecting individuals for particular educational-training programs or positions in the business world. Thus the rise of the trait approach was closely tied to the development of such allied fields as test theory, statistics, and measurement theory.

The relationship between the study of traits and the study of personality also deserves special mention. Without being completely arbitrary, we can form a dichotomy between those personality theorists who place measurement (particularly the measurement of traits) first, and those who place theory without measurement first. In a strict sense, of course, either route to understanding behavior must begin with some degree of observation. However, the first approach places a great deal of emphasis on observation-measurement, whereas the latter places relatively less emphasis in this area and more on the development of theory. Cattell and Butcher (1968), as a representative of the first approach, have stated the importance of careful prior measurement in these terms:

> Take away the scientifically, carefully constructed instruments of a dozen investigators—of whom Cattell, Com-

rey, Eber, Eysenck, Guilford, Horn, Hundleby, Meredith, Nesselroade, Porter, Schaie, Thurstone, Warburton, and Zimmerman may be taken as representative—and one is left in the catalogues with nothing but a crowded shop window of ad hoc scales. These are unrelated to any systematic and extensive experimental work on structures and development—we are convinced—that the future lies with structured measurement (p. viii).

As it is seen later, Cattell's approach may be viewed as an attempt to take certain concepts from such personality theorists as Freud and McDougal and provide a sound measurement basis, that is, quantifying personality concepts and anchoring them to a solid empirical base.

Historically it has been generally true that the development of psychological tests designed to measure traits have followed from concepts in personality theories. However, in the post-World-War-II era, the system of traits built up over a number of years of careful measurement and test construction has come to stand on its own. As represented in particular by psychologists working with the technique of factor analysis for the extraction of traits, this approach to the total study of the individual has come to develop a distinctive philosophy of human nature; that is, man's psychological attributes may be quantified. It may now be argued that trait psychology stands as a separate personality system along with the other major systems: behavioristic, psychoanalytic, and self-actualization approaches. There are points of conflict as well as points of agreement among these approaches which are discussed in a later chapter.

FURTHER READING:

Anastasi, A. (Ed.) *Individual differences.* New York: Wiley, 1965.

Buss, A. R. Galton and the birth of differential psychology and eugenics: Social, political and economic factors. *Journal of the History of the Behavioral Sciences,* 1976, *12,* 47-58.

Edwards, A. J. *Individual mental testing: Part I, history and theories.* San Francisco: Intext Educational Publishers, 1971.

Jenkins, J. J. and Paterson. *Studies in Individual Differences.* New York: Appleton-Century-Crofts, 1961.

Chapter 2

SEARCHING FOR ELEMENTS OF INDIVIDUALITY: FACTOR ANALYSIS

Measurement versus Nonmeasurement

Individuals differ from one another in a great number of ways —in fact—in thousands of ways. As an illustration of this point, Allport and Odbert (1936) found nearly 18,000 words in the English language to describe traits (which would be considered primarily in the temperament domain). A similar proliferation of individual differences has taken place in the area of intelligence testing. In this case, however, the situation is due more to the efforts of psychologists than to the layman. Since intelligence testing has been going on (for around 75 years), psychologists have had ample opportunity to develop a great variety of tests and measures of intelligence. The problem presented by this "embarrassment of riches" is that it is difficult to work with many thousands of trait descriptors. It could be argued, of course, that if we are ultimately to develop a truly comprehensive system for understanding behavior, we must deal with every one of these concepts. In other words, each trait descriptor is unique to some degree and must be maintained as a separate entity for study. However, we also know, on common sense grounds, that there is considerable overlap in meaning for a number of these concepts. Thus it is logically justifiable to attempt to collapse the number of variables we are dealing with into a more manageable basic taxonomy. In addition, it is much more convenient to deal with several dozen trait descriptors than with several thousand. Furthermore, reducing the number of traits to a workable subset appeals to the scientific principle of *parsimony,* that is, the attempt to avoid redundancy in dealing with phenomena. Also, many of the individual units of behavior that could be assessed would inevitably be considered as trivial. For example, one's "back-scratching inclinations" may be psychologically trivial, but a trait of compulsiveness (perhaps related to back scratching) may be very important because it relates to many different behaviors.

Having established the desirability of reducing our variables to a manageable number, we must now ask the question of how to go about it. The most direct way, perhaps, is to undertake an analysis of the obvious surface characteristics of the variables. For example, a semantic analysis of trait descriptors from the vernacular reveals that adjectives such as happy and cheerful or assertive and dominant are similar in meaning. Thus they could logically be subsumed under a single concept. This kind of reduction of concepts carries a certain risk in that the semantic similarity on which it is based is not synonymous with psychological similarity. For example, actual measures of assertiveness and dominance may yield different results. Thus the prima facie utility of trait reduction via semantic similarity is not worth the risk, and we must pass to the next stage, where we attempt to group variables by psychological similarity. For example, the adjectives anxious, guilt prone, and depressed would not be semantically grouped together; psychologically, however, they may be part of a similar process and might form a single broad trait of, say, emotional instability.

These considerations lead to the first major controversy in identifying traits in that there are basically two ways of tackling this problem. On the one hand, we can consider the formulation of traits to be essentially a process of conceptualization carried out by the psychologist, who abstracts whatever trait is useful to his thinking (theorizing on personality). We can call this the conceptualization approach to trait formulation. On the other hand, the psychologist may believe that by mathematical analysis it is possible to abstract traits from a number of variables. The most popular version of the latter is the factor-analytic approach. The factor analyst may criticize the conceptualization approach on any of the following grounds: (a) He argues that conceptualization does not really solve the problem of reducing many variables to fewer basic traits, because the psychologist's abstractions are limited only by his own imagination and may proliferate beyond all reasonableness. The hundreds of psychological tests currently available (as listed, for example, in various editions of Buros' *Mental Measurements Yearbook*) seems to support this contention. (b) He may argue that conceptualization is essentially an "arm-chair" process that lacks sufficient contact with actual observation. Although this would contribute to the proliferation of the foregoing traits, it also carries the risk of leading to traits with little basis in reality—traits that are almost impossible to measure and study systematically. (c) The factor analyst may also argue that in more established sciences, sound measurement and description tends to precede theory. Because the conceptualization approach abstracts those traits it believes will be useful to a theory, it tends to reverse this process. The danger here is that neither theory nor traits will prove to be valid.

In its rebuttal, the conceptualization approach can argue: (a) If the theorist is sufficiently skilled in his work, the theory will be viable and the abstraction of traits will be limited to those that are useful to the theory. (b) Conceptualization of traits requires thinking, although it is not completely an "arm-chair" process. Traits develop out of theory (for example, in clinical psychology) which is based to some extent on observations of individuals. (c) Although some degree of measurement precedes theory, most scientists work in both directions, that is, from observation to theory and from theory to observation. Factor analysis may, in fact, be accused of focusing too much on observation.

An example of the conceptualization approach applied to the development of traits is found in the work of Adorno, Frenkel-Brunswick, Levinson and Sanford (1950), on the "authoritarian personality." These researchers were concerned with the personality type that supported the fascist regimes of World War II. As one facet of their work they set out to develop scales that could assess the important traits involved in the authoritarian and antidemocratic personality. The most important of these scales, the fascism scale (F scale), includes a number of characteristics such as conventionalism, authoritarian submission, authoritarian aggression, vilification of those outside the ingroup, sexual repression and denial, and preoccupation with power and toughness.

A factor analyst would approach the same issue with a certain amount of scepticism about the F scale itself. He would wonder whether the trait of fascism is, in fact, a unitary construct. In other words, concepts such as conventionalism and authoritarian aggression may be separable traits. Moreover, the factor analyst would wonder whether the concept of fascism is not simply a subset of some broader trait. He would be more likely to approach this area of research by beginning with a large pool of items designed to measure fascism and related concepts. He would then administer the questionnaire to a large number of subjects and, mathematically, extract traits from the items. This approach has been taken by Poley (1974) who found important broad factors such as authoritarianism (involving punitiveness, repression, and denial) and restrictiveness (involving restriction of one's own life style and those of others in society) underlying many of the items developed to measure constructs in this area.

We thus come to a point where the difference between the two schools of thought becomes a matter of personal philosophy on how best to do science. Logical distinctions do not weigh decisively in favor of one approach or the other. However, we can observe the progress of psychology historically and attempt to make a judgement from that vantage point. Thus many psychologists are dissatisfied with the progress of those personality theories derived from clinical observation and which have been active since the turn of the century. For example, Cattell (1966b) states:

> Relative to the numbers, the intelligence and the perseverence of those engaged in research, the progress of psychology as a science has scarcely reached in this half-century the standards expected by its devotees. Soothing words could be uttered, stressing the intractable and unusually complex subject matter and certain other inherent difficulties of our study. But it would be more constructive in the long run to subject ourselves to the cold shower of a realistic recognition that the trouble may be in ourselves and our methods. Is it not possible that the workman has brought along the wrong tools, or that the expositor is persistently talking the wrong theoretical language? (p. 4).

The factoranalytic school, really strong only since World War II, has probably had insufficient time to prove itself. In extracting traits (by mathematical methods) that can be interpreted and replicated, it has met with considerable success. But the movement to date has been admittedly slow in developing robust theory.

The Logic of Factor Analysis

The logic of factor analysis may, for convenience, be treated here as a separate topic from the mathematical basis of the factor analytic model considered subsequently. Basically, the logic underlying factor analysis is that it is a way of reducing the complex interrelationships of a number of variables to a smaller subset of latent constructs or factors, where the intervariable relationships are expressed in the form of correlation coefficients. That is to say, the factor analyst wishes to sample extensively a given domain, such as the abilities or temperament, with the purpose of arriving at the basic constructs or dimensions of individual differences that will faithfully be able to reproduce the original complexity of intervariable relationships. Thus the factor analyst achieves considerable parsimony by being able to reproduce the original variable intercorrelations from a much smaller number of basic factors.

To get a clearer idea of the relationship between the original test variables and the hypothetical underlying factors extracted to account for the original intervariable correlations, consider the following. In Figure 2.1 the geometric representation of the intercorrelations of three tests is illustrated. The hatched area represents the underlying common component or the hypothetical factor. Thus the correlation between test 1 and test 2 is accounted for by what they have in common, that is, factor A, whereas the correlation between test 2 and 3 is accounted for by a different commonality, factor B. There is no correlation between test 1 and test 2 because they share no underlying common component. In terms of describing the underlying commonality (or common variance) of these three tests, factors A and B will do the job completely, thereby achieving the identification of a smaller subet of more basic variables or factors. Armed with his more basic set of two factors, it is now mathematically possible for the factor analyst to assign estimated scores on each of the two factors to each individual. In

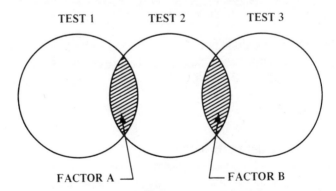

Figure 2.1   Geometric representation of the intercorrelations of three tests, where the hatched area represents the underlying common component or hypothetical factor.

this way it is further possible to specify the score on each of the original tests (more correctly, the common variance part of each score—see below) in terms of the underlying two factors. Thus the common part of test 1 is specified by factor *A*, whereas the common part of test 2 is specified by equal parts of factors *A* and *B*, and the common part of test 3 may be specified by factor *B*. In this simple example, then, we have intercorrelated three tests and have identified two more basic or underlying factors that can account for the commonality or the overlapping parts of the tests. Thus the intercorrelations between the original variables (dependent on the commonalities) may be faithfully reproduced by a smaller subset of factors. Parsimony thereby is achieved.

Mathematical Basis of the Factor Model

This section develops the mathematical basis underlying factor analysis by explaining the major equations of the model. However, a step-by-step progression from one equation to the next will not be included, and the reader is referred to more detailed treatments of factor analysis listed at the end of the chapter.

First of all, factor analysis assumes that individual differences in any psychological variable *(x)* is determined by three sets of influences: those common to other variables (*common factor variance*, symbolized by h^2); those *specific* to this variable, that is, not shared by other variables (symbolized as s^2); and *error* variance (symbolized as e^2). Thus *all* the variability or variance (σ^2) for a given response *x* is accounted for by these influences:

$$\sigma_x^2 = h^2 + s^2 + e^2 \tag{2.1}$$

For example, consider the hypothetical case of the goal-scoring ability of hockey players as variable *x*. Individual differences (or for mathematical convenience, the variance) in this variable might be determined partly by the aggressiveness of the player, where this aggressiveness is a trait entering into a variety of other acts as well such as control of the puck, body checking, and penalty time. Thus aggressiveness is part of the common factor variance or h^2. Scoring ability might also be influenced by conditions specific to this act. It may be possible to further analyze the specific variance or s^2 (e.g., by studying various conditions prior to a game), but any conclusions could not be generalized to other behaviors. Finally, if we are measuring any variable there will be some degree of error variance or e^2, that is, error of measurement or chance influences. The variance which is not common variance (i.e., $s^2 + e^2$) is known as the uniqueness or u^2.

It is the common factor variance, h^2, which is of most interest to us, because h^2 enters into many responses and is therefore of great theoretical and practical significance. Focusing again on the example given above, we can also note that the common factor variance is not limited to a single trait such as aggressiveness. There is every reason to believe that other traits are involved in scoring ability, and these traits may enter into other acts as well (including behaviors expressed off the ice). For example, physical perseverence, eye-hand co-ordination, intelligence, and attentiveness are all hypothetical traits that may be important. Thus we can expand h^2 in Equation 2.1 and get what is known as the basic factor equation, pattern equation, or what Cattell (1965, pp. 78–81) refers to as a *specification equation,* so designated because it specifies the combination of traits determining individual differences in a response, that is

$$z_{xi} = b_{x1}\, F_{1i} + b_{x2}\, F_{2i} + b_{x3}\, F_{3i} + \ldots b_{xk}\, F_{ki} \qquad (2.2)$$

Expressing this otherwise we find that any standard score response z on a variable x for individual i is determined by a set of traits (or factors $F_1, F_2, F_3 \ldots F_k$). But these traits or factors are not all of equal importance in determining z_{xi}. Thus we allow for a set of weights, $b_{x1}, b_{x2}, b_{x3} \ldots b_{xk}$ to designate this fact. (Actually, if we completed the equation, in combining Equations 2.1 and 2.2 we would add s^2 and e^2 terms, but since we are most interested in the underlying common variance or h^2, we can leave out that proportion of variance due to specificity and error).

In actually carrying out a factor analysis, we start with data gathered on a number of individuals for a number of psychological variables. Designating the number of individuals as N and the number of variables as n, our data would be arranged as an $n \times N$ table of scores (see Figure 2.2 and the Z matrix). This table is referred to as a *matrix,* more formally defined as any rectangular arrangement of numbers. More important for immediate purposes is the $n \times n$ (square) matrix of correlations (among variables) which can be calculated from this. The *correlation matrix* is designated as R and is illustrated in Table 2.1. Remember that the purpose of factor analysis is to extract the common factors that influence a number of variables, or more precisely, determine covariation between the original variables. Thus a reasonable starting point is to calculate R, which represents all the relationships among variables. Theoretically, these relationships among variables also represent the influence of the underlying common factors, but at this stage of analysis we don't know what the factors are. The computational procedure of factor analysis (which won't be elaborated upon here) takes us from the $n \times n$ correlation matrix to an $n \times k$ matrix of factor loadings referred to as a *factor pattern matrix* or P matrix (see Table 2.1). The relations among the n variables are now expressed in terms of k factors instead of the other $n - 1$ variables as is true of the R matrix. The size of the numbers (loadings) entered in the P matrix differ, depending on, for example, whether they are expressed as correlations between variables and factors or as weights of variables on factors. In either case, it is the overall pattern of the magnitudes of the loadings that gives us the *interpretation* of the factor, or its psychological meaning. In particular, we look at the largest loadings of the variables on a given factor and ask what it is that these variables have in common in a psychological sense. Interpretation, then, is not a mathematical but a psychological undertaking.

Table 2.1
Demonstration of How a Factor Matrix P,
Multiplied by Its Transpose P′ Gives a Correlation Matrix R

	Factors			Tests								Tests					
	A	B		1	2	3	4	5	6		1	2	3	4	5	6	
1	.9	.0	A	.9	.8	.0	.3	.0	.7	=	(.81)	.72	.00	.27	.00	.63	1
2	.8	.2	B	.0	.2	.8	.8	.6	.0		.72	(.68)	.16	.40	.12	.56	2
3	.0	.8									.00	.16	(.64)	.64	.48	.00	3
4	.3	.8									.27	.40	.64	(.73)	.48	.21	4
5	.0	.6									.00	.12	.48	.48	(.36)	.00	5
6	.7	.0									.63	.56	.00	.21	.00	(.49)	6
	P	X			P′					=			R				
	(Factor matrix)			(transpose of factor matrix)							(correlation matrix)						

Table 2.1 (modified from Guilford, 1954) represents the relationship between the correlational matrix and the factor pattern matrix. Thus in matrix algebra language, the correlational matrix R is equal to the factor pattern matrix P post multiplied by the transpose of the factor pattern matrix P, where the transpose of a matrix P involves making each successive row a column. The operation involved here is *matrix multiplication*, and although the finer

points of what this entails do not concern us here, the reader can get some basic idea by the following equation and its explanation:

$$r_{lm} = a_l a_m + b_l b_m + c_l c_m + \ldots + q_l q_m \qquad (2.3)$$

where a_l equals the loading on factor A in test l, a_m equals the loading on factor A in test m, and so on. Equation 2.3 states that the correlation between two test variables l and m is an additive function of the product of the factor loadings of the two tests on each of the factors. Thus in Table 2.1 the correlation of test 1 with test 2 is equal to $(.9 \times .8) + (.0 \times .2) = .72$, where there are only two factors involved in this simple example (the reader can verify the remaining entries as an exercise). In other words, the correlation between two test variables is a function of the nature and extent of their common factor loadings. The greater the commonality two test variables share in terms of factor loadings, the greater the correlation between the two variables. One can perform the operation of Equation 2.3 for all possible combinations of variables (i.e., row-by-column multiplication for matrices P and P', which is technically known as matrix multiplication). In this way one can go from the factors underlying a set of variable intercorrelations (once they have been extracted, of course) to the variable intercorrelations themselves. Row-by-column multiplication involves taking each element in a given row of matrix P and multiplying it by the respective element in a given column of matrix P', then adding the products. Thus the correlation between tests 1 and 4 in Table 2.1 is found by $(.9)(.3) + (.0)(.8) = .27$.

Once we have extracted the common factors underlying a matrix of correlations, it is possible to specify the common part of a particular test score of an individual in terms of the factor loadings

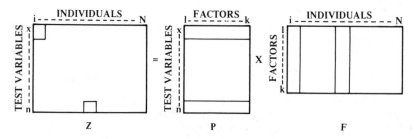

Figure 2.2   Relationship between the original test scores (the score data matrix Z), the factor loadings (the factor pattern matrix P), and the factor scores (the factor score matrix F).

of that test and the individual's factor scores. This relationship was previously expressed in Equation 2.2, but it is also possible to reformulate it in terms of matrices in order to grasp the total situation. Figure 2.2 represents the relationship between the original test scores (the score data matrix Z), the factor loadings (the factor pattern matrix P), and the factor scores (the factor score matrix F). Thus just as Equation 2.3 was a single instance of row x column matrix multiplication, Equation 2.2, or the specification equation, can also be seen as a special instance of a single row x column matrix multiplication, where the score of person i on test variable x is an additive function of the product of the respective k factor loadings of the test and the k factor scores of the individual. Thus for factor 1 the factor loading for test x (from matrix P) is multiplied by the factor score for factor 1 of individual i (from matrix F), and so on across the row of factor loadings and down the column of factor scores, respectively, as indicated in Figure 2.2 and represented by Equation 2.2. The resultant score, z_{xi}, is placed in row one, column one of matrix Z. Also indicated in Figure 2.2 and matrix Z is the result of the last test in matrix P row by column multiplied with the middle individual in matrix F. The reader should not dispair at this point, and a rereading of this section several more times may be necessary to grasp the fundamental relationships discussed. The remainder of the text may be understood, however, without a firm understanding of this section.

Rotation and Transformation

Rotation and *transformation* are two other basic concepts in factor analysis that require explanation through the mathematical approach. The P matrix which is initially obtained in a factor analysis is difficult to interpret. To obtain more interpretable factors, the loadings must be transformed or multiplied by a *transformation matrix*. The reason for this is difficult to explain conceptually in matrix multiplication terms, but may be clarified by the equivalent geometrical process of rotation.

The geometric model of factor analysis begins by expressing variables in terms of *vectors* (which is a projection having magnitude and direction, i.e., an "arrow"), and correlations in terms of angles between vectors. When the row scores have been transformed into z scores, the common factor variance of a variable is equal to 1.0 only when it has no specific or error variance (i.e., its uniqueness is zero).

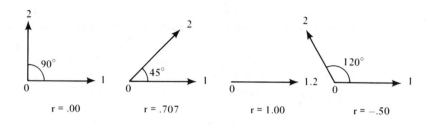

$$r_{12} = V_1 V_2 \cos \phi_{12}$$

Figure 2.3 Vectorial representation of correlation coefficients (from Fruchter, 1954).

In this case the vectors are then of unit length, as in the examples illustrated here. If there is unique variance then a vector will be less than unity, that is, some fraction of one. Geometrically, the formula for the correlation between two variables *1* and *m* is given as:

$$r_{lm} = V_l V_m \cos \phi_{lm} \tag{2.4}$$

where V_l is the length of the vector for variable *1*, V_m is the length of the vector variable *m*, and ϕ is the angle between the vectors (see Figure 2.3). Of course, if the vectors are of unit length, the correlation coefficient can be calculated simply from the cosine of ϕ. Thus, as one would expect, the greater the commonality of two vectors at a given angle, the greater will be the length of the vectors and hence the greater will be the correlation, as Equation 2.4 demonstrates. The cosine of an angle is the ratio of the adjacent side to the hypotenuse of a right angled triangle. Thus $r = 0$ will be represented by a right-angle between two vectors and, at the other extreme, $r = 1.0$ will be represented by vectors which exactly coincide.

An example of a correlation matrix (from Fruchter, 1954) involving 10 variables is illustrated in Figure 2.4. Geometrically, all these relationships can be represented in three-dimensional space since, as will be seen, three orthogonal factors account for all the commonality. In situations involving more than three factors, the sample principle applies, that is, the relationships are contained in a multispace, although we can, of course, only imagine and represent a three-dimsional space geometrically. The three factors extracted in the present example are represented both algebraically (by a factor pattern matrix of factor loadings) and geometrically. The full geo-

INTERCORRELATIONS OF TEN VARIABLES

	1	2	3	4	5	6	7	8	9	10
1	1.00	.96	.60	.48	.64	.80	.36	.48	.00	.70
2	.96	1.00	.80	.36	.48	.60	.48	.64	.00	.70
3	.60	.80	1.00	.00	.00	.00	.60	.80	.00	.50
4	.48	.36	.00	1.00	.96	.60	.64	.48	.80	.86
5	.64	.48	.00	.96	1.00	.80	.48	.36	.60	.82
6	.80	.60	.00	.60	.80	1.00	.00	.00	.00	.50
7	.36	.48	.60	.64	.48	.00	1.00	.96	.90	.86
8	.48	.64	.80	.48	.36	.00	.96	1.00	.60	.82
9	.00	.00	.00	.80	.60	.00	.80	.60	1.00	.70
10	.70	.70	.50	.86	.82	.50	.86	.82	.70	1.00

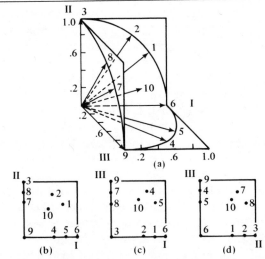

Graphical representation of correlation coefficients

FACTOR LOADINGS

Variable	Factor I	II	III	h^2
1	.8	.6	.0	1.0
2	.6	.8	.0	1.0
3	.0	1.0	.0	1.0
4	.6	.0	.8	1.0
5	.8	.0	.6	1.0
6	1.0	.0	.0	1.0
7	.0	.6	.8	1.0
8	.0	.8	.6	1.0
9	.0	.0	1.0	1.0
10	.5	.5	.7	1.0

Figure 2.4 The table of intercorrelations of 10 variables, the graphical representation of the intercorrelations in a three dimensional *(a)* and two dimensional *(b, c, and d)* frameworks, and the table of factor loadings (from Fruchter, 1954).

metric model in Figure 2.4a corresponds to inserting three new vectors into the original vectors that represent the interrelationships of the 10 variables. The three new vectors are designated as I, II, and III. Factor loadings for each original variable are found by dropping perpendiculars from the end of the variable vectors to the factor vectors. Thus variable 4, for example, loads factor I by .6 and factor III by .8. Variables close together in the space are highly correlated, and not surprisingly, load on the same factors to a similar degree. The factor loadings, then, correspond to correlations between the original variable vectors and the hypothetical vectors of the three factors (strictly speaking, this holds only for uncorrelated *"orthogonal"* factors—see below). In the present example, the resultant pattern of loadings is quite different for each factor, thereby facilitating interpretation.

In the second problem (Figure 2.5), however, too many high loadings in the upper matrix fail to bring out the contrast important for interpretation. A rotation through 50 degrees of the two axes remedies this problem. The resultant factor loadings in the lower matrix permit easier interpretation of the factors. It has good simple structure (see below). In both of the illustrations just presented, the factors are at right angles to one another, or *orthogonal*. In orthogonal *rotations,* as in the second example, this right-angled relationship is maintained. Many factor analysts prefer to relax this restriction and locate factors at various oblique angles to one another. Such rotations serve the purpose of allowing the investigator to rotate freely in order to maximize the contrast of loadings, a process referred to as rotation to oblique *simple structure.* Oblique factors are thus correlated: They can then be treated in the same way as the original variables and again factor analyzed to produce *higher-order factors* (factors of the factors so to speak). This type of analysis results in a *hierarchical model* of psychological dimensions and is preferred by some researchers, as contrasted with the single-level model from orthogonal analyses (see Chapter 3 for a discussion of hierarchical factor models in the abilities domain).

The Concept of Simple Structure

Historically, the concept of simple structure is an important one within factor analysis, and a few additional comments are necessary to appreciate more fully its meaning. Mathematically speaking, there are an infinite number of fully equivalent factor solutions possible

FACTOR MATRIX

Variable	Factor I	II	h^2
1	.6	.4	.52
2	.6	.6	.72
3	.7	−.3	.58
4	.4	−.5	.41

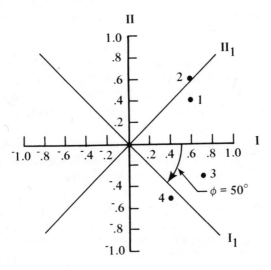

Graphical representation
and rotation

ROTATED FACTOR LOADINGS

Test	Factor I_1	II_2	h^2
1	.08	.72	.52
2	−.07	.85	.73
3	.68	.34	.58
4	.64	−.02	.41

Figure 2.5 The original factor loadings, the graphical representation of rotation, and the new rotated factor loadings (from Fruchter, 1954).

that account for the common variance. This point can be appreciated when it is recalled that rotation to *any* degree desired will still faithfully reproduce the original variable interrelationships as expressed by the R matrix. So that one might arrive at the most useful factor solution, it is desirable to have factors that are easily interpretable, that is, meaningful psychological constructs. Because factor interpretation is based on the factor loadings, and because the interpretation of a factor is most unambiguous when there are a few high loadings and many low or near zero loadings for the variables, the concept of a simple structure was invoked by Thurstone to facilitate arriving at scientifically useful constructs. Rotating to the criterion of simple structure may best be summed up by the statement "maximize the high and minimize the low loadings for a given factor." Ideally, after rotation to simple structure a given factor would have high loadings for three to five test variables and low or near zero loadings for the remaining test variables. Thereafter, factor interpretation requires that the factor analyst decide what the three to five test variables with high loadings on the factor have in common.

Basically, the concept of rotating to simple structure permits the factor analyst to arrive at a *unique* factor solution. In this way, the numerous possible factor solutions that will reproduce equally well the original correlation matrix may be dispensed with—and the unique (one and only) solution that best approaches simple structure will be preferred. Besides the criterion of arriving at interpretable factors, the concept of simple structure is important to the extent that it allows for replicating the pattern of a given factor across several experiments. Rotating to simple structure enhances the possibility of achieving *factor invariance,* that is, replicating the pattern of a given variable on different occasions. In other words, to the extent that different factor analyses incorporate a similar criterion of rotation (i.e., simple structure), the possibility of different investigators replicating the same factors exists, provided, of course, that they use the same tests. In order that factors provide us with useful psychological constructs, it is crucial that it be possible for different investigators to reproduce or identify the same factor. Replicability is an important condition for any scientific construct, and the factor analyst can best meet this scientific requirement by invoking the concept of simple structure.

Replicability of a given factor must occur across conditions of change. For example, if the same test battery is given to two different groups of individuals, there are techniques for determining the degree of similarity of the two sets of factors. Other kinds of indices and statistical models exist for determining factor similarity across two different test batteries given to the same group of individuals. In the toughest case, in which both the variables and individuals are different, no direct quantitative index of factor similarity is possible, although recently (Buss, 1975a) an indirect solution has been offered. The reader should appreciate, however, that the issue of factor invariance is crucial if different researchers want to work with the same constructs.

Plasmodes and Factor Analysis

Having developed the essential features of factor analysis, we now turn to empirical support for the usefulness of the procedure. We cannot prove mathematically that factors correspond to real entities, but we can support this empirically in an interesting way. Two classic examples of empirical support for factor analysis are referred to as the *Thurstone Box Problem* (Thurstone, 1947) and Cattell's *Ball Problem* (Cattell and Dickman, 1962)—both examples of *plasmodes* or concrete models whose intercorrelational structures are actually known in advance so that they provide a true test for the capability of factor analysis to recover the known factors or sources of influence. In the case of the box problem, Thurstone reasoned that the three physical dimensions, length, width, and height, determined all the various dimensions one could think of for measuring a set of boxes. Examples of such dimensions included height $\times$ width, girth, various diagonals,—in other words, various combinations of the height, width, and/or length of each of the boxes. The three basic physical dimensions of length, width, and height are analogous to k common factor traits sought in a factor analysis; all the various dimensions measured are analogous to n variables or tests; a collection of N boxes would be analogous to N individuals in a study. The resultant factor analysis with 26 dimensions, in fact, yielded three, more basic factors after rotation to simple structure that corresponded to the physical dimensions of length, width, and height.

Cattell's ball problem comes a little closer to a behavior example, because in this study physical measures (e.g., diameter) on a number of balls were combined with measures of performance (e.g., rolling balls up an inclined plane). We would expect factors in this case to correspond to dimensions such as size, weight and elasticity —and this is exactly what was found. Of course, in conducting an original exploratory factory analysis we do not have a priori knowledge of the factors, since otherwise there would be little point in doing the analysis. In other words, factor analysis is a technique that aids the process of discovery with respect to identifying useful theoretical constructs. The two studies cited, however, add to our belief that, after rotation to simple structure, the resultant factors will correspond to real influences.

Cattell's Covariation Chart

Thus far we have largely illustrated the basics of factor analysis by assuming that one was correlating various test variables across persons to yield factors that are basic attributes of people. Of course, the reader should realize that the factor model is substantively empty, that is, it is a formal mathematical model that can be used to deal with various kinds of data. In terms of the specific psychological content, the factor model is quite capable of treating data from various domains such as the abilities, temperament, and motivation —this statement is supported in the following chapters. In fact, we should note in passing that factor analysis is not restricted to psychological data, as the previous plasmodes illustrated. Although developed by psychologists, factor analysis may be applied to any situation in which the investigator is attempting to arrive at the underlying structure or theoretical constructs that account for the observed covariation or corelationships (co-relate, hence, correlation), among numerous variables. Thus people within various fields such as sociology, economics, geography, meteorology, and biology have all used factor analysis.

In this section we will illustrate the generality of the factor model with respect to psychology—more specifically—developing the idea that there are at least five other ways one may proceed other than by correlating test variables across persons. Some time ago Cattell (1946, 1952) presented his covariation chart for purposes of explicating the various factor analytic research designs. Figure 2.6 illustrates Cattell's original covariation chart, which is essentially a three-dimensional "data box" defined by persons, variables, and occasions. Now the usual procedure found in psychological research is to correlate the different variables across persons at one occasion— known as R technique. This technique is illustrated in Figure 2.6 by correlating variables j_{10} and j_8 across persons i_1, i_2, i_3, and so on at occasion k_1. In R technique we are after common traits characteristic of the population of individuals from which we drew our sample

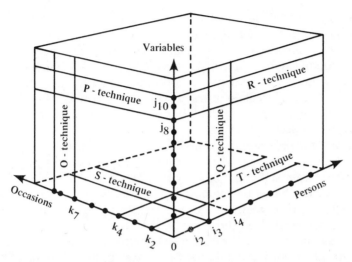

Figure 2.6 Cattell's covariation chart, indicating the various factor techniques in terms of "what one correlates with what" (from Cattell, 1957).

and which are from a domain determined by the kinds of variables we have selected. The transpose of R technique, that is, Q technique, involves correlating persons across variables at one occasion. As such, this is a useful design for grouping or clustering people into *types*, hence the factors extracted refer to prototype factors (see Chapter 4). Another useful factor analytic design is P technique—correlating variables across occasions for one individual. Because time is included in this design, it is especially useful for identifying *states*, that is, factors that fluctuate over time. One problem of P technique is that the factors refer to only one specific individual, and it is necessary to determine the generality of a given factor by carrying out further analyses on other individuals. This limitation of P technique, however, may also be viewed as a strength, because this method allows for the identification of factors that may be truly unique to the individual, that is, not shared by any other person.

The remaining three factor designs, O, T, and S techniques, have, to date, been little used. Perhaps in time factor analysis will be used to explore the various data relationships implied by Cattell's variation chart. In passing it can be noted that Cattell (1966a) has expanded the original three-dimensional data frame to a full 10 dimensions! This revised "data box" is a veritable gold mine for the researcher seeking to explore innovative relationships. Although this newer model would be of special interest to factor-analysis, the data indexed by the full 10 dimensional model are in principle amenable to other kinds of data analyses. Finally, before leaving Cattell's three-dimensional covariation chart, mention should be made of a recent modification of this data frame (Buss, 1974a) which provides a general developmental model for simultaneously considering interindividual differences, intraindividual differences, and intraindividual changes. Because the latter model is quite complex conceptually, it is best left to be pursued by the reader interested in exploring possible developmental data relationships.

In summary, then, what are factors, and what do they give us? (a) Factors can be thought of as hypothetical constructs; that is, they are constructs based on the data but postulated by an investigator. In the geometric model, for example, factors correspond to hypothetical vectors located by the investigator. (b) Factors are sources of individual differences. Just as weight, size, and elasticity can be thought of as causing individual differences in the behavior of balls in various situations, psychological factors cause individual differences in the behavior of living organisms. Thus Cattell refers to factors as source traits, that is, the sources of individual differences in behavior, rather than just the surface traits as represented by manifest clusters of source trait influences (e.g., scholastic performance). (c) Factors are classificatory devices and they enable us to express n variables in terms of a smaller number of k dimensions or factors. (d) Factors are functional unities. In questionnaire measures, for example, items are retained only if they cluster so that they explicitly relate to or "tap" a factor. Other methods of constructing psychological tests may lead one to retain unrelated items, and such tests may be poorer because they carry around "excess baggage."

FURTHER READING:

Coan, R. W. Facts, factors and artifacts: The quest for psychological meaning. *Psychological Review*, 1964, *71*, 123–140.

Gorsuch, R. L. *Factor analysis.* Toronto: U. B. Saunders, 1974.

Lykken, D. T. Multiple factor analysis and personality research. *Journal of Experimental Research in Personality*, 1971, *5*, 161–170.

Mulaik, S. A. *The foundations of factor analysis.* New York: McGraw-Hill, 1972.

Royce, J. R. The development of factor analysis. *Journal of General Psychology*, 1958, *58*, 139–164.

Royce, J. R. Factors as theoretical constructs. *American Psychologist*, 1963, *18*, 522–528.

Chapter 3

MENTAL ABILITIES

From Univariate to Multivariate

Intelligence testing began around the turn of the century. Early progress was impeded by the approach to psychological experimentation which was popular at the time; that is, research was dominated by studies on sensation and perception. From earlier philosophical notions, it was assumed that all mental processes could be analyzed in terms of units of sensation and perception. Thus it seemed reasonable to approach intelligence as if it were just a composite of sensations.

Binet, however, decided that if psychologists were to measure a complex process such as intelligence, they needed complex measuring devices. This led to the Binet-Simon test of general intelligence, which was later revised by Lewis Terman of Stanford University to the Stanford-Binet test of general intelligence. The Stanford-Binet consists of a number of items at each age level from 2 to adult. There is no grouping of items that are alike into scales; rather, there is a mixture of various types of items at each age level. There is, however, a heavy predominance of verbal stimuli and verbal responses required at most age levels. When an individual is tested, the psychologists will start at a level of difficulty at which the person can answer all items, then work up to a level at which no items are correctly answered. A score is then calculated which is called a mental age. This is converted into an *intelligence quotient* or IQ, which is defined as the mental age *(MA)* over the chronological age *(CA)* times 100, that is, $MA/CA \times 100$. This definition has proven inadequate, because beyond the age of 16 it does not make much sense, owing to the inappropriateness of the concept "mental age" at more advanced ages (e.g., what does a mental age of 43 mean in relation to the mental age of 41?). IQ is now defined as a score on an intelligence test that by convention has a mean of 100 and a standard deviation of 16. The advantages of defining IQ statistically as a deviation score (which is actually a misnomer, because it is no longer a "quotient") include doing away with the concept of mental age, as well as providing for a constant standard deviation across all ages. In any case, the net result is a single score designed to reflect mental ability.

A second popular test of "general" intelligence used even more widely than the Stanford-Binet was developed by Wechsler. The Wechsler-Bellevue scale was prepared in 1939, and later revised to the *WAIS* (Wechsler Adult Intelligence Scale) and *WISC* (Wechsler Intelligence Scale for Children). Wechsler divided his test into 11 scales to represent different types of thinking, although they would still all serve to identify general intelligence. In the test there are two major scales, called verbal and performance. The former has six subtests, the latter five subtests. Verbal subtests include: (a) information (e.g., "What is the population of the U.S."); (b) comprehension (e.g., "What does the saying "Shallow brooks are noisy" mean?); (c) digit span, in which the subject is given a series of digits and is asked to repeat these, forward and backward; (d) similarities (e.g., "How are an orange and a banana alike?"); (e) arithmetic (e.g., "How many oranges can you buy for 36 cents if one orange costs 4 cents?"); and finally, (f) vocabulary, which asks for definitions. Thus the verbal scale requires verbal responses to verbally presented material. The performance scale, on the other hand, requires "abstract psychomotor" kinds of responses. Subtests for the latter include: (a) block design, which requires the subject to duplicate the pattern in a diagram with a set of red and white blocks; (b) object assembly, which requires the subject to fit cut-out cardboard portions of an object to produce the object—like a jigsaw puzzle: (c) picture completion, which requires the subject to discover what is incomplete in a picture; (d) picture arrangement, which requires the subject to put a randomly arranged set of pictures involving a sequence of actions into the proper sequence; and finally (e) digit symbol, in which the subject is given a code relating different symbols to different numbers after which he must then fill in the proper symbol under each number in a new table of numbers.

The Stanford-Binet and Wechsler are considered as tests of "general" intelligence. That is, the different items or subtests represent a varied sampling of problems, all of which tend to correlate significantly with overall performance on the test. There is no attempt to explicitly partition intelligence into its more basic components, and a single score is typically of *most* interest, although Wechsler's tests do provide for separate scores on the various subtests which permit more detailed analysis of intellectual functioning. As expected from the notion of general intelligence, Wechsler and Stanford-Binet scores intercorrelate quite highly (about .80), and both predict academic achievement quite well (correlations are commonly in the order of .60).

Wechsler's partitioning of general intelligence into subtests is of some help in identifying the diversity of the components of intelligence. However, finding more basic units of abilities was not explicitly his goal, and the first major contribution in this direction was not made until Thurstone began his work on primary mental abilities. It is instructive to refer back to the above brief discussion of WAIS scales after considering the primary mental abilities. The true complexity of the WAIS can then be seen in terms of the various primary ability factors which run through the subtests, such as verbal comprehension, numerical facility, memory, and spatial relations.

Thurstone's Work on Primary Mental Abilities

Thurstone is a significant figure in the history of factor analysis. He was one of the first investigators to take a multifactor approach to the abilities domain—identifying ability factors which are still widely used today. Consistent with the philosophy behind the application of factor analysis, Thurstone notes:

> One of the oldest psychological problems is to describe and to account for individual differences in human abilities. How are these abilities and the great variations in human abilities to be comprehended? And just what is an ability? For centuries philosophers have been free to set up arbitrary classifications of personality types and lists of abilities, and there have been almost as many classifications as there have been writers. The factorial methods have for their object to isolate the primary abilities by objective experimental procedures so that it may be a question of how many abilities are represented in a set of tasks, and whether a particular objective performance represents an ability that is in some fundamental sense primary (1938, p. 1).

In introducing Thurstone's work, we must also note that even as early as the 1930s, the fertile imagination of psychologists had created a considerable array of devices for testing mental abilities. In Thurstone's words:

> The present investigation was made with a battery of fifty-six psychological tests that were given to a group of 240 volunteers. . . . In preparing this battery, the tests were assembled so as to represent a fairly wide range of the mental activities that are typical in current psychological tests, with special emphasis on those tests which are used as measures of general intelligence (1938, pp. 10–11).

The value of the factor analytic study is also emphasized by noting that it would have been virtually impossible to correctly classify the tests in this battery by any other means. Prior to the investigation, Thurstone did attempt to classify tests; using the best available psychological knowledge of mental abilities. However,

Table 3.1
Factor Matrix for Seven Primary Mental Abilities
(from Thurstone and Thurstone, 1941, p. 91)

		I (P)	II (N)	III (W)	IV (V)	V (S)	VI (M)	VII (R)	RESIDUALS
1.	Identical numbers	**.42**	**.40**	.05	−.02	−.07	−.06	−.06	.08
2.	Faces	**.45**	.17	−.06	.04	.20	.05	.02	−.12
3.	Mirror reading	**.36**	.09	.19	−.02	.05	−.01	.09	.12
4.	First names	−.02	.09	.02	.00	−.05	**.53**	.10	.02
5.	Figure recognition	.20	−.10	.02	−.02	.10	**.31**	.07	−.17
6.	Word-number	.02	.13	−.03	.00	.01	**.58**	−.04	.04
7.	Sentences	.00	.01	−.03	**.66**	−.08	−.05	.13	.07
8.	Vocabulary	−.01	.02	.05	**.66**	−.04	.02	.02	.05
9.	Completion	−.01	.00	−.01	**.67**	.15	.00	−.01	−.11
10.	First letters	.12	−.03	**.63**	.03	−.02	.00	−.00	−.08
11.	Four-letter words	−.02	−.05	**.61**	−.01	.08	−.01	.04	−.05
12.	Suffixes	.04	.03	**.45**	.18	−.03	.03	−.08	.10
13.	Flags	−.04	.05	.03	−.01	**.68**	.00	.01	−.07
14.	Figures	.02	−.06	.01	−.02	**.76**	−.02	−.02	.07
15.	Cards	.07	−.03	−.03	.03	**.72**	.02	−.03	.13
16.	Addition	.01	**.64**	−.02	.01	.05	.01	−.02	−.03
17.	Multiplication	.01	**.67**	.01	−.03	−.05	.02	.02	.01
18.	Three-higher	−.05	**.38**	−.01	.06	.20	−.05	.16	−.12
19.	Letter series	−.03	.03	.03	.02	.00	.02	**.53**	.02
20.	Pedigrees	.02	−.05	−.03	.22	−.03	.05	**.44**	−.02
21.	Letter grouping	.06	.06	.13	−.04	.01	−.06	**.42**	.06

there was considerable discrepancy between this classification and the factor analytic result.

> The primary factors that have appeared have a general relation to the tentative categories with which we started, but they are not identical with the tentative categories. We had postulated a verbal factor, but we found two distinct verbal factors in the analysis. We found that the number factor is highly restricted. We had postulated different reasoning factors for verbal, numerical, and spatial material; but this tentative classification was not sustained. The reasoning tests revealed two factors that we have called "induction" and "deduction", the latter being less clearly indicated than the inductive factor. From the methodological standpoint these findings give strength to the factorial methods in that they do not merely reproduce the classifications that we had in mind (1935, p. v).

Thurstone worked not only at extracting ability factors but also in replicating them in different samples of subjects and for different age levels. Seven of the better-established factors are presented in

Here is a row of faces. One face is different from the others. The face that is different is marked.

Look closely to be sure that you see why the middle face is marked. The mouth is the part that is different.

Here is another row of faces. Look at them and mark the one that is different.

You should have marked the last face.

Here are more pictures for you to practice on. In each row mark the face which is different from the others.

The test contains sixty rows of faces.

Figure 3.1 The faces test (from Thurstone and Thurstone, 1941).

factor matrix form in Table 3.1, where factor loadings that are salient for identifying the factors (above .30) are italicized. A more complete description of these factors is given.

The following descriptions of factors are based on the work of Thurstone and Thurstone (1941) with eighth grade children. The factors have been isolated, however, at both higher and lower age levels by using tests that are more appropriate to these age levels. The first factor in Table 3.1 is *P*, perceptual speed. Three tests have major leadings on this factor: identical numbers, faces, and mirror Reading. A common element in these tests appears to be the ability to rapidly identify a perceptual configuration set in a confusing perceptual environment. For example, identical numbers involves selecting a given number from a large set of numbers. Faces involves selecting a face that is different in some minor detail from a set of faces (Figure 3.1). Mirror reading, just as the name implies, requires the reversal of figures from a mirror image, in order that they may be recognized.

Tests identifying *N*, the numerical factor, tend to be numerical in nature, such as addition, multiplication and three-higher (e.g., "Identifying the numbers in a row of numbers which are three more than the preceding number). These three tests have in common some

The following sentence has a word missing at the place indicated by the parentheses. You are to think of the word that best completes the meaning of the sentence. The number in parentheses is the number of letters in the missing word.

A (4) is a contest of speed . . . .

B ⚌ F ⚌ M ⚌ P ⚌ R ▬

The missing word is *race*. The number in the parentheses is the number of letters in the missing word. The letter *R* has been marked because it is the first letter in the missing word.

Do the following example:

A (9) is a place or building for athletic exercises . . . .

C ⚌ D ⚌ G ⚌ H ⚌ T ⚌

You should have marked *G* because it is the first letter in the missing word *gymnasium*. This word has nine letters and it completes the sentence.

Do the following examples in the same way:

A (5) is an organized company of singers in church service . . . . . .

B ⚌ C ⚌ D ⚌ F ⚌ G ⚌

The thin cutting part of an instrument, as of a knife or sword, is called its (5) . . . .

A ⚌ B ⚌ E ⚌ H ⚌ W ⚌

A mark made with a hot iron, as to indicate ownership, quality, etc., is called a (5) . . . .

B ⚌ L ⚌ P ⚌ S ⚌ V ⚌

Figure 3.2 The completion test (from Thurstone & Thurstone, 1941).

fairly elementary arithmetic manipulations. The fact that identical numbers also loads on this factor suggests that in this test both the recognition of arithmetic forms as well as arithmetic manipulations may be involved in producing individual differences.

Factor *W,* word fluency, has major loadings from the following tests: First letters (e.g., "Write as many words as you can which begin with P"); four-letter words (e.g., "Write as many words as you can which begin with B and have four letters"); and suffixes (e.g., "Write as many words as you can which end with -tion"). Thus the focus of this factor is on quantity of verbalization rather than understanding per se.

Factor *V,* Verbal Comprehension, on the other hand, is focused upon the understanding of words. It loads sentences (a sentence completion test), vocabulary (a synonym test) and completion (see Figure 3.2).

Here is a picture of a card. It looks like an *L*, and it has a hole in one end.

Ŀ

The two cards below are alike. You can slide one around on the page to fit the other exactly.

Now look at the next two cards. They are different. You cannot make them fit exactly by sliding them around on the page.

Here are more cards. Some of the cards are marked. The cards which are like the first card in this row are marked.

Below is another row of cards. Mark all the cards which are like the first card in the row.

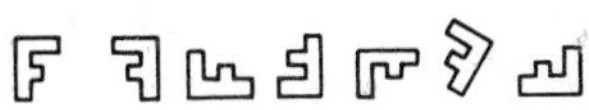

You should have marked the second and third cards. They are like the first card.

Here are some more cards for you to mark. In each row mark every card that is like the first card in the row.

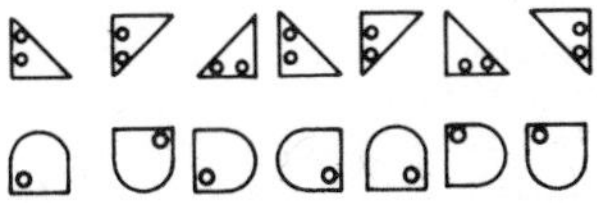

The test contained twenty rows of seven figures.

Figure 3.3   The cards test (from Thurstone and Thurstone, 1941).

Factor *S,* Spatial, loads primarily three tests. The flags test involves mentally rotating a flag in two dimensions to determine whether it will match the pattern of another target flag design. The Figures tests requires a similar manipulation in two dimensions, although the target is a figural design rather than a flag. In the cards test (Figure 3.3), the problem is to mentally rotate an object to determine whether it is identical to a target. Thus the common characteristic of the tests that load on Thurstone's spatial factor is that they require the ability to imagine the transformation of an object or figure in space.

Factor *M,* memory, relates to the recall of relatively simple information or paired-associates. For example, the first-names test requires memorization of a list of first names with their associated last names. Word-number recall involves memorization of a list of words associated with numbers. Because figure recognition has a somewhat smaller loading on this factor than the above two tests, we can hypothesize that the factor is closest to an associative type of memory ability.

Factor *R,* inductive reasoning, tends to involve the ability to extract a general principle (or pattern) from a test and apply it to draw a conclusion. For example, letter series is a test with a sequence of letters arranged according to a preconceived pattern. The subject

Look at this chart.

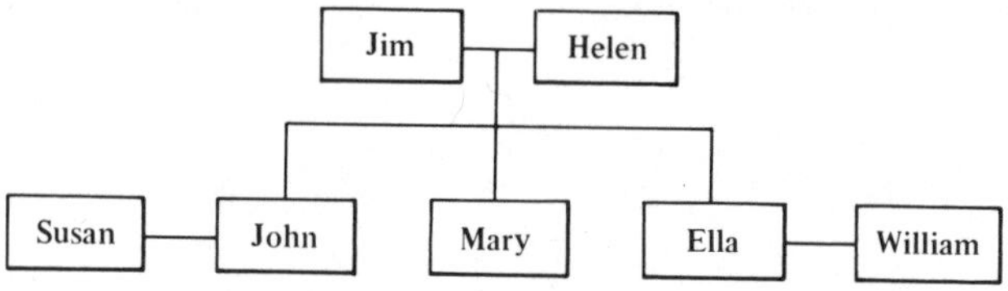

This chart tells you that Jim and Helen were married and had three children, John, Mary, and Ella. John married a girl named Susan, and Ella married a man named William.

Now answer these questions by consulting the chart.

Mary's brother is _____
How many children did Helen have? _____
How many brothers-in-law does Mary have? _____
How many brothers-in-law does Ella have? _____
Jim's daughter-in-law is _____
William's mother-in-law is _____
How many daughters has Jim? _____
Helen's husband is _____
Susan married _____
Ella's sister-in-law is _____

Figure 3.4 The pedigrees test (from Thurstone and Thurstone, 1941).

is required to discover this pattern and use it to determine the next letter in the series. Letter grouping requires determining a different kind of "code." In this case, letters are grouped in sets of four according to a pattern, and the subject must discover a set that does not conform to this pattern. In the pedigrees test (Figure 3.4), the subject must be able to determine a pattern of family relationships.

Much research has been done since Thurstone first proposed his primary mental abilities. Table 3.2 consists of an updating of this work, where 19 primary or first-order factors are outlined.

Table 3.2
Nineteen Primary Mental Abilities
(adapted from Pawlik, 1966)
Illustrating Some of the Finer Distinctions which Have Been Made among
Primary Mental Abilities
since Thurstone's Work in This Area

Factor	Brief Description	Marker Tests
Perceptual Speed (*P*)	"The essential characteristic of factor *p* is fast speed in comparing visual configuration—Petceptual Speed is restricted to speed of performance on tests emphasizing quick apprehension of a visual pattern and/or its identification among similar and therefore distracting configurations."	(1) Speed of mirror reading (2) Identical forms: Indicate which of five figures is identical to a standard
Spatial visualization (*Vi*)	"—the ability to imagine properly the movement or spatial displacement of a configuration or some of its parts."	Mechanical movements: Given a drawing of a mechanisms, indicate the direction of the resulting movement of one of the parts
Spatial relations (*S*)	"Unlike Vi, tasks with high saturation in S do not require thesubject to imagine spatial transformations of a configuration but to recognize 'the identity of an object when it is seen from different angles' or in different positions."	Cubes: Given two drawings of a cube and assuming no cube will have two faces alike, indicate for each pair of drawings whether it shows the same or two different cubes.
Spatial orientation (*SO*)	"—relates to aptitude differences in thinking about those spatial problems in	Complex instrument comprehension (as in navigating an airplane).

Table 3.2 (cont'd)

	which the body orientation of the observer is an essential part of the problem."	
Speed of closure (Cs)	"—involves organizing hitherto unrelated configurations into a structured pattern exhibiting familiar Gestalt qualities."	(1) Gestalt completion: speed of organizing 'mutilated words' (2) Speed of dark adaptation.
Flexibility of closure (Cf)	"—the task is to abstract a given Gestalt from a distracting field in which it is embedded."	Hidden figures: a familiar though hidden configuration has to be detected.
Verbal comprehension (V)	"—relates to knowledge of words and their meaning as well as to application of this knowledge in understanding corrected discourse."	Vocabulary; verbal analogies
Numerical facility (N)	"—the facility in performing elementary arithmetical operations (typically under speeded conditions)."	Tests of addition, multiplication, etc.
Word fluency (W)	"—the ability to rapidly produce words fulfilling specific symbolic or structural requirements."	Four-letter words: Give as many four-letter words as possible.
Ideational fluency (IF)	"—represents the ability which provides for rapid production of ideas fitting a given specification."	Topics: List as many ideas as possible relating to a given topic.
Associational fluency (AF)	"—concerns the facility of producing isolated words meeting specific requirements of meaning."	Simile insertion: e.g. complete the simile 'as——as a fish'.
Expressional fluency (EF)	"—the subject's task is not to produce ideas but to supply proper verbal expressions for ideas already stated or to find a suitable expression which would fit a given semantic frame of reference."	Picture description: The subject is shown a picture for two minutes and subsequently has to talk about it for two minutes; score is rated quality of verbal expression.
Deduction (D)	"—involves reasoning from the general to the specific, the ability to test the correctness of a meaningful	Syllogisms test: given two premises, indicate which one of several alternative conclusions is correct.

	conclusion by applying general principles to the individual case."	
Induction (*I*)	"—relates to reasoning from the specific to the general, in the sense of discovering a rule or principle in a given material and subsequently applying it correctly."	Series continuation: e.g. What number comes next in the series 3, 5, 7, 9 ?
General reasoning (*R*)	"—The Reasoning factor R is still difficult to interpret psychologically—it may simply represent a general convergent reasoning factor."	Tests of arithmetic reasoning, which require little specific mathematical training.
Associative memory (*M*)	"—primarily loads retention scores from paired-associate memory tests."	Memory for word-number pairs, figure-word pairs, etc.
Meaningful memory	"—a factor of memory for meaningful material." (vs. rote learning as in factor M.)	Memory for material which is meaningful to the subject.
Visual memory	"—restricted to memory for visual material."	Visual memory tests.
Span memory	Involves capacity of memory or span of units retained.	Digit span: Memory of a given set of numbers which may be varied in length.

Guilford's Structure of Intellect Model

Guilford's major contribution to the domain of intelligence and abilities is his *structure of intellect* or SI Model (Guilford, 1967). A major property of the SI model is that it is a significant effort to consider both the categorization of individual differences in mental abilities (factors) with an attempt to understand and describe the underlying mental processes (the way the factors are organized or the SI model itself). Guilford's model is derived from both empirical and logical considerations. Thus he draws from the empirical work on mental abilities (primarily from Thurstone's onward) as well as the logical expectations of what might be predicted to be ultimately measureable in the domain of abilities.

At first glance, Guilford's model might seem to be primarily a classification scheme for abilities—and could perhaps be criticized as arbitrary and excessively large and unwieldy (see Figure 3.5). On closer examination, however, it does go beyond simple classification

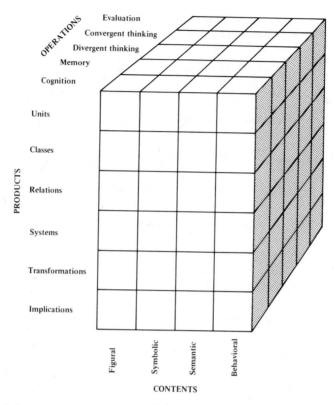

Figure 3.5 Guilford's structure of intellect model (from Guilford, 1959b).

and attempts to explain cognitive functioning. Moreover, because of the classification-explanation duality, the model is not arbitrary or overly extensive. The SI model may be seen as an information-processing or, in traditional psychological paradigms, an *S-O-R* model. In these terms, what Guilford calls *contents* may be thought of as information-input, stimuli *(S)*, or the mode of presentation for various kinds of problem solving. *Operations,* may be thought of as mediating between *S* and *R*; having to do with the manner or strategy by which the organism *(O)* operates or processes the contents of a problem. Finally, *products* represent the final form or response *(R)* that characterizes the required solution. Each act of processing information, then, may be thought of as involving a particular content, operation, and product. A total of 120 factors are hypothesized to account for the various kinds of mental abilities. Approximately three-quarters of these abilities have been empirically verified to date;

the remaining one-quarter represent an active area of research. Let us now consider Guilford's *SI* model in greater detail.

Contents: Refer to the type of information being processed. There are four contents, which may be seen as varying in complexity of input.

1. Figural: The information is simply a figure of some description (i.e., a direct representation of an object).

2. Symbolic: Symbolic input may superficially resemble "figural" but if so, the figure is used as symbolic or representative of something else.

3. Semantic: The information is presented verbally.

4. Behavioral: The information consists of the behavior of others. These abilities tap what has been called social intelligence; they refer more to the abilities we use in daily interaction with people. How do we judge peoples' motives, intentions, feelings, and the like and react appropriately to these? Of course, at this point Guilford is getting close to the ability to judge personality traits.

Operations: Refer to the manner in which the information is processed. There are five operations:

1. Cognition: This is a matter of discovering information or recognizing information.

2. Memory: Memory abilities involve relatively direct recall of information.

3. Convergent Production: Taking information and producing one correct answer.

4. Divergent Production: Taking information and producing many appropriate responses, as in creative thinking.

5. Evaluation: Evaluating information along the dimension of good-bad or right-wrong. Once again, here we may be approaching the area of personality, particularly in dealing with such evaluation processes as moral-judgement.

Products: Refer to the outcome of the operations on different contents; that is, the results of thinking. There are six products, ordered in terms of the complexity of the product.

1. Units: A single response, e.g., *(A)*.

2. Class: A group or class of responses, e.g., *(A, B, C)*.

3. Relation: Involves interrelating units, e.g., *(A > B > C)*.

4. System: An organized total structure.

5. Transformation: Involves converting one type of product into another form.

6. Implication: Involves producing results which go beyond the data.

Table 3.3
Examples of Marker Tests from Guilford's Structure of Intellect Model
(Examples taken from Guilford, 1959b; 1967)

	Category of Factor	Marker Test
Contents	Figural *(F)*	Gestalt completion test (see Figure 9,a) [cognition of figural units]
	Symbolic *(S)*	Analogies test (in symbolic form) e.g. JIRE: KIRE:: FORA: ? (KORE) (KORA) (LIRE) (GORA) (GIRE) [cognition of symbolic relationships]
	Semantic *(M)*	Analogies test (in verbal form) e.g., poetry: prose:: dance: ? (music) (walk) (sing) (talk) (jump) [cognition of semantic relationship]
	Behavioral *(B)*	Any information regarding the behavior of others (i.e., the domain of 'social intelligence')
Operations	Cognition *(C)*	See the three examples above (under 'contents)
	Memory *(M)*	Digit span test: requires recall of a given set of digits of specified length. [memory of symbolic units]
	Convergent Thinking *(N)*	Reasoning tests would be included in this category
	Divergent Thinking *(D)*	Fluency tests would be included in this category
	Evaluation *(E)*	Clerical aptitude test: Are the following pairs identical? 825170439_____825176493 C.S. Meyerson_____C.E. Meyerson [evaluation of symbolic units]
Products	Unit *(U)*	Several examples of units are given above
	Class *(C)*	Figural classification test: Identifying the group or class to which a figure belongs (see Figure 9,b) [cognition of figural classes]
	Relation *(R)*	Figure matrix test: Identifying the figure which should appear as next in a given arrangement of figures. (see Figure 9,c) [cognition of figural relations]
	System *(S)*	Unusual details test: Identifying internal inconsistencies in a picture (See Figure 9,d) [evaluation of figural system]
	Transformation *(T)*	Hidden figures test: Requires identifying simpler figures in a more complex figure (see Figure 9,e) [divergent production of figural transformation]
	Implication *(I)*	Apparatus test: Asks for two needed improvements with respect to each of several common devices, such as the telephone. [evaluation of figural implication]

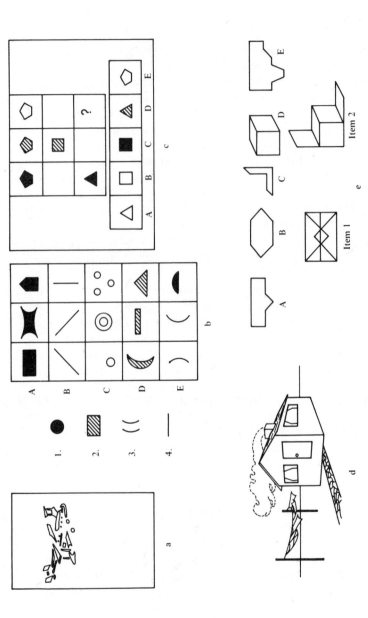

Figure 3.6 (a) Sample item from the Street Gestalt Completion test. What is the object? (b) Sample items from a test of figural classification. To which group at the right does Figure 1 belong? Figure 2 and so on? (c) A sample item from the figure matrix. What kind of figure should appear in the cell with the question mark? (d) A sample item from the test unusual details. What two things are wrong with this picture? (e) Sample items from the hidden figures test. Which of the simpler figures is concealed within each of the more complex figures?

Examples of marker tests that represent different factors of the Guilford model are in Table 3.3 and Figure 3.6. Of course, these tests are not to be equated with the factor, because a factor represents a unitary process underlying a variety of tests. Parallels with Thurstone's work may be especially seen among the operations (Table 3.3), where we have memory abilities, convergent thinking (e.g., reasoning factors) and divergent thinking (e.g., fluency factors).

In considering the implications of Guilford's *SI* model for general psychological theory, it is important to appreciate that his model provides a framework for taking a new look at such things as learning, problem solving, and creativity. Critical here is the idea that the content and product categories provide a taxonomy of different kinds of information that is processed via the various operations. Information is more generally defined as that which an organism discriminates. In considering learning and the question what is learned, Guilford considers that it is the products of information rather than stimulus response connections which is acquired. Problem-solving behavior is viewed in terms of a flow chart model (see Figure 3.7). In Figure 3.7, information is received at the left-hand side, and there is a series of operations that act on this input. Thus there is a recurrent feedback loop going from cognition → memory store → evaluation-production → cognition, and so forth. In other words, information is first received and evaluated, additional information is then retrieved from memory store which is evaluated in terms of relevancy to the problem at hand, the problem is then cognized or formulated, and a solution is produced. The solution then undergoes additional transformations by the operations of evaluation, memory retrieval, and cognition. Critical here is the cybernetic principle of feedback loops, in which evaluation permits the major operations to recur until an adequate solution to the problem has been produced.

In considering creativity, Guilford has closely identified this phenomena with two major categories—the divergent production abilities and the transformation abilities. The divergent production abilities are most critical for characterizing individual differences in creativity, because these abilities involve the notion of generating ideas where variety is important. Some of the more important divergent production abilities involve various kinds of fluency, flexibility, and elaboration. In considering the transformation category of abilities, it is important for effective creative thinking that one be able to revise and modify available information. Thus transforming the information available in memory story will facilitate the restructuring,

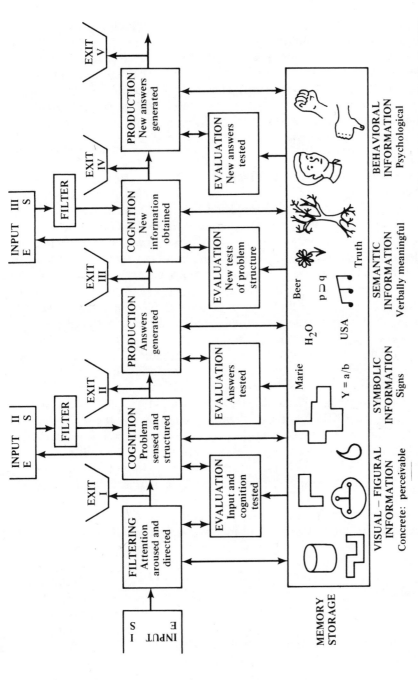

Figure 3.7   A model representing the operations and flow of information in a general instance of problem solving (from Guilford, 1967).

reorganization, and reinterpretation of material; which is critical for successful creative thinking.

These considerations of Guilford's SI model serve to illustrate a very important approach within the field of individual differences. Thus Guilford has not been content merely to provide a descriptive taxonomy of dimensions of individual differences, but, rather, he has taken such dimensions and put them within a theoretical model that attempts to explain some rather complex cognitive activity.

Hierarchical Models of Intelligence

It is a well-established observation that most tests of intelligence correlate positively with one another. This in itself is obviously not a satisfactory theoretical argument for dispensing with a multivariate approach to intelligence. It does indicate, however, that a concept of general intelligence, G, is warranted, although factor-analytic research indicates that the influence of G is less than would be suggested by the use of testing devices such as the Wechsler and Stanford-Binet. Of the leading multivariate researchers in the present discussion, only Guilford is opposed to a hierarchical model of intelligence. The logic of Guilford's model necessitates a commitment to orthogonal rotation and tends to rule out the possibility of a hierarchy of factors.

Early work on a hierarchical model of intelligence was done by Spearman. In 1904, Spearman began working on his theory of the organization of intelligence. According to this theory, as it was developed in 1927, there is a single general factor of mental ability or G that is contained in different degrees in all tests of mental ability. In addition, there are specific factors, called S, which require an ability specific to the task at hand. Later, Spearman also suggested an intermediate class of factors, not as specific as S or as general as G. These are the group factors and include such dimensions as arithmetical, mechanical, and linguistic abilities. Later Spearman also included other factors at the G level, including P (perseveration), O (oscillation) and W (will). However, these factors were interrelated with the functioning of G, which was considered to be of overwhelming importance in determining mental ability. Although Thurstone considered his work on primary mental abilities to be compatible with a hierarchical model such as Spearman's, there was some conflict related primarily to the question of the relative importance of G. Workers in the Thurstone tradition tended to place less emphasis

TABLE 3.4

Averaged Correlations among Twelve Primary
Mental Abilities

(from Pawlik, 1966, p. 552)

		P	S	Cs	Cf	M	V	N	W	IF	I	D	R
P	Perceptual speed	—	+27	(+47)	(+12)	+14	+13	+14	+21	(+08)	+08	(+28)	−02
S	Spatial relations		—	+05	+60	+14	+15	+20	+15	(−07)	+28	(+05)	+10
Cs	Speed of closure			—	+13		(−06)	(−38)	−15		+08		
Cf	Flexibility of closure				—		(−01)	(+26)	+24	−04	+13	(+26)	
M	Associative memory					—	+15	+14	+23	+11	+12		+04
V	Verbal comprehension						—	+23	+23	(−01)	+26		+15
N	Numerical facility							—	+28	+13	+13	(−07)	−04
W	Word fluency								—	+13	+16	(−05)	+12
IF	Ideational fluency									—	(+08)		
I	Induction										—	(+50)	(+18)
D	Deduction											—	
R	Reasoning												—

on *G* than is given by the Spearman model. Table 3.4, from Pawlik (1966), is based on a review of intercorrelations of some of the primary mental abilities from 14 studies. Most of the correlations are positive, thus indicating that if one were to factor the primary abilities one would obtain higher-order factors. Those few correlations that are negative are quite small and probably due to measurement error.

The next issue that arises concerns identifying the factors in the ability hierarchy between *G* and the primary mental abilities. Research along these lines has simultaneously considered the relative effect on abilities of genetic-biological and environmental-cultural influences. Aside from the theoretical importance of this distinction, there are also practical implications for the assessment of abilities. It is of obvious importance to be able to separate the effects of environmental-cultural advantage or disadvantage from more "native" ability, and such issues are further considered in Chapters 7, 9, and 10. But let us now examine attempts to identify factors of more generality than the primaries yet less general than *G*.

Cattell (1957, 1971) and his colleagues (Horn, 1968) have developed a theory of fluid *(Gf)* and crystallized *(Gc)* general intelligences along these lines. According to the theory, based on little empirical support at the time of its origin, crystallized intelligence relates to cognitive performance, in which skilled judgements have become "crystallized" or consolidated as a result of the cumulative effects of early learning. Fluid intelligence, on the other hand, is thought to depend more on the ability to adapt to a new problem or situation. Thus if we think of intelligence in terms of the processing of information involved in a particular problem, *Gc* reflects the influence of previously learned abilities on information processing. The latter could be considered in terms of learning sets, or, in Cattell's terms, aids. They may range from simple codes for memorizing details to complex, learned, mathematical equations. The role of *Gf* in information processing, on the other hand, does not reflect the influence of previously acquired aids, in which the individual must rely more on unlearned ability to deal with information or problem solving.

Fluid and crystallized intelligence are both *general* abilities, entering into many separate functions at the level of primary mental abilities. However, they are thought to have a common origin in a more general factor of intelligence *(G)* at the third-order of the hierarchy. General intelligence, *G*, is also thought to be the original source of all abilities; developmentally, giving rise to a *differentiation hypothesis* of the origin of abilities. Expressing the relationships between *Gf* and *Gc* another way, we can say that the individual who has a high level of native endowment *(Gf)* will also tend to develop, in the course of life experience, a greater repertoire of aids *(Gc)*. Of course, we should not ignore the possibility that the facility of acquiring aids, learning sets, or executive functions is a separate ability in itself, perhaps also determined by innate influences and to some extent independent of *Gf.*

Predictions based on the distinction between *Gf* and *Gc* have also been made by Cattell (1963b). For example, *Gf* is thought to reach its peak at age 14 to 15 with completion of the maturation of the brain, whereas *Gc* will develop to ages 18 to 28 or beyond, depending on the duration of the learning process (education in the broadest sense). Fluid intelligence is hypothesized to have greater *heritability* (extent of genetic influence determining individual differences—see Chapter 8) than crystallized intelligence, although *both* will still be highly heritable. Similarly, cortical brain damage will be expected to affect both *Gf* and *Gc,* but *Gf* to a greater extent.

TABLE 3.5
Second-Order Factors of Mental Abilities
(from Horn and Cattell, 1967)

Primary factor symbol and name		Second-order factors and loadings					
		Gf	Gc	Gv	Gs	C	F
I	Inductive reasoning	50		28			
CFR	Figural relations	46		43			
Ma	Associative memory	32					
ISp	Intellectual speed	40			−21		
IL	Intellectual level	51					
R	General reasoning	23	30				
CMR	Semantic relations	33	50				20
Rs	Formal reasoning	34	40				
N	Number facility	24	29			34	
V	Verbal comprehension		69				26
Mk	Mechanical knowledge		48	25			
EMS	Experiential evaluation		43		23		
Fi	Ideational fluency		25		25		42
Fa	Associational fluency		35				60
S	Spatial orientation			50			−20
Vz	Visualization			58			
Cs	Speed of closure	21		36			
Cf	Flexibility of closure			48			
DFT	Figural adaptive flexibility			40			
P	Perceptual speed				48		
Sc	Speed copying				63		
Pf	Productive flexibility		23		46		
C	Carefulness					60	

In terms of actual test construction, heavily verbal tests such as the Stanford-Binet and the verbal scale of the Wechsler would be oriented toward Gc, whereas the culture-fair intelligence tests would be oriented toward Gf. Examples of items from culture-fair tests are given in Figure 3.8. The work Cattell began on Gf and Gc has been taken up by John Horn, with the result that we now have a more complete description of second-order factors of ability in terms of primaries. What we find, in fact, (see Table 3.5) is that there are additional second-order factors than just Gf and Gc. We have, in addition, Gv (general visualization), identified by spatial and closure factors; Gs (general speed), reflecting the influence of speed in test performance; and F, a general fluency dimension.

The theory of fluid and crysallized intelligence has reached a fairly well-developed stage at present. However, we must note that Cattell, Horn, and co-workers are not the only researchers to have made developments along these lines. Hebb (1949), for example, has developed a two-factor model of intelligence based on physiological theory and observations of brain-damaged patients. He points out that:

> The clinical evidence has indicated, in effect, that there are two components in intelligence-test performance and in any intelligent behavior. One is diminished by damage to the brain, and amounts to a factor of heredity; one is related more to experience, consisting of permanent changes in the organization of pathways in the cerebrum (in the present theory, these changes are the establishment first of assemblies of cells, and secondly, of interfacilita-tion between assemblies). The heredity factor is essentially the capacity for elaborating perceptions and conceptual activities; the experiential factor is the degree to which such elaboration has occurred. . . . (p. 294).

Thus cortical brain damage in infancy or early childhood is much more detrimental to intellectual performance than the same damage in adulthood because it impairs the development of assem-blies of brain cells. After these assemblies have been developed, on the other hand, Hebb's physiological theory proposes that they be-come, to some extent, redundant. That is, more paths of transmission are established than are usually necessary to process information. Early damage impairs what Hebb refers to as intelligence A or innate potential, but damage later in life (if not too extensive) may primarily

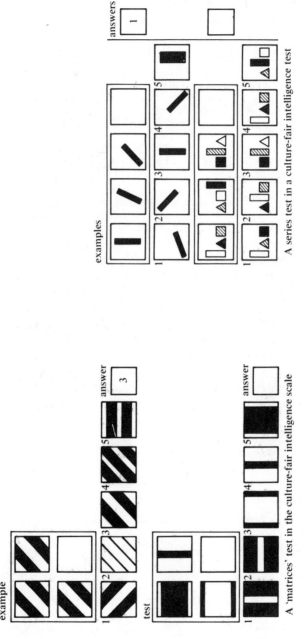

A series test in a culture-fair intelligence test

A 'matrices' test in the culture-fair intelligence scale

Figure 3.8 Some problems in the culture-fair intelligence test (from Cattell, 1965).

impair intelligence *B* or "average level of performance or compre-hension by the partly grown or mature person."

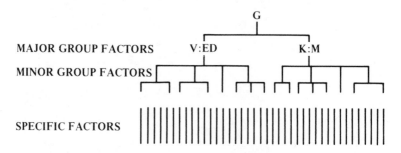

Figure 3.9   Vernon's hierarchical model of intelligence (from Vernon, 1950).

Vernon (1950) has also developed a model of intelligence involv-ing two major general factors, though his factor-analytic methods have been closer to the Spearman tradition and his work, in general, has been oriented closer to educational and practical applications than the other researchers discussed. Vernon (see Figure 3.9) states that after *G* is extracted, there are two major group factors, which he identifies as *v:ed* and *k:m*. The former corresponds to a verbal-numerical-educational grouping; the latter corresponds to a practi-cal-mechanical-spatial grouping. What Vernon refers to as minor group factors would be analagous to primary mental abilities and would include (under *v:ed*) factors of numerical and verbal facility, and (under *k:m*) factors of mechanical aptitude and spatial ability.

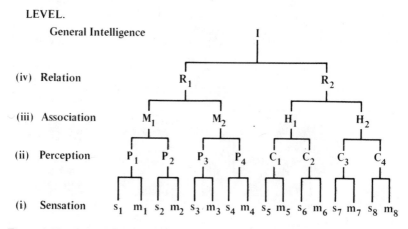

Figure 3.10   Burt's hierarchical model of intelligence (from Burt, 1949).

Another British psychologist, Cyril Burt (1949), also considered ability factors to be organized hierarchically, and he considered several distinct levels: a general factor, broad-group factors, narrow-group factors, and finally, specific factors. Burt's view on the organization of the "mind" was heavily influenced by Sherrington's anatomical and physiological studies of the brain and nervous system. According to Sherrington, the "mind" is hierarchically organized, in that there are systems within systems that vary as to the complexity of information processed. Burt's hierarchical model of mental levels (see Figure 3.10) bears a strong affinity to a functional hierarchy ordered in terms of cognitive complexity, in which the lowest level is concerned with elementary sensory and motor process *(s,m)* subsumed by the higher-order level of perceptual processes and coordinated movement *(P,M)*, in turn subsumed by the relatively more complex processes of association involving memory and habit formation *(M,H)*, in turn subsumed by relational processes *(R)*, leading finally to general intelligence *(I)* at the apex of the hierarchy. General intelligence is thought to serve an integrative role—being involved at every level in the hierarchy. Burt's hierarchical model of intelligence is a logical one—based more on extra factor analytic considerations rather than arrived at inductively from empirical studies.

Mention has already been made that Guilford's model of the structure of mental abilities is the only "maverick" with respect to accepting a hierarchical view of intelligence. Guilford's adoption of orthogonal rotation procedures precludes arriving at correlated primary factors that permit further factoring and therefore the building of a pyramid. Guilford has been able to arrive at orthogonal factors with some ease because the sample of subjects are highly homogeneous with respect to age, overall ability, education, and so on. However, it should be noted that orthogonal rotation in and of itself does not preclude a kind of hierarchical model of intelligence. Guilford's model is a logical model in the same manner that Burt's is; that is, the model is postulated based on extra factor theoretic considerations—and then the empirical work begins in trying to identify the postulated factors. More to the point is the observation that the British tradition of mapping out structure has tended to involve orthogonal factors—where a centroid factor is successively placed through the test variables. What this entails is that all tests will load on the first centroid (the *G* factor), and the next set of factors will be smaller bipolar group factors accounting for less variance, and so on. Rotation is typically not carried out, thus resulting in orthogonal factors that are hierarchically arranged. Thus the British hierarchical models of abilities have typically been arrived at in a very different manner than, say, the North American procedure of oblique rotation of primaries, followed by further factoring, and so on. These two procedures of building hierarchies are radically different and based on different rationales. More recently, there has been a move underway for constructing hierarchical models based on what has traditionally been the North American approach. Vernon (1965), for example, as well as a former student of his, MacArthur (1968), acknowledge that one may just as well start from the bottom and move up (oblique with rotation) or go from the top to the bottom (orthogonal without rotation). Similar results are obtained with both procedures, although the former method is to be preferred to the extent that one finds the arguments for rotating to oblique simple structure compelling.

Abilities and Creativity

The area of creativity has received increased attention from psychologists ever since Guilford's presidential address to the American Psychological Association in 1950 (Guilford, 1950). Guilford served to establish acceptance that the study of creativity may be considered as a legitimate problem amenable to psychological and especially psychometric analysis. Mention has already been made of Guilford's general problem-solving model—which may be viewed as an attempt to represent the creative process with respect to its cognitive aspects. Especially important in Guilford's view of creativity is the operation of divergent thinking, including such abilities as fluency, flexibility, and elaboration. Transformation abilities are also thought to be especially important in the creative process in which new products are produced.

Although many of Guilford's abilities thought to be related to creativity have a convincing amount of face validity (i.e., would appear to tap creativity), the more important questions pertains to their construct validity (i.e., do these abilities actually get at important aspects of creativity). Unfortunately, the evidence on the latter is not convincing. Guilford has been mainly content to measure what he considers to be creative abilities with little if any follow-up concerning how well such abilities do in fact predict individual differences in creative productivity. In recent reviews of the adequacy of Guilford's divergent productive abilities as related to other indices of creative performance, both Dellas and Gaier (1970) and Nicholls (1972) conclude that the evidence weighs heavily against considering divergent thinking tests as measuring meaningful aspects of creativity. Part of the problem here is that Guilford considers creative abilities as normally distributed traits within the general population, and to the extent that the majority of individuals are not creative in the sense of producing outstanding creative products, there is little hope of relating Guilford's measures, as given to samples from the general population, to future creative performance. Because the very definition of creativity (unusual but effective outstanding accomplishments, say, in the fields of science and the arts) would seem to argue against normally distributed traits within the general population, Nicholls (1972) goes so far to suggest we should give up the trait approach to studying creativity and concern ourselves more with creative products and the differing conditions for creative achievements.

Nicholls' criticisms of a trait approach to creativity are compelling, and they are reinforced by a further distinction. Although some investigators have reported very low correlations between punative measures of creativity and general intelligence, and thus arguing for their distinctiveness, these findings have been criticized by Wallach and Kogan (1965), who in review of the empirical evidence, conclude that few studies adequately satisfy the dual requirements of both convergent validity (i.e., high intercorrelations between measures of creativity) and divergent validity (low intercorrelations between creativity and intelligence measures). To the extentent both of these requirements are not sufficiently met (a distinction pointed out by Campbell and Fiske, 1959), it is questionable whether one may speak of creativity as distinct from general intelligence.

Guilford's view is, of course, that creativity measures are not identical to general intelligence. Those factor analysts who have a heavy commitment to the concept of *G* or general intelligence consider creativity tests as tapping overall intelligence (e.g., Burt, 1962; Vernon, 1964). However, this view is defended partly on the grounds that one should sample individuals from a wide range of general intelligence, and psycholmetric considerations would indeed predict a high correlations between general intelligence and putative measures of creativity in such cases. Those who argue that general intelligence and creativity are distinct abilities have done so partly on the basis of reported differential correlations between the two abilities at different levels of general intelligence. This idea involves the notion that for lower levels of general intelligence creativity may well be correlated with *G*, but at higher levels of general intelligence there is a low correlation. The reason for the latter is that, although a high level of general intelligence is a necessary condition for high creativity, the former does not guarantee the latter. There are many highly intelligent individuals who lack creative abilities. This relationship between creativity and intelligence is illustrated in Figure 3.11, where the scatter plot illustrates that low general intelligence necessitates low creativity, but at high levels of general intelligence, the full range of creativity values are possible. This state of affairs supports Nicholl's conclusion that it is not meaningful to speak of creativity as a normally distributed trait within the general population because it is indistinguishable from *G* at low levels of general intelligence. At high levels of general intelligence, it is differences in temperament and motivation that discriminate best between those who do and do not achieve high creativity. These aspects are taken up in the following chapter.

In an interesting article by Albert (1975) concerning the nature of "genius," he advances a strictly behavioral definition. In his view, genius should be defined in terms of one's productivity and, further, the influence of one's creative products on one's discipline. Thus scientific genius may depend on certain kinds of abilities, temperament traits, and motivational factors, but the concept of genius should be defined strictly in terms of the impact of one's creative

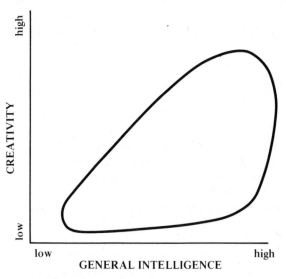

Figure 3.11 Relationship between creativity and general intelligence.

products on the scientific community. In avoiding a trait view of genius, then, there are no "might-have'been's" who have been prevented from "flowering." Of course, one may still look at the traits that enhance the possibity for the occurrence of genius.

Before leaving the topic of the relationship between creativity and intelligence, mention should be made of a combined factor-analytic study of creativity and intelligence tests. Thus Cave (1970) found three factors rotated to oblique simple structure: verbal intelligence, reasoning, and creativity. The rationale of this study was to give both intelligence and creativity tests to individuals at the *same time,* because previous studies reporting no correlation between these two constructs may be faulted in that the separate measures of creativity and intelligence were separated in time. Because the three primary factors were highly intercorrelated, higher-order factor analysis was indicated. Cave found a single general factor or *G.* Thus Cave's study supports the notion that there is a trait of creativity that is distinct from verbal and reasoning ability factors, although creativity is highly correlated with traditional measures of intelligence. In his own words,

> The results of this study differ from the claims of those who propose that creativity does not correlate with intelligence and also it differs from the ideas of those who propose that creativity is essentially the same as intelligence. This study indicates that the truth is midway between the two extremes (Cave, 1970, pp. 190–191).

Abilities and Cognitive Styles

Brief mention should be made of the distinction between traditional ability factors and a growing concern with individual differences in cognitive styles in information processing. The latter may be considered as spanning the three traditional domains of abilities, temperament, and motivation. The most extensive study of one particular cognitive style is Witkin's et al. (1962) field dependence-independence. Field dependence is measured by the inability to overcome the effects of an embedded context. For example, in the body adjustment test, the subject attempts to adjust a tilted chair in a tilted room to the true upright position. In the rod and frame test, the subject must adjust a luminous rod in a dark room to the true vertical against the background of a frame in various positions. A third test which has been used as a measure of field dependence-independence is the embedded figures test, which involves locating a simple geometric figure embedded in a more complex one. This dimension has been related to various psychological measures. For example, field dependents are found to be more passive and dependent as measure by personality tests than are field independents.

Another cognitive style receiving attention is extensiveness of scanning. Extensive scanners tend to "take in" large amounts of information before making a response. Such being the case, scanners are less susceptible to making a quick first-impression type of judgement. It has been found that scanners are more likely to engage in such ego defenses as isolation of affect and projection, and in terms of pathology, are more likely than nonscanners to be paranoid schizophrenics, undoubtedly related to their cautious, uncertain, distrustful approach to cognizing the world.

Other cognitive styles that have been studied include: conceptual differentiation, involving differentiating more analytic concepts (e.g., height and weight) from global ones (e.g., size); leveling versus sharpening, or the loss of information versus the emphasis of detail; tolerance for the unconventional, or the acceptance of experience that is at variance with other beliefs; constricted versus flexible control, or the proneness to interference by perceived contradictory cues; category width, referring to the inclusiveness of a category; and finally, reflection versus impulsivity, referring to the tendency to consistently make slow or fast response times to problem situations which are uncertain. Other cognitive styles have been proposed (reviewed by Kagan and Kogan, 1970; Royce, 1973), but the above-mentioned dimensions have the strongest empirical support.

Although there have been some factor-analytic studies of cognitive styles (see Royce, 1973, for a taxonomy), most of the research in this area has evolved from other considerations. Indeed, two major factor analysts have questioned the value of cognitive styles as a useful approach to individual differences in cognition (Cattell, 1971; Vernon, 1973). Both Cattell and Vernon see little to be gained from cognitive styles that more traditional concepts cannot handle. Thus differences in abilities, perception, temperament, and motives would seem to be able to accommodate the findings from the cognitive style literature. Although this argument has some merit, it should be noted that the work on cognitive styles may add substantially more to our understanding of individual differences in cognition to the extent such work is embedded in a theoretical framework as opposed to being merely descriptive dimensions. Klein's (1970) work on cognitive controls fits this requirement in that his dimensions are based upon neopsychoanalytic theorizing. Different theoretical bases exist (reviewed by Kagan and Kogan, 1970) as background for developing explanations of individual differences in cognitive styles. It is in this respect that the growing style literature may further enhance the study individual differences in cognitive functioning.

Applied Value of Multivariate Models of Intelligence

Finally, we must consider the extent to which the multivariate approach to intelligence has had an impact on psychological assessment in applied psychology. Multivariate researchers are often dismayed at the limited application of their work. For example, Horn (1966a) has stated:

> Sixty years after Spearman's tremendous methodological contribution, fifty years after Burt's lucid refinements of statement, and thirty years after Thurstone's general restructuring of the ability field, the intelligence tests still most popularly used in schools and clinics remain on relatively crude "omnibus" designs and rest on a priori subtests, factored, if at all, after the construction (p. 552).

Although the notion of a gross separation of mental abilities (along the lines of fluid and crystallized intelligence) has been accepted, particularly for the meaningful testing of culturally deprived social groups, Horn's lament is essentially accurate. The primary reason for this situation is not due to the inadequate psychometric training of intelligence test users (as some multivariate workers think), or to the inadequacy of the multivariate models (as some general intelligence test users think). As is the case of many cultural lags, there is a question of whether society *needs* a particular new "product" at a given time. Binet would have been frustrated if he had produced his general intelligence test for a medieval society, in which mental ability was less important than social position at birth for purposes of entering a trade or guild. In the case of contemporary testing of abilities, we find that the omnibus test predicts academic achievement very well, with correlations of .6 being quite common, and it is easier and less expensive to administer one test than a complete battery. Multivariate assessment does not currently add enough to the prediction of general achievement to warrant the expense in many cases. This is a function of the tendancy of most factors of intelligence to intercorrelate positively. Thus an omnibus test with a sufficiently varied sampling of the different facets of intelligence will be a good index of general intelligence, in itself, and there is seldom a practical need to explicitly partition the components.

What then can we say of *differential* predicition? Can we use the multivariate approach to devise different prediction equations for different occupations or training or educational programs? McNemar (1964) believed not. Tyler (1965) drew a similar conclusion:

> It seemed reasonable to expect that some kinds of school work would be related to verbal ability, others to memory, and others to facility with numbers—these hopes have not been supported by the correlation findings. Most of the work has been done with the Thurstone Primary Mental Abilities battery at the college level, but what evidence there is from high school studies corroborates the conclusion. Verbal and Reasoning factors are the only ones giving consistently significant correlations with scholastic achievement, and they correlate about equally well with everything (p. 112).

In spite of this "pessimistic" pronouncement, Vandenberg (1973) has pointed out that the optimal kinds of evidence needed is not available because schools or companies do not administer a sizable battery of tests to students in different types of classes or different types of jobs. We can also offer the following defense for the use of multivariate models (aside from the fact that they "exist" according to the data). (a) In some situations, the extra predictive power for predicting general achievement from a systematic assessment of the components of general intelligence may prove to be warranted. If a great expense and a great number of individuals are involved, any small but reliable improvement in prediction will be economically practical. Such a situation might occur in an extensive armed-services training program in which the goal is to predict who will maximally benefit from training. (b) Similarly, any slight advantage of the multivariate approach in differential prediction could be justified on a large scale if we were channeling many individuals into a number of *different* programs. (c) In individual assessment and counseling, *extreme* assymmetries of abilities should not be ignored. If an individual's profile of abilities reveals that spatial-mechanical abilities, for example, are highest, this is not in itself justification for channeling the person into an engineering program. All educational programs are composite in nature. But, if the spatial-mechanical portion of the profile is quite extreme, this person may well have an advantage over another person with the same general ability but low spatial-mechanical ability. (d) In general, we should not ignore the possibility of individuals developing *compensatory* functioning during the educational process for those abilities that are strongest. For example, a student with good memory abilities can often compensate for other inadequacies. (e) The multivariate approach is highly useful in helping us to understand the intellectual processes. A notion of general intelligence as the sole dimension in mental ability tends to lead to confusing and conflicting definitions of the nature of mental ability, while the multivariate model actually specifies the different processes involved (particularly the Guilford model). (f) Even those who subscribe to omnibus tests of intelligence such as the Wechsler, often speak of different mental abilities within the test such as spatial or reasoning. If this is going to be common practice, it may easily be argued that these conclusions should be based on the results of formal factor analytic work rather than the armchair factor analysis of the individual user of the test.

FURTHER READING

Butcher, H. J. *Human intelligence: Its nature and assessment.* London: Methuen, 1968.

Cattell, R. B. *Abilities: Their structure, growth, and action.* Boston: Houghton Mifflin, 1971.

Guilford, J. P. *The nature of human intelligence.* New York: McGraw-Hill, 1967.

Horn, J. L. Structure of intellect: Primary abilities. In R.M. Dreger (Ed.), *Multivariate personality research: Contributions to the understanding of personality in honor of Raymond B. Cattell.* Baton Rouge, Louisiana: Claitor, 1972.

Wiseman, S. (Ed.) *Intelligence and ability.* New York: Penguin Books, 1967.

Chapter 4

TEMPERAMENT

Temperament or Personality?

Researchers in the general area of trait psychology or individual differences have not been consistent in their terminology for designating what aspects of the person are under investigation. The concept of *temperament* is rather straightforward and presents little difficulty—referring as it does to individual differences in "temper," that is, characteristics which are largely stylistic ways of behaving in social situations. Contrasting the temperament domain with the abilities brings out the essential defining properties of the former. Whereas the measurement of abilities may be characterized as involving unipolar scales, the measurement of temperament traits are based on bipolar scales. A unipolar scale is one that ranges from low to high or from poor performance to good performance. In the abilities it makes good conceptual sense to view differences in behavior as being ordered along a continuum bounded by poor and good performance, that is:

trait *x:* _____

low	average	high
(poor)	(medium)	(good)

In contrast to abilities, temperament traits may best be thought of as a range from a minus pole to a plus pole in which the middle values are best thought of as neutral, that is:

trait *y:* _____

(−)	neutral	(+)

For example, the trait Extraversion-Introversion is a bipolar trait in which the extremes represent two poles, that is, it is normally not desirable to label one pole as low or high in the sense that one's performance is poor or good, respectively, as is done for abilities. Such judgments *may* be made with respect to temperament, but these judgments would be largely personal, stemming from preferred styles of behavior rather than part of the logic of temperament traits. The labeling of the two poles of a temperament trait is arbitrary, that is, extraversion, for example, may be considered as the negative or positive pole of the bipolar dimension of extraversion-introversion. Such arbitrary labeling is not possible for ability traits, which further clarifies the distinction between temperament and ability traits.

Many persons working in the area of trait psychology employ the term personality as synonymous with the term temperament. This practice leads to some confusion, however, to the extent that others reserve the term personality to cover a broad spectrum of behavior. Thus Cattell (1965) subsumes under personality the study of abilities, temperament, motives, moods, roles, interests, and so on. Guilford (1959) has a similar approach in painting personality with a broad brush, including such traits as morphological (body structure) and physiological, aptitude, temperament, needs, interests, abilities, values, and so on all under the rubric of personality. Eysenck's (1967) use of the term personality is a little less clear, because he appears to equate it with temperament, yet he has made a bold attempt to relate individual differences in temperament (i.e., extraversion-introversion) to individual differences in physiological measures, conditioning, perception, attitudes, and so on. In summary, then, we will follow the practice of reserving the term personality for referring to the multiple aspects of individual differences, that is, subsuming the various psychological domains or modalities, rather than equating it to the more restricted term temperament.

Historical Precedents

The classification of persons in terms of temperament has had a long history, going back as far as the ancient Greek philosophers Hippocrates and Galen (see Eysenck and Eysenck, 1969, Ch. 3). Kant (1798), in his *Antropologie,* presented us with a formal description of "the four temperaments" as these concepts had developed to that point in history. These character types are described by Kant (quoted in Eysenck & Eysenck, 1969) as follows:

The Sanguine Temperament   The sanguine person is carefree and full of hope, attributes great importance to whatever he may be dealing with at the moment, but may have forgotten all about it the next. He means to keep his promises, but fails to do so because he never considered deeply beforehand whether he would be able to keep them. He is good-natured enough to help others, but is a bad debtor and constantly asks for time to pay. He is very sociable, given to pranks, contented, doesn't take anything very seriously and has many, many friends. He is not vicious, but difficult to convert from his sins; he may repent, but this contrition (which never becomes a feeling of guilt) is soon forgotten. He is easily fatigued and bored by work, but is constantly engaged in mere games—these carry with them constant change, and persistence is not his forte.

The Melancholic Temperament   People tending toward melancholia attribute great importance to everything that concerns them. They discover everywhere cause for anxiety, and notice first of all the difficulties in a situation, in contradistinction to the sanguine person. They do not make promises easily, because they insist on keeping their word and have to consider whether they will be able to do so. All this is so not because of moral considerations, but because interaction with others makes them worried, suspicious and thoughtful; it is for this reason that happiness escapes them.

The Choleric Temperament   He is said to be hot-headed, is quickly roused, but easily calmed down if his opponent gives in; he is annoyed without lasting hatred. Activity is quick, but not persistent. He is busy, but does not like to be in business, precisely because he is not persistent; he prefers to give orders, but does not want to be bothered with carrying them out. He loves open recognition, and wants to be publicly praised. He loves appearances, pomp and formality; he is full of pride and self-love. He is miserly; polite, but with ceremony; he suffers most through the refusal of others to fall in with his pretensions. In one word, the choleric temperament is the least happy, because it is most likely to call forth opposition to itself.

The Phlegmatic Temperament   Phlegma means lack of emotion, not laziness; it simply implies the tendency to be moved, neither quickly nor easily, but persistently. Such a person warms up slowly, but he retains the warmth longer. He acts on principle, not by instinct; his happy temperament may supply the lack of sagacity and wisdom. He is reasonable in his dealing with other people, and usually gets his way by persisting in objectives while appearing to give way to others.

A major difficulty with Kant's system is that it is *typological;*

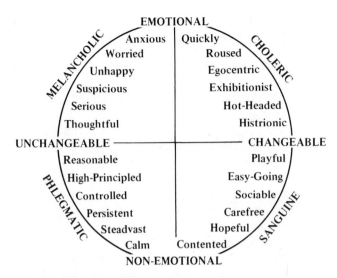

Figure 4.1 Classical theory of the four temperaments according to Kant and Wundt (from Eysenck and Eysenck, 1969).

that is, individuals are pigeon-holed according to the particular temperament that best fits their character. However, it is clear that not everyone can be readily placed in one of four mutually exclusive categories. Thus this approach lacks a fundamental property of science in general: the quantification or measurement of attributes of "things." Wundt (1903) attempted to modify the earlier typological scheme for temperament in order to provide for greater precision— a development that was, implicitly at least, based on a quasimeasurement point of view. Wundt proposed superimposing the dimensions of strength of feeling and changeability of feeling on Kant's types, with the attendant ordering indicated by the verbal designations within the circle. This combination of models has been presented by Eysenck and Eysenck (1969) and is represented in Figure 4.1. The example of Wundt's typological system hints at the idea that "type" thinking is not necessarily incompatible with "trait" thinking or a dimensional approach, and later in the chapter we return to this topic in light of modern developments.

Modern Q Data, L Data and T Data

The modern period of temperament assessment has been marked by attempts at rigorous quantification of personality and research designed to understand the causes of individual differences in personality. The most commonly used test device for assessing temperament has consisted of questionnaires, largely because of the efficiency and ease of administration in this approach. Other methods of personality assessment include objective tests (e.g., physiological indices and other laboratory devices) and behavior ratings in everyday interactions. This distinction is of importance for experimental work, of course, but it is also important for validating the frequently used questionnaire approach. That is, if traits abstracted from questionnaires are real in some sense, that is, valid, they should correspond to traits derived from the other methods.

One well-known set of temperament factors that was based upon questionnaire data is that of Guilford and Zimmerman (1956). These factors, quoted in full from that report, were:

G.   *General activity:* Energetic, rapid-moving, rapid-working person, who likes action and may sometimes be impulsive.

A.   *Ascendance:* The person who upholds his rights and defends himself in face-to-face contacts; who does not mind being conspicuous, in fact may enjoy it; who through social initiative gravitates to positions of leadership; who is not fearful of social contacts; who is not inclined to keep his thoughts to himself. There is little to indicate that 'submission' accurately describes the negative pole, as was formerly believed.

M.   *Masculinity vs. femininity:* Has masculine interests, vocational and avocational; not emotionally excitable or expressive; not easily aroused to fear or disgust; somewhat lacking in sympathy.

I.   *Confidence vs. inferiority feelings:* Feels accepted by others, confident, and adequate; socially poised; satisfied with his lot; not self-centred.

N.   *Calmness, composure vs. nervousness:* Calm and relaxed rather than nervous and jumpy; not restless, easily fatigued, or irritated; can concentrate on the matter at hand.

S.   *Sociability:* Likes social activity and contacts, formal or informal; likes positions of social leadership; has social poise, not shy, bashful, or seclusive.

T.   *Reflectiveness:* Given to meditative and reflective thinking; dreamer, philosophically inclined; has curiosity about and questioning attitude towards behaviour of self and others.

D. *Depression:* Emotionally and physically depressed rather than cheerful; given to worry and anxiety and to perseverating.

C_1. *Emotionality:* Emotions easily aroused and perseverating, yet shallow and childish; daydreamer.

R. *Restraint vs. rhathymia:* Self restrained and self controlled; serious minded rather than happy-go-lucky; not cheerfully irresponsible.

O. *Objectivity:* Takes an objective, realistic view of things; alert to his environment and can forget himself; not beset with suspicions.

Ag. *Agreeable:* Low-scoring individual is easily aroused to hostility; resists control by others; has contempt for others; and may be aroused to aggressive action. High-scoring person is friendly and compliant.

Co. *Co-operativeness, tolerance:* Low-scoring person is given to critical fault-finding generally; has little confidence or trust in others; self-centred and self pitying.

The investigator who has contributed most to the study of the relationship among the three methods is Raymond B. Cattell, who refers to "the three data bases of psychometry" (Cattell, 1965, Chap. 3). Cattell refers to Q data, obtained from ". . . questionnaires which are answered by the person himself, from his own observations and introspecting." Objective tests give us T data ". . . miniature situations set up for a person to react to, in which he does not really know in what aspect of his behavior he is being scored (hence 'objective')." Finally, we have L data obtained from ". . . ratings made by observers of the frequency and intensity with which specific kinds of behavior occur in the people they observe." Cattell has found that there is a high degree of matching between traits from L data and *Q* data. On the other hand, *T* data factors do not match as well, perhaps because of the relatively underdeveloped stage of this research. In other words, with the construction of new devices and further factor analytic work, more matchings may be established. Enough matchings have been established at the present time, however, to be of considerable assistance in validating some of the *L* data and *Q* data factors.

It is important to consider the background to the development of *L* and *Q* data factors because this background most strongly supports Cattell's claims to have covered comprehensively the source traits of personality. Cattell refers to this comprehensive coverage as the personality sphere. His initial attempts to extract or distill traits from the personality sphere were based on the assumption that the natural language would include all the important trait names. Thus Allport and Odbert (1936) found 17,954 trait names in the language, which they then reduced to a more-basic 4,504 terms on semantic grounds. Cattell then reduced these to 171 terms by eliminating what he considered to be synonymous forms. Empirical work then began. A cluster analysis from a study of peer ratings reduced the 171 terms to 36 clusters.

Finally, additional factor analysis of the 36 scales led to the present inventory of approximately 16 factors. This process of distillation is important, because it represents the only major contribution toward extensively sampling the personality domain and discovering the number of source traits required to account for it. A list of the major source traits that can be identified from Cattell's 16 *PF* (*Q* data), together with key adjectives for descriptive purposes, is found in Table 4.1. These factors have also been identified in *L* data.

TABLE 4.1
Factors *A* to *Q*4, From The 16 P.F. Test: Key Descriptive Adjectives.
(from Cattell, Eber, and Tatsuoka, 1970, chap. 9)

CHARACTERISTIC EXPRESSIONS OF SOURCE TRAIT
Factor A
U.I.(L&Q)1

Low Score Sizothymia, A− (Reserved, Detached, Critical, Aloof, Stiff)	versus	High Score Affectothymia, A+ (Warmhearted, Outgoing, Easygoing, Participating)
Critical	vs.	Good natured, easygoing
Stands by his own ideas	vs.	Ready to cooperate, likes to Participate
Cool, aloof	vs.	Attentive to people
Precise, objective	vs.	Softhearted, casual
Distrustful, skeptical	vs.	Trustful
Rigid	vs.	Adaptable, careless, "goes along"
Cold	vs.	Warmhearted
Prone to sulk	vs.	Laughs readily

Factor B
U.I.(L&Q)2

Low Score Low Intelligence, B− (Crystallized, Power Measure, Dull)	versus	High Score High Intelligence, B+ (Crystallized, Power Measure, Bright)

Low mental capacity	vs.	High general mental capacity
Unable to handle abstract problems	vs.	Insightful, fast-learning, intellectually adaptable

The measurement of intelligence has been shown to carry with it, as a factor in the personality realm, *some of the following ratings;* the correlations, however, are quite low.

Apt to be less well organized	vs.	Inclined to have more intellectual interests
Poorer judgment	vs.	Showing better judgment
Of Lower Morale	vs.	Of higher morale
Quitting	vs.	Persevering

Factor C
U.I.(L&Q)3

Low Score Emotional instability or Ego Weakness, C− (Affected by Feelings, Emotionally Less Stable, Easily Upset, Changeable)	versus	High Score Higher Ego Strength, C+ (Emotionally Stable, Mature, Faces Reality, Calm)

Gets emotional when frustrated	vs.	Emotionally mature
Changeable in attitudes and interests	vs.	Stable, constant in interests
Easily perturbed	vs.	Calm
Evasive of responsibilities, tending to give up	vs.	Does not let emotional needs obscure realities of a situation, adjusts to facts
Worrying	vs.	Unruffled
Gets into fights and problem situations	vs.	Shows restraint in avoiding difficulties

Factor E
U.I.(L&Q)5

Low Score Submissiveness, E− (Obedient, Mild, Easily Led, Docile, Accommodating)	versus	High Score Dominance or Ascendance, E+ (Assertive, Aggressive, Competitive, Stubborn)

Submissive	vs.	Assertive
Dependent	vs.	Independent-minded
Considerate, diplomatic	vs.	Stern, hostile
Expressive	vs.	Solemn
Conventional, conforming	vs.	Unconventional, rebellious
Easily upset by authority	vs.	Headstrong
Humble	vs.	Admiration demanding

Factor F
U.I.(L&Q)6

Low Score Desurgency, F− (Sober, Taciturn, Serious)	versus	High Score Surgency, F+ (Enthusiastic, Heedless, Happy-go-lucky)
Silent, introspective	vs.	Talkative
Full of cares	vs.	Cheerful
Concerned, reflective	vs.	Happy-go-lucky
Incommunicative, sticks to inner values	vs.	Frank, expressive, reflects the group
Slow, cautious	vs.	Quick and alert

Factor G
U.I.(L&Q)7

Low Score Low Superego Strength or Lack of Acceptance of Group Moral Standards, G− (Disregards Rules, Expedient)	versus	High Score Superego strength or Character, G+ (Conscientious, Persistent, Moralistic, Staid)
Quitting, Fickle	vs.	Persevering, Determined
Frivolous	vs.	Responsible
Self-indulgent	vs.	Emotionally disciplined
Slack, Indolent	vs.	Consistently ordered
Undependable	vs.	Conscientious, dominated by sense of duty
Disregards obligations to people	vs.	Concerned about moral standards and Rules

Factor H
U.I.(L&Q)8

Low Score Threctia, H− (Shy, Timid, Restrained, Threat-sensitive)	versus	High Score Parmia, H+ (Adventurous, "Thick-skinned," Socially Bold)
Shy, withdrawn	vs.	Adventurous, likes meeting people
Retiring in face of opposite sex	vs.	Active, overt interest in opposite sex
Emotionally cautious	vs.	Responsive, genial
Apt to be embittered	vs.	Friendly
Restrained, rule-bound	vs.	Impulsive
Restricted interests	vs.	Emotional and artistic interests
Careful, considerate, quick to see dangers	vs.	Carefree, does not see danger signals

Factor I
U.I.(L&Q)9

Low Score Harria, I− (Tough-minded, Rejects Illusions)	versus	High Score Premsia, I+ (Tender-minded, Sensitive, Dependent, Overprotected)
Unsentimental, expects little	vs.	Fidgety, expecting affection and attention
Self-reliant, taking responsibility	vs.	Clinging, insecure, seeking help and sympathy
Hard (to point of cynicism)	vs.	Kindly, gentle, indulgent, to self and others
Few artistic responses (but not lacking in taste)	vs.	Artistically fastidious, affected, theatrical
Unaffected by "fancies"	vs.	Imaginative in inner life and in conversation
Acts on practical, logical evidence	vs.	Acts on sensitive intuition
Keeps to the point	vs.	Attention-seeking, flighty
Does not dwell on physical disabilities	vs.	Hypochondriacal, anxious about self

Factor L
U.I.(L&Q)12

Low Score Alaxia, L− (Trusting, Accepting Conditions)	versus	High Score Protension, L+ (Suspecting, Jealous)
Accepts personal unimportance	vs.	Jealous
Pliant to changes	vs.	Dogmatic
Unsuspecting of hostility	vs.	Suspicious of interference
Ready to forget difficulties	vs.	Dwelling upon frustrations
Understanding and permissive, Tolerant	vs.	Tyrannical
Lax over correcting people	vs.	Demands people accept responsibility over errors
Conciliatory	vs.	Irritable

Factor M
U.I.(L&Q)13

Low Score Praxernia, M— (Practical, Has "Down to Earth" Concerns)	versus	High Score Autia, M+ (Imaginative, Bohemian, Absent-minded)
Conventional, alert to practical needs	vs.	Unconventional, absorbed in ideas
Concerned with immediate interests and issues	vs.	Interested in art, theory, basic beliefs
Prosaic, avoids anything far-fetched	vs.	Imaginatively enthralled by inner creations
Guided by objective realities, dependable in practical judgment	vs.	Fanciful, easily seduced from practical judgment
Earnest, concerned or worried, but steady	vs.	Generally enthused, but occasional hysterical swings of "giving up"

Factor N
U.I.(L&Q)14

Low Score Naïvete, N— (Forthright, Unpretentious)	versus	High Score Shrewdness, N+ (Astute, Worldly)
Genuine, but socially clumsy	vs.	Polished, socially aware
Has vague and injudicious mind	vs.	Has exact, calculating mind
Gregarious, gets warmly emotionally involved	vs.	Emotionally detached and disciplined
Spontaneous, natural	vs.	Artful
Has simple tastes	vs.	Esthetically fastidious
Lacking self-insight	vs.	Insightful regarding self
Unskilled in analyzing motives	vs.	Insightful regarding others
Content with what comes	vs.	Ambitious, possibly insecure
Has blind trust in human nature	vs.	Smart, "cuts corners"

Factor O
U.I.(L&Q)15

Low Score Untroubled Adequacy, O— (Self-assured, Placid, Secure, Complacent)	versus	High Score Guilt Proneness, O+ (Apprehensive, Self-reproaching, Insecure, Worrying, Troubled)
Self-confident	vs.	Worrying, anxious
Cheerful, resilient	vs.	Depressed, cries easily
Impenitent, placid	vs.	Easily touched, overcome by moods
Expedient, insensitive to people's approval or disapproval	vs.	Strong sense of obligation, sensitive to people's approval and disapproval
Does not care	vs.	Scrupulous, fussy
Rudely vigorous	vs.	Hypochondriacal and inadequate
No fears	vs.	Phobic symptoms
Given to simple action	vs.	Lonely, brooding

FACTOR Q_1
U.I.(Q)16

Low Score		High Score
CONSERVATISM OF TEMPERAMENT, Q_1-	versus	RADICALISM, Q_1+
(Conservative, Respecting Established Ideas, Tolerant of Traditional Difficulties)		(Experimenting, Liberal, Analytical, Free-thinking)

FACTOR Q_2
U.I.(Q)17

Low Score		High Score
GROUP DEPENDENCY, Q_2-	versus	SELF-SUFFICIENCY, Q_2+
(Sociably Group Dependent, A "Joiner" and Sound Follower)		(Self-sufficient, Resourceful, Prefers Own Decisions)

FACTOR Q_3
U.I.(Q)18

Low Score		High Score
LOW SELF-SENTIMENT INTEGRATION, Q_3-	versus	HIGH STRENGTH OF SELF-SENTIMENT, Q_3+
(Uncontrolled, Lax, Follows Own Urges, Careless of Social Rules)		(Controlled, Exacting Will Power, Socially Precise, Compulsive, Following Self-image)

FACTOR Q_4
U.I.(Q)19

Low Score		High Score
LOW ERGIC TENSION, Q_4-	versus	HIGH ERGIC TENSION, Q_4+
(Relaxed, Tranquil, Torpid, Unfrustrated, Composed)		(Tense, Frustrated, Driven, Overwrought, Fretful)

Four examples of important traits from *T* data are designated as *U.I.* 19: critical practicality, *U.I.* 22: corticalertia, *U.I.* 24: anxiety and *U.I.* 32: extraversion-introversion [for further details of attempts to code factors according to a universal index *(U.I.)* system, refer to Cattell, 1957]. These factors are very difficult to interpret from the loadings of variables on factors (see Cattell and Warburton, 1967). The reason for this is that the manifestation of temperament in laboratory tests and physiological measures is not readily apparent to us. What does a test such as tapping speed or an EEG (electroencephalography) pattern mean in terms of temperament? Fortunately, we are able to use statistical techniques to aid in factor interpretation by correlating factors from *T* data with those from *Q* data. In doing this, we find that *T* data factors tend to correlate best with second-order factors from Q data. Thus we must ask what higher-order factors mean in questionnaires.

Higher-Order Factors and Eysenck's Contribution

What then are the higher-factor factors of personality? Cattell (1973) and Cattell, Eber and Tatsuoka (1970) have gone into considerable detail on the nature of second-order and even third-order factors. However, only the four major second-order factors are described here (Table 4.2). Factor QI is the best match to U.I. 32 in T data. It is readily interpretable from the major first-order factors that are involved. Factors A, E, F, H, and Q_2 have in common their relationship to an internal (introverted) versus external (extraverted) frame of reference. Cattell uses the trait name exvia versus invia to denote this. Factor QII matches $U.I.$ 24 in T data. It loads primaries (first-order factors) which relate to states of emotional stability, guilt-

TABLE 4.2
Four major Second-order Factors
Measured by the 16P.F. Test

Standard Index	Bipolar Title	Chief Primaries Involved	Equivalent in Factors from T Data
$Q1$	Invia vs. exvia	$A+,E+,F+,H+,$ Q_2-	U.I.32
QII	Adjustment vs. Anxiety	$C-,H-,L+,O+,$ Q_3-,Q_4+	U.I.24
$QIII$	Pathemia vs. cortertia	$A-,I-,M-$ $(E+,L+)$	U.I.22
QIV	Subduedness vs. Independence	$E+,L+,M+,Q_1+,$ Q_2+	U.I.19

TABLE 4.3
Indexes of Relationship between Second-order Factors from
Hundleby-Connor (1968) and Gorsuch-Cattell (1967)
(Adapted from Hundleby and Connor, 1968, Table 3).

		HUNDLEBY-CONNOR SECOND-ORDER FACTOR			
		F1	F2	F3	F4
GORSCH-CATTELL SECOND-ORDER FACTOR	I Anxiety	$+.97$	$-.07$	$+.29$	$-.08$
	II Exvia	$-.04$	$+.99$	$+.17$	$+.02$
	III Pathemia	$+.18$	$-.07$	$+.94$	$+.01$
	IV Independence	$-.09$	$-.02$	$+.01$	$+.95$

proneness, extrapunitiveness, tension, and so on. Cattell identifies this factor as adjustment versus anxiety. Factor QIII, cortertia versus pathemia, also has a corresponding factor from objective test data — *U.I.* 22. Cortertia is an abbreviated form of the term cortical alertness. It is related to a reserved, detached orientation toward people $(A-)$, tough-mindedness $(I-)$ and practicality $(M-)$. Factor QIV is independence versus subduedness, matching *U.I.* 19. The independence component can be directly found in factors Q_2 (self-sufficiency), $Q_1 +$ (radicalism), and $M +$ (imaginativeness). There are additional indications of dominance $(E+)$ and suspiciousness toward others $(L+)$. It is also worth noting that these factors have been well replicated by independent investigators. The matchings between the Cattell factors and those found in an analysis of a separate population by Hundleby and Connor (1968) are presented in Table 4.3. In this table we see high similarity indices in the main diagonal (.97, .99, etc.) and low ones in the off-diagonal entries. In other words, each of the factors in one study is highly related to one and only one of the factors from the other study. This kind of evidence for factor invariance provides strong support for factors as useful theoretical constructs.

The Hundleby and Connor work also interrelates Cattell's higher-order factors with the factors of Hans J. Eysenck as measured by the *EPI* (Eysenck Personality Inventory). Eysenck has been concerned with the two broad factors of extraversion-introversion *(E)* and neuroticism-stability *(N)*. There is considerable agreement between Eysenck's factors and Cattell's first two second-order factors (Table 4.4). However, as we can see, either Cattell's anxiety contains a mixture of *N* with some *E* (i.e., introversion) or conversely, Eysenck's *E* contains a mixture of exvia and some QII (i.e., stability). Samples of items from the *EPI* are given in Table 4.5

Eysenck has made considerable use of objective tests in his work, and intensive study of *N* and *E* (particularly *E*) has led to the development of a highly stimulating (and controversial) theory of personality. Eysenck identifies individual differences in the neuroticism or anxiety factor with individual differences in the activity of the autonomic nervous system, particularly the sympathetic branch. The autonomic nervous system, in turn, is aroused by the limbic region of the brain, particularly the hypothalamus. Thus Eysenck's strategy is to offer a theory that ties individual differences in temperament to individual differences in physiological functioning. Because this aspect of Eysenck's theory, however, is not as well developed as his work on the extraversion factor, for further theorizing

TABLE 4.4

Correlations between 16 P.F. Factors and Eysenck's N and E Factors
(Adapted from Hundleby and Connor, 1968, Tables 1 and 4)

	N	E
Second-order $F1$ Anxiety	+.60	−.26
Second-order $F2$ Exvia	−.04	+.73
Second-order $F3$ Pathemia	+.04	+.03
Second-order $F4$ Independence	+.05	−.26

TABLE 4.5

Sample items for Measuring Factors N and E
(from Eysenck and Eysenck, 1969, p. 83)

		Key
A.	Do you sometimes feel happy, sometimes depressed, without any apparent reason?	N
B.	Do you have frequent ups and downs in mood, either with or without apparent cause?	N
C.	Are you inclined to be moody?	N
D.	Does your mind often wander while you are trying to concentrate	N
E.	Are you frequently 'lost in thought' even when supposed to be taking part in a conversation?	N
F.	Are you sometimes bubbling over with energy and sometimes very sluggish?	N
G.	Do you prefer action to planning for action?	E
H.	Are you happiest when you get involved in some project that calls for for rapid action?	E
I.	Do you usually take the initiative in making new friends?	E
J.	Are you inclined to be quick and sure in your actions?	E
K.	Would you rate yourself as a lively individual?	E
L.	Would you be very unhappy if you were prevented from making numerous social contacts?	E

on the N factor we will subsequently consider Jeffrey Gray's work.

Eysenck is better known for his well-developed theory of extra-version-introversion (Eysenck, 1967). Eysenck began with the concepts of excitation and inhibition which Pavlov had postulated to be fundamental to activity of the central nervous system. (For a review of Pavlov's theory as applied to personality, see Berlyne, 1968.) Pavlov applied the terms excitation and inhibition to dogs to explain individual differences in their temperaments and related these in turn to differential conditioning. For example, Pavlov's earlier work (which formed the basis for Eysenkian concepts) postulated that the more "choleric" dog would have a nervous system in which excitation predominated over inhibition. Such a dog would be difficult to discipline, forming positive conditioned associations readily but inhibitory associations more slowly. The "melancholic" dog, on the other hand, would be described by a predominance of inhibition over excitation. Consequently, this kind of dog could be readily disciplined and would typically appear as quite timid.

Although Eysenck borrowed the terms excitation and inhibition from Pavlov, he developed his own usage of them. Thus, Eysenck (1957) proposed the hypothesis that *"introverted people are characterized by strong excitatory and weak inhibitory potentials, whereas extraverted people are characterized by weak excitatory and strong inhibitory potentials."* Although this hypothesis tends to conflict with common-sense usage of the terms excitation-inhibition, it can be more readily understood if we think of the processes involved in more literal physiological terms. Thus:

> In its strong form the law of excitation/inhibition has been linked by Eysenck with the notion of the ascending reticular formation . . . others have recently put forward the hypothesis of a continuum of cortical arousal which is attained in response to corticopetal impulses from lower centers. The continuum extending from deep sleep at the low arousal end to 'excited' states of the high arousal end is a function of the amount of cortical bombardment by the ascending reticular activating system such that the greater the corticular bombardment, the higher the activation (Eysenck and Eysenck, 1969, p. 52).

The introvert therefore is hypothesized (in physiological terms) to be marked by strong excitation of the cortex by the reticular formation but weak inhibition of this arousal pattern. Because he is in a high state of arousal, he will tend to avoid external stimulation (i.e., extraverted behavior) that would lead to too high a level of arousal for optimum functioning. Conversely, the extravert, because of his low arousal state, will seek out external stimulation to raise his level of cortical arousal to a more optimal level. Eysenck has pointed out that extraversion involves more than just social extraversion and includes the pursuit of sensory stimulation in general.

Clearly, all the above is posed as a hypothesis. However, the hypothesis is stated clearly and leads to experimental predictions. Because of the success of these predictions, the theory (hypothesis) has gained considerable validity. For example, if extraverts are characterized by strong cortical inhibition (i.e., low arousal) they should also exhibit the low-frequency, high-amplitude alpha rhythm on EEG recordings, whereas introverts, because of high cortical arousal, will be expected to exhibit desynchrony of the alpha rhythm. This in fact is supported by research findings (Eysenck, 1967).

A number of more psychological kinds of predictions can also be made. For example, we can make predictions about the socialization process in general. A well-established formulation in psychology holds that response is a function of drive $\times$ habit, that is, $R = D \times H$. Thus conditioning depends in part on the arousal (D) level of the organism. Because the introvert is in a relatively high state of arousal (excitation), he should, generally speaking, condition well. Developmentally speaking, there is a risk that the introvert will be oversocialized (condition too readily the "do's" and "don'ts" of society) and may develop neurotic symptoms, particularly obsessive-compulsive, phobic, and anxiety problems. The extravert, on the other hand, risks under-socialization (lack of conditioning society's moral strictures) which, in its pathological form, would be manifested as criminal and antisocial behavior, that is, psychopathic or sociopathic behavior. Eysenck predicts that both of these tendencies will be exacerbated by high N scores, which would accentuate the autonomic responses to be conditioned in neurosis and energize the antisocial tendencies of the extravert. On the whole, these predictions have been confirmed. Neurotic-anxiety patients with these symptoms appear as high N–low E individuals, whereas criminals appear as high N–high E individuals. That these personality constellations are in fact predisposing persons to the correlated disorder has been confirmed by Burt (1965). Burt obtained the personality ratings of 763 children at the age of 10 in terms of N and E. Over a 35-year follow-up, 15% became habitual offenders and 18% became neurotic. Of the former, 63% were rated as high on N; 54% as high on E. Of the latter (neurotics), 59% were rated as high on N; 44% as low on E (only 1% were rated as high on E).

Another prediction which has been made in regard to individual differences in extraversion-introversion is that introverts will react more strongly than extraverts to the same stimulus. Corcoran (1964) has stated "if introverts are in general more highly aroused than extraverts, then, assuming that arousal is synonymous with a state of high cortical facilitation, it follows that the output of an effector of an introvert should be greater than the output of an effector of an extravert when both are equally stimulated" (p. 299). Corcoran

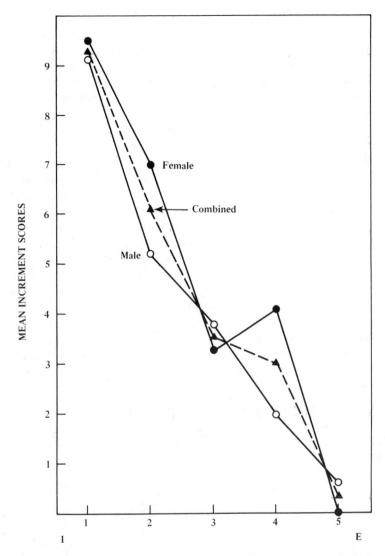

Figure 4.2 Increment in salivation in five groups of subjects ordered according to E. Four drops of lemon were used to induce salivation (from Eysenck, 1970).

tested this prediction by devising the lemon-drop test in which several drops of lemon are placed on the subject's tongue while cotton pellets absorb the resulting salivation. As predicted, introverts salivate to a greater degree. Figure 4.2 is from a replication of this study by Eysenck and Eysenck (1967). We can also predict that introverts should be more tolerant of sensory deprivation, and extraverts should be more tolerant of pain. Figure 4.3, from Eysenck (1963), shows the relationship between level of stimulation (sensory input) and "hedonic tone" or the degree of pleasantness-unpleasantness of the stimulation. The inverted-U function between arousal and performance is well established in the psychological literature. Eysenck has added the distinguishing functions for both introverts and extraverts with respect to hedonic tone and level of stimulation. For the general population curve note that very low stimulation at point A (sensory deprivation) is as aversive as is very high stimulation at point B (pain), but this is not the case for introverts and extraverts. Thus at low levels of stimulation (point A) introverts are in a higher state of arousal than extraverts, because introverts are already in a relatively higher arousal state. As stimulation level increases, introverts reach their optimum level of arousal much sooner than do extraverts. With further increases of stimulation, arousal increases to yield negative hedonic tone for introverts at a much faster rate than for extraverts. In summary, then, a given amount of stimulation will lead to greater arousal in the introvert, who will thus tend to reach both his optimum level of arousal and nonoptimal level of high arousal sooner than the extravert.

In passing it can be noted that Eysenck's theorizing on extraversion-introversion has passed through three distinct phases. The first

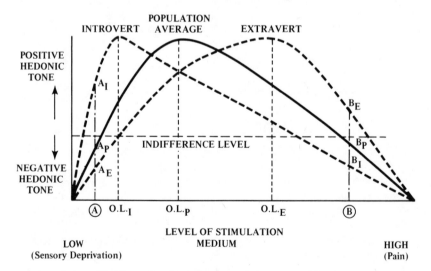

Figure 4.3 Relationship between sensory stimulation and hedonic tone in introverts, extraverts, and the population average (from Eysenck, 1963).

phase involved the initial identification of the two major dimensions of E and N (Eysenck, 1947). The second phase involved invoking the concepts of excitation and inhibition in explaining individual differences in E (Eysenck, 1957) in which these concepts were framed within a Hullian learning framework. And finally, the most recent phase identified the concepts of excitation and inhibition as having a specific neurological basis, that is, tentatively identified with the reticular activating system (Eysenck, 1967). This latter phase also has seen some preliminary work on linking the neuroticism dimension to the autonomic nervous system and in turn, to the limbic system, although by far the major experimental research has been carried out on the E dimension. In addition to the examples already cited, which reflect Eysenck's hypothetical-deductive approach to theory construction, that is, predicting on the basis of the theory, differences between extraverts and introverts on various experimental tasks, there has been a mammoth amount of similar research. The diversity and richness of deductions possible are reflected in Table 4.6 which summarizes many of the relationships found thus far for extraversion-introversion.

Jeffrey Gray's Theory of N and E

As we have stated, Eysenck's theory gives us considerable insight into the cause of individual differences in E, but not in N. The hypothesized physiological underpinnings of N refer to the physiological system that may mediate the response pattern. However, it does not explain individual differences in this response pattern. Gray's theory (see Gray, 1973), which explains individual differences in both N and E, rests heavily on concepts of sensitivity to signals of reward and sensitivity to signals of punishment (see Figure 4.4). The concept of signals of reward and punishment refers to the focus of the theory on conditioned stimuli rather than unconditioned stimuli. According to learning theory, conditioned stimuli should be more important to daily human functioning than unconditioned stimuli. We can state the theory verbally in three propositions: (1) As we move in a direction from introvert to extravert, sensitivity to reward increases and sensitivity to punishment decreases; (2) as we move in a direction from low N to high N, both sensitivity to reward and punishment will increase; (3) the rate at which these increases and decreases take place is not constant. Thus, moving from introvert to extravert, the increase in sensitivity to reward is greater for

TABLE 4.6
Experimental Studies of Extraversion-Introversion
(from Eysenck and Rachman, 1965)

Variables	Introversion	Extraversion	Reference
Neurotic syndrome	Dysthymia	Hysteria: psychopathy	Eysenck (1947)
Body build:	Leptomorph	Eurymorph	Eysenck (1947)
Intellectual function	Low I.Q.— vocabulary ratio	High I.Q.— vocabulary ratio	Himmelweit (1945) Foulds (1956)
Perceptual rigidity	High	Low	Canestrari (1957)
Persistence:	High	Low	Eysenck (1947)
Speed:	Low	High	Foulds (1953)
Speed/accuracy ratio:	Low	High	Himmelweit (1946)
Level of aspiration:	High	Low	Himmelweit (1947) Miller (1951)
Intra-personal variability:	Low	High	Eysenck (1947)
Sociability:	Low	High	Eysenck (1957)
Repression:	Weak	Strong	Eriksen (1954)
Social attitudes:	Tender-minded	Tough-minded	Eysenck (1954)
Rorschach test	High M%	High D	Eysenck (1956)
T.A.T.:	Low productivity	High productivity	Foulds (1953)
Conditioning:	Strong	Weak	Franks (1956, 1957)
Reminiscence:	Low	High	Eysenck (1962b)
Figural after-effects:	Small	Large	Eysenck (1955b)
Stress reactions:	Overactive	Inert	Davis (1948) Venables (1955)
Sedation threshold:	High	Low	Shagass (1956)
Perceptual constancy:	Low	High	Ardis et al. (1957)
Time judgment:	Longer	Shorter	Claridge (1960) Eysenck (1959)
Verbal conditioning:	Good	Poor	Eysenck (1959b) Sarason (1958)
Response to therapy:	Good	Poor	Foulds (1959)
Visual imagery:	Vivid	Weak	Costello (1957)
Necker cube reversal:	Slow	Fast	Costello (1957)
Perception of vertical:	Accurate	Inaccurate	Taft & Coventry (1958)
Spiral after-effect:	Long	Short	Claridge (1960) Willett (1960c)
Time error:	Small	Great	Claridge (1960)
Vigilance:	High	Low	Claridge (1960) Bakan (1957)
Motor performance decrement:	Little	Much	Ray (1959)
Problem solving; performance decrement:	Little	Much	Eysenck (1959e)
Smoking:	No	Yes	Eysenck, Tarrant & England (1960) Eysenck, Claridge & Eysenck (1960)
Car-driving constancy:	High	Low	Venables (1955)
Cheating:	No	Yes	Keehn (1956)

high *N* than low *N* persons and the decrease in sensitivity to punishment is greater for high *N* than low *N* persons. Similarly, moving from low *N* to high *N*, the increase in sensitivity to punishment is greatest for introverts, whereas the increase in sensitivity to reward is greatest for extraverts.

The interactions that follow from proposition (3) lead to the diagonals superimposed in Figure 4.4. Each diagonal represents the steepest rate of increase in either sensitivity to punishment and reward and are identified by Gray as anxiety and impulsivity, respectively. Gray suggests that these dimensions are occasionally assessed

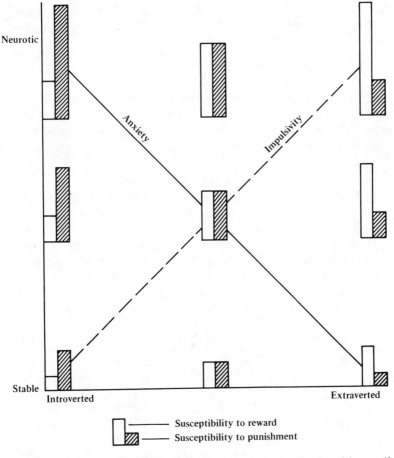

Figure 4.4 Gray's model of N and E as a function of reward and punishment (from Gray, 1973).

by investigators in such a way that anxiety may be confused with
N, and impulsivity may be confused with E.

Gray's theory enables us to make many of the same predictions
that would be made from Eysenck's theory. For example, a risk of
oversocialization would be predicted in the high N–low E individual,
primarily because of his high sensitivity to punishment. Similarly, a
risk of undersocialization would be predicted in the high N–high E
individual because of his relatively high sensitivity to reward. This
would seem to be a more straightforward explanation of neurosis and
antisocial behavior than that offered by Eysenck. Gray's theory has
the additional advantage in that it provides an explanation of individual differences in both N and E within a single framework—sensitivity to signals of reward and sensitivity to signals of punishment.

Five Major Factors From T-Data

The following five factors are obtained from analyses of T data.
As temperament factors, four of these are important because they
seem to be the counterparts in T data of the four major second-order
factors of temperament obtained from Q data. Of particular interest
is the fact that the interpretation of these factors from objective tests
alone is not as obvious as is interpretation from questionnaire items.
Thus the studies Cattell and co-workers have done to directly relate
T data and Q data factors are very important for confirming the
identification of the former. The fifth factor described below ($U.I.$
23) is important in establishing the distinction between the concept
Neurotic Regression and another dimension with which it is often
confused (Anxiety or $U.I.$ 24).

$U.I.$ 19: Independence vs. Subduedness   Cattell and Warburton
provide the following verbal description for this factor:

> U.I. 19 is characterized by its overall character of con-
> scientiousness, exacting criticalness, reliability, restraint,
> control, concern for accuracy and standards, indepen-
> dence, and refusal to make errors. Tests with positive
> loadings in this factor include more accuracy in several
> perceptual tests, quicker response in irregularly fore-
> warned reaction time, high accuracy in gestalt comple-
> tion, good performance in Gattschaldt figures, higher
> muscle tension, more acceleration of performance when
> placed in a competitive situation, and high social critical-

ness. It contributes to intellectual, but not to social, success (Cattell & Warburton, 1967, p. 198).

Thus the factor tends to combine elements of criticalness toward others (consistent with the notion of 'independence') with equally exact standards for oneself. The term exacting would not be inaccurate as an overall description of the pattern.

U.I. 22: Cortertia vs. Pathemia   Cattell and Warburton describe this factor as follows:

> The evidence points clearly to this being a sheer speed factor in basic neural proceses . . . it shows itself chiefly in reacting times, in alternative perspective, in flicker fusion and also in some responses that could be interpreted as lack of inhibition . . . On the whole, it is best expressed as an alert, eager controlled contact with internal events. We shall hypothesize that it is a condition of high general cortical alertness, determined partly by good integration, and accompanied by higher cortical metabolism rates. The opposite trait to cortertia is one of depressed cortical reactivity with slow reaction time as in oxygen or glucose deficiency, showing as a retreat to hypothalamic, emotional and unadaptive behavior (Cattell & Warburton, 1967, p. 199).

Cattell's term "cortical alertness" appears to be quite satisfactory as a summary of this factor.

U.I. 24: Anxiety vs. Adjustment   According to Cattell and Warburton:

> The notion of anxiety is shown by high annoyability and irritability, high emotionality of comment, strong desire to do the right thing, uncertainty regarding untried performances, greater fluency about self than others, greater decrement in performance through noise, lower basic metabolic rate, and greater restlessness in the figetometer (Cattell & Warburton, 1967, p. 200).

This factor is well matched with its corresponding second-order factor from *Q* data.

U.I. 32: Exvia (Extraversion) vs. Invia (Introversion)   This factor is described as follows:

At the introversion pole we have a 'lack of self confidence in regard to overt reaction' and an inattention to outer requirements, together with greater memory for one's own views than for outer presentations, e.g., ratio of guidance by memories to guidance by external cues in solving a problem. The basic explanation appears to be that the introvert has a higher ratio of internal to external reactivity, owing to differences in the speed and strength of reactive inhibition (p. 201).

TABLE 4.7
Major Loadings for U.I. 23 (Regression) and U.I. 24 (Anxiety)
(from Cattell, 1963)
U.I. 23

Variable	Loading
Inability to do simple addition and Subtraction mentally	.57
Stuttering and upset of speech with delayed auditory feedback	.57
Slow and erratic recognition of upside-down forms	.57
Aspiration-level high relative to performance	.55
Poor ability to co-ordinate simultaneous spatial cues	.55
Low metabolic rate change in response to stimuli	.50
Low readiness to tackle unpleasant activities	.47
Numerous "indecisive" responses in questionnaires	.44
Errors in reciting alphabet with prescribed skipping	.42
Rapid increase of errors when made to hurry	.31
High motor-perceptual rigidity	.29
Affected more by color than form in artistic preferences	.25
High body sway in suggestibility sway test	.20

U.I. 24

Variable	Loading
High susceptibility to annoyance	.56
High willingness to admit common faults	.47
High tendency to agree	.38
High heart rate	.30
Slow reaction time	.28
Low writing pressure	.28
Low total physical strength	.27
High critical severity	.25
High autonomic conditioning rate	.25
Low hand-steadiness	.22
High emotionality of comment	.20
High self-criticism	.19
Less alkaline saliva	.19
Slow speed of perceptual judgment	.18

This factor is also well correlated with its counterpart for Q data.

U.I. 23: Mobilization of Energy vs. Regression This factor is considered as more closely related to neurotic disorders than any other. Thus neurosis is, according to Cattell, marked by more regression than it is by anxiety itself (*U.I.* 24).

> The general evidence points to low U.I. 23 as a state of exhaustion and debility, not in the sense of physical fatigue, but as some neuro-endocrinal product of emotional and mental stress. The main manifestations of U.I. 23 are: a withdrawal of interest in the psychoanalytic sense, distractability, more decrement in performance due to noise, more verbal rigidity, less persistence with previously successful responses in the face of failure, less ability to 'work in one's head', lower correct word rate in reading, poorer performance in simple numerical problems, less saliva secretion, less alkaline saliva, and higher absolute skin resistance (p. 199).

Cattell considers Eysenck's N factor to be a combination of *U.I.* 23 (which would be related to the validity of N in predicting neurosis) and *U.I.* 24 (which is closer, conceptually to general tension, and irritability). Table 4.7 gives some of the major variables loading on the two factors, *U.I.* 23 and *U.I.* 24.

Traits and States

Cattell makes the distinction between relatively stable traits and fluctuating states. The latter would be conceptually close to the term mood as it is used in the vernacular. State factors should be expected to match trait factors. However, state research is comparatively recent, and only some of these matchings have been well confirmed to date. Table 4.8 presents major loadings for three of the seven state factors recognized in objective tests. These three factors, elation versus pathemia, mobilization versus regression, and anxiety, can also be recognized in trait data. Because of the strong physiological nature of these factors, of course, it is difficult to assign complete verbal descriptions without simply describing the tests that load themselves on the factors. The identifying labels are then used largely for convenience.

Mefferd (1966) also describes a second-order pattern to inte-

TABLE 4.8
Three State Factors That Can Also be Identified in Traits
(from Mefferd, 1966)

P.U.I. 2. Elation vs. Pathemia (Depression)

Independent Researches:	1	2	3	4	5	6	7	8
Short reaction time	−75	−35	−67	−21	—	−09	−67	−16
Fast reversible perspective	43	—	61	(−05)	—	25	16	07
Acidity of saliva (low *pH*)	−56	−33	−10	—	—	−44	—	—
Food memorization	45	00	61	13	—	—	—	07
Many figures added correctly in two minutes	—	—	61	49	—	—	—	—
High cholinesterase in serum	—	—	78	—	—	—	—	—
High body temperature	—	—	—	70	—	03	07	24
Fast tempo	—	—	66	—	—	—	—	—
Lengthy dream recall	—	48	—	—	—	—	—	—
Fast arm-shoulder tempo	—	—	—	—	—	55	01	64
Fast leg circling tempo	—	—	—	—	19	30	—	71
Faster ideomotor speed	—	—	—	—	—	—	41	35

P.U.I. 8. Mobilization vs. Regression

Independent Researches:	2	4	5	6	7	8
Low disposition rigidity (motor)	−54	(−17)	−30	−56	—	—
Many hours of sleep previous night	51	26	—	—	—	—
Large movements in myokinesis	44	—	26	23	—	—
Fast reaction time	−41	−14	—	−43	—	—
High fluency of association	07	38	—	—	—	—
Early in day	—	−21	—	—	—	—
Higher ratio accuracy to accomplishment	—	—	40	33	—	—
C+, High Ego Strength, 16 P.F. Scale	—	—	21	—	—	—
Less errors made in complex reaction time	—	—	−21	−49	—	—
Small minimum body displacement, ataxic sway	—	—	—	−29	—	—

P.U.I. 9. High Anxiety vs. Low Anxiety

Independent Researches:	3	5	6	9	10
Low cholinesterase in serum	−78	—	—	—	—
High pulse pressure	71	30	37	08	08
High basal metabolic (estimated)	59	—	—	—	—
Low initial PGR resistance	−25	−26	—	—	—
Fast rate of respiration	—	—	17	45	—
High plasma 17-hydroxycorticosteroids in blood	10	—	—	43	22
High level of anxiety (questionnaire responses only)	41	—	—	37	—
Faster heart rate	(−04)	—	51	30	20
Much lack of confidence in skill in untried performances	—	−35	—	22*	—
High level of psychiatrically evaluated anxiety	—	—	—	20	—
O4+, Higher Ergic Tension	—	40	—	—	—
−, Low Ego Strength	—	−29	—	—	—
Higher anxiety score on IPAT Verbal Anxiety scale	—	—	33	—	—
High m-OH-phenylhydracrylic	—	—	—	—	74
High m-OH-hippuric acid	—	—	—	—	74
High p-OH-hippuric acid	—	—	—	—	57
High histidine	—	—	—	—	52

grate the seven states into two broader dimensions (Figure 4.5). These dimensions are identified as general stress response and general frustration response. This description suggests that states are very much related to the ways in which we can handle stressors in everyday life. The general stress response ranges on a continuum from the ability to meet a challenge directly and effectively (though not without difficulty) implied in effort stress, to the ineffectiveness of anxiety. Thus we have in this state an active-passive continuum. The pattern of general frustration response implies a state of conflict in dealing with difficulties, leading to an inability to act effectively and resolve the cause of the stress.

Predicting Behavior: Traits versus Situations

At some point in this book it is necessary to consider an important controversy that has been gaining increased attention over recent years—a controversy no trait psychologist can choose to ignore. Because the argument as to the relative importance of traits versus situations in predicting behavior has centered mainly on tempera-

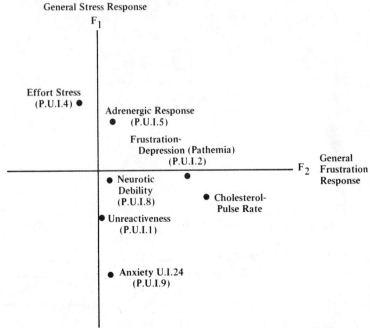

Figure 4.5 Second-order state factors (from Mefferd, 1966).

ment kinds of behavior, now is as good a time as any to briefly examine the issues involved here. Putting the issue in proper perspective requires distinguishing between the role of the environment in, say, the development of traits, where traits in this instance are the dependent variables, and the role of the environment (more specifically, a specific situation) in accounting for behavior variability or predicting behavior as opposed to traits (as independent variables).

The modern form of the controversy regarding traits versus situations in predicting temperament behavior may, without gross distortion, be said to begin with Mischel's (1968) highly influential book. In that book, Mischel argues forcefully for the position that, whereas there is considerable evidence for consistency of individual differences in abilities, that is, cross-situational consistencies in behavior, a similar state of affairs does not exist in the temperament domain. In his own words:

> Response patterns even in highly similar situations often fail to be strongly related. Individuals show far less cross-situational consistency in their behavior than has been assumed by trait-state theories. The more dissimilar the evoking situations, the less likely they are to produce similar or consistent responses from the same individual. Even seemingly trivial situational differences may reduce correlations to zero. Response consistency tends to be greatest within the same response medium, within self-reports to paper-and-pencil tests, for example, or within directly observed non-verbal behavior. Intra-individual consistency is reduced drastically when dissimilar response modes are employed. Activities that are substantially associated with aspects of intelligence and with problem solving behavior —like achievement behaviors, cognitive styles, response speed—tend to be most consistent (Mischel, 1968, p. 177).

More recently, Mischel (1973) has tempered his original stance, arguing that he does not deny the existence of traits, but, rather, that the utility of traits (and traits alone) for predicting behavior remains to be demonstrated. Undoubtedly traits do account for some of the behavior variance, but the specific situation is a powerful additional source of variability in responses that must not be forgotten. The value of Mischel's analysis is to temper the overzealous endorsement of traits by trait theorists in carrying the major burden for predicting behavior.

In fairness to trait theorists there has been at least one major researcher who has been aware of the importance of the situation in predicting behavior. Thus Cattell (1963) has outlined a rather elaborate model for incorporating both traits and situations into the specification equation (see Equation 2.2, Chapter 2). Essentially, the model involves integrating traits, roles, moods, and situations by the use of modulators, that is, distinctive weights that modulate or modify the trait scores. The total or global situation is conceptualized in terms of two components: the focal and the ambient or contextual situational aspects. Roles involve the capacity to react to the focal stimulus differently in a global situation. In this way the situation determinants (focal and ambient situation, roles) of a response are represented within the basic factor model by incorporating a series of weights or modulators that theoretically enable much more precise prediction of behavior than afforded by a consideration of only traits.

The practical utility of Cattell's elaborate mathematical models for accommodating both the person and the situation in predicting behavior remains to be seen. Mischel (1973) has been critical of such schemes, stating:

> The more moderators required to qualify a trait, the more the "trait" becomes a relatively specific description of a behavior-situation unit. That is, the more highly circumscribed, "moderated", and situation specific the trait, the more it becomes indistinguishable from a specific behavior-situation description (Mischel, 1973, p. 257).

In any case, the issue of traits versus situations in predicting behavior has now moved on to a new and more meaningful phase. Researchers in this area (e.g., Bowers, 1973; Endler, 1975) are now asking the question: What is the interaction of persons and situations in predicting behavior? Thus it is recognized that knowledge of a person's disposition to behave (traits) and the specific situation in which the behavior occurs are both necessary and interactive in predicting behavior. This more enlightened approach was actually anticipated 10 years earlier by Cattell in so far as he provided a quantitative model for dealing with person × situation interactions. Of course, interactionism as a theoretical notion has a long history within psychology (reviewed by Ekehammer, 1974), although it is only recently that formal models have been developed to test it. Cattell's solution to the person × trait interaction problem, however, has not been widely accepted, probably because of the technical complexity of his model. Still, perhaps it is time for those psychologists specifically interested in the person × situation interaction to look back to the earlier insights of Cattell and test the usefulness of his formal model.

Types Reconsidered

At the outset of this chapter the notion of types was briefly considered and dispensed with in favor of a trait approach, that is, ordering individuals along a dimension or dimensions rather than attempting to classify them into mutually exclusive categories. Because typologies of an older vintage typically involve nominal measurement, that is, classification into mutually exclusive categories, they are logically opposed to quantification of man's attributes. But one might well wonder if there are alternative conceptions of types that are compatible with a measurment or quantitative approach to individual differences.

Cattell, Coulter, and Tsujioka (1966) have considered three different usages of the type concept that are based on measurement models. Figure 4.6 illustrates the three major measurement models underlying the type concept. The polar type refers to the extremes of a normally distributed bipolar trait, where it is assumed that the trait in question is a broad one (e.g., extraversion-introversion). The modal type is defined by a clustering of individuals along a single trait continuum, where each clustering or mode represents a type. The species type is a multidimensional definition of type, where individuals are grouped into classes or types on the basis of the similarity of their profiles.

The identification of species types within a multidimensional framework is indeed a complex process as set out by Cattell et al. (1966), although the logic is not difficult to grasp. Essentially, the problem is to identify clusters of individuals by first determining the similarity of different trait profiles, where a trait profile is defined as the unique pattern of scores for a particular individual on a set of traits. Any two profiles may differ in terms of elevation (the mean of all scores in a profile), scatter (the square root of the sum of squares of the subject's deviation scores about its own mean), and shape (the residual information after equating profiles for both elevation and scatter). At first glance one might think that an appropriate strategy would be simply to correlate the various profiles. However,

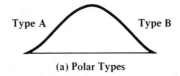

(a) Polar Types

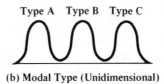

(b) Modal Type (Unidimensional)

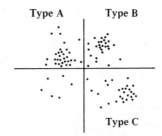

(c) Species Type (Modal Multidimensional)

Figure 4.6 The three major measurement models underlying the type concept (from Cattell, Coulter, and Tsujioka, 1966).

the properties of the correlation coefficient are such that, although it takes into account shape, it ignores elevation and scatter because it cancels out means and variances. A useful index of similarity that takes into consideration all three of the parameters along which profiles may differ is Cattell's pattern similarity coefficient (r_p). In reviewing 10 distance measures for determining the similarity between two objects, Bolz (1972) concludes that Cattell's r_p is superior for various reasons (has a known distribution, has a test for significance—Horn, 1961, etc.). The r_p is the basis for a computer program called *taxinome* for identifying temperament types. The model consists essentially of operating on a square Q matrix where persons define the rows and columns with r_ps as entries.

Although the identification of temperament types within a multitrait or multidimensional framework is still at an early stage of development, preliminary findings have been reported by Bolz (1972) illustrating the usefulness of type analysis. Using Cattell's 16 *PF* as the basis for constructing temperament profiles, Bolz identified the following six types:

> *Type One*—The men in Type One are low on factors C and F, and high on factors I, M, O, and Q. This particular pattern is very similar to the general profile of neurotics. It turns out that the composite neuroticism scale score (Cattell, Eber, and Tatsuoka, 1970) is a sten of 9.79. This is in effect saying that the men are a group of "normal neurotics". This type represented approximately six percent of the total sample.

> *Type Two*—Type Two is low on factors C, E, and F and high on factors O and Q. In other words, they are characteristically affected by feelings, have low ego strength and are humble, mild, sober, apprehensive and tense.

> *Type Three*—Type Three men are low on factors A and M, and high on factors B, C, N, Q. They are very reserved, highly intelligent, and emotionally stable, while somewhat practical, shrewd, self-sufficient and controlled.

> *Type Four*—Type Four men are notably low on factors C and G and high on factors O and Q. They are emotionally less stable, expedient, have weak super-ego strength, and are apprehensive and frustrated.

> *Type Five*—Type Five is low on factor F and high on factor A. This type of man is sober and serious but still outgoing and warmhearted.

> *Type Six*—Type Six men are low on factor E and high on factor A. These men are characteristically humble and mild but are also outgoing and warmhearted.

Future research may further explore the identification of temperament types, in which the power of structured measurement of traits may be usefully brought to bear on rejuvenating an earlier strategy in differentiating persons.

That the location of types based on traits may be applied to novel and important problems in experimental design is illustrated in a recent study by Becker (1973). The issue of concern here is the extent to which sampling bias is introduced in that typical situation in which introductory psychology students are permitted to voluntarily sign up for various experiments during the term as part of the course requirement. Working on the assumption that different personality types may be eager to sign up early and complete their experimental requirements, whereas others may be more disposed to put off signing up until the end of the term, Becker attempted to see if such differences in time of signing up were accompanied by distinguishable differences in temperament. To the extent that such differences could be found, there would be a serious sampling bias operating in such (typical) situations.

Becker employed Q technique in his analysis, that is, correlating persons across test variables. The test variables consisted of seven scales which from previous research were known to mark well-known factors. Three of the scales were measures of various aspects of the second-order factor extraversion-introversion, that is, restraint versus rhathymia *(R)*, sociability *(S)*, and thoughtfulness (of reflectiveness) *(T)*. Two of the scales measured two aspects of approval-seeking motivation: social desirability *(SD)* and social reinforcement *(SR)*. The final two scales tapped different aspects of femininity: "conscious" aspects (femininity scale or *Fe*) and "unconscious" aspects (Franck drawing completion test or *Fr*). Although the results of this study are rather complicated and difficult to summarize, five different type factors were extracted that corresponded to different points in time of signing up. Thus (say) those individuals who chose to complete their experimental requirement early in the term revealed a trait profile quite different from (say) those persons deferring signing up until the end of the term.

The importance of Becker's study is to emphasize that different and conflicting findings on a similar research problem from different universities may be due in part to differential sampling biases. Thus one investigator may conduct a study early in the term, whereas another located at a different setting may test subjects late in the term. To the extent that the dependent variable or variables are similar across studies, and to the extent that the personality types distinguishing between early and late "signer uppers" are related to the dependent variables, then in the above situation part of the conflicting results will be due to differential sampling of subjects. This problem may be circumvented by randomly assigning subjects to experiments conducted throughout the term. Becker, at the University of Winnipeg, has implemented such a procedure. It is hoped that other psychology departments will follow his lead in an area of general concern to all those researchers engaged in the study of temperament related dependent variables.

Temperament and Creativity

In the previous chapter it was noted that temperament and motivational traits are important for discriminating between creative and noncreative people. The importance of temperament and motivational factors becomes apparent once it is recalled that at relatively high levels of general intelligence, creativity and intelligence correlate virtually zero. Many researchers working in the area of creativity have thus come to place increasing importance on relating temperament to creativity, in which creative individuals are identified by actual performance (say of artists and scientists) and such ratings are made by persons knowledgeable of the specific area. In summarizing the literature in this area, Dellas and Gaier (1970) concluded

> Despite the various approaches and heterogeneity of instruments, many similarities in the results can be seen across samples differing in cultural background, eminence, and profession. Independence, manifested not only in attitudes but also in social behavior, consistently emerged as being relevant to creativity, as did dominance, introversion, openness to stimuli, and wide interests. Self-acceptance, intuitiveness, and flexibility also appeared to characterize the creatives, and though they had social presence and poise, they exhibited an asocial attitude and an unconcern for social norms. This may reflect antipathy toward anything encroaching on individuality or compelling conformance. Some of these characteristics appear more pronounced in aesthetic creativity—radicalism, rejection of external restraints—as opposed to scientific creativity; but the data reflect that the majority of these qualities appear to differentiate the creative from his noncreative counterparts. This evidence points up a common pattern of personality traits among creative persons and also that these personality factors may have some bearing on creativity in the abstract, regardless of field (p. 65).

Cattell and Butcher (1968) have investigated creative researchers using the 16 *PF*—reporting similar findings as above. The mean

Personality dimension label at lower pole	Mean stens	Plotted Mean Sten Scores 1 2 3 4 5 6 7 8 9 10	Personality dimension label at upper pole	
A — Sizothymia	3.36		Affectothymia	A +
B — Low intelligence	7.64		High intelligence	B +
C — Low ego strength	5.44		High ego strength	C +
E — Low dominance	6.62		High dominance	E +
F — Desurgency	3.15		Surgency	F +
G — Low group superego	4.10		High group superego	G +
H — Threctia	6.01		Parmia	H +
I — Harria	7.05		Premsia	I +
L — Low protension	5.36		High protension	L +
M — Prazernia	5.36		Autia	M +
N — Simplicity	5.50		Shrewdness	N +
O — Low guilt-proneness	4.38		High guilt-proneness	O +
Q₁— Conservatism	7.00		Radicalism	Q_1+
Q₂— Low self-sufficiency	7.52		High self-sufficiency	Q_2+
Q₃— Low self-sentiment	6.44		High self-sentiment	Q_3+
Q₄— Low ergic tension	4.91		High ergic tension	Q_4+

Figure 4.7 The mean 16PF profile for eminent scientists in physics, biology, and psychology (from Cattell and Butcher, 1968).

16 *PF* profile for eminent scientists in physics, biology, and psychology is illustrated in Figure 4.7, where extreme sten scores are the factors of interest. Thus in Cattell's terminology, creative scientists tend to be more sizothyme $(A-)$, more intelligent $(B+)$, more dominant $(E+)$, more inhibited or desurgent $(F-)$, more emotionally sensitive $(I+)$, more radical (Q_1+), and more self-sufficient (Q_2+). With respect to second-order temperament factors, the creative researcher is found to be lower on all those primaries involved in extraversion. This finding of high introversion for creative scientists is explained by Cattell and Butcher in terms of information theory and brain action:

> As long as you use a lot of the channels for input, you have too few free channels for scanning. That could explain a good deal here. The typical extravert conceivably has too many channels taking in information—or at least, alert to the external trivia of everyday life—and not enough for scanning accepted material. Or, to quote Wordsworth instead of information theory: 'The world is too much with us.' And if we paraphrase his next line: 'Talking and visiting, we lay waste our powers' (p. 279).

Important in Cattell's concern with creativity is *prediction*. Thus he and Butcher have developed various specification equations (see Chapter 2 and Equation 2.2) for predicting creativity in various fields, in which factors from the abilities, temperament, and dynamic motivation domains are all thought to be of equal importance. Related to this work is the concern for predicting school achievement on the basis of traits from various domains.

Cattell, Eysenck, and Guilford: Similarities and Contrasts

To conclude this chapter it may be of value to point to some similarities and contrasts between three of the major multivariate people who have done work on temperament. Whereas Guilford's (1959a) approach may be termed largely taxonomic, that is, identifying the major temperament traits, Eysenck goes much beyond description in attempting to explain individual differences. Cattell's work has also involved considerable theory, drawing from such areas as learning and genetics in accounting for individual differences in traits. Cattell and Guilford share a similar conviction—that it is the primary or first-order factors which are of prime interest. Eysenck (Eysenck and Eysenck, 1969) has argued strongly that the temperament factors at the primary level are not sufficiently replicable to warrant serious attention. One must turn to higher-order factors which have some breadth to adequately demonstrate the invariance of factors, that is, replication across different investigators. Cattell and Eysenck share certain common characteristics in terms of strategy. Cohen (1966) has identified the following:

1. Both value procedures in proportion to their objectivity.

2. Both have identified extraversion and neuroticism as major dimensions.

3. Both stress hereditary factors in explaining individual differences, although both recognize the importance of environmental influences as well.

4. Both emphasize the need for basing clinical psychology on an adequate taxonomy of traits. In addition to the above, Howarth (1971) lists the following:

1. Both share a solid grounding in science, both having been thoroughly trained in chemistry and physics, which leads them to be nomothetic and quantitative.

2. Both were trained in the same department of psychology at the University of London.

3. Both are empiricists and neither has been content to sit in an armchair. "Active exploration" of the world of behavioral observation is the keynote.

For a more detailed discussion of the contrasts and similarities of Cattell and Eysenck in aspects of their work other than the temperament domain, see Howarth (1971).

FURTHER READING

Cattell, R. B. *Personality and mood by questionnaire.* San Francisco: Jossey-Bass, 1973.

Dreger, R. M. (Ed.). *Multivariate personality research: Contributions to the understanding of personality in honor of Raymond B. Cattell.* Claitor Press, 1971.

Eysenck, H. J. *The biological basis of personality.* Springfield, Illinois: Charles C. Thomas, 1967.

Guilford, J. P. *Personality.* New York: McGraw-Hill, 1959a.

Wiggens, J. S. *Personality and prediction: Principles of personality assessment.* Reading, Massachusetts: Addison-Wesley, 1973.

Chapter 5

MOTIVATION

Motivational traits can be defined as those that involve some element of goal directedness. Individual differences in motivation appear in terms of variability in strength of response or perseverance of response toward the goal object. This area of study includes research on values, needs, interests, and attitudes. Values involve preferential modes of behaving either as a means directed toward the attainment of some goal or as an end itself. Needs are the basic (largely biological) driving force behind our patterns of interest and our attitudes. Interests and attitudes involve the cultural (environmental) channeling of these biologically based needs and drives. Interests have been of less factor analytic interest (although Guilford, 1959a, has summarized some of the literature on the factor analysis of interests), possibly because they are of a high degree of specificity in most cases, such as those factors involved in vocational interest patterns. The search for broader patterns of interest by factor-analytic techniques, however, has been carried out to some extent. At present, we can define groupings that correspond to factors such as "liking for adventure versus security" or "liking for variety" or "reflectiveness" and "scientific interest" or "business interest" in the vocational area (Guilford, 1959a, Chap. 17). A recent factor analysis of the Strong vocational interest blank for men revealed seven principal factors (Navran and Posthuima, 1970). Attitudes have aroused more factor-analytic interest, however, possibly because of the psychological breadth as well as the social implications of such patterns as liberalism versus conservatism.

TABLE 5.1
Major Ergs and Sentiments Found in Adults and Children
(from Horn, 1966b)

Erg or Sentiment	Major Attitudes Begin Each With "I Want"	Adult	Children
Security-fear erg	More protection from nuclear weapons	48	
	To reduce accidents and diseases	33	22
	To stop powers that threaten our nation	38	
	To go to mother when things go wrong		43
	To be at home safe		38
	To grow up normally		31
Mating (sex) erg	To love a person I find attractive	52	
	To see movies, TV shows, etc.		
	with love interest	34	
	To satisfy mating needs	52	
	To enjoy fine foods, desserts, drinks	37	38
	To spend time with opposite sex		38
	To dress to impress opposite sex		32
	To go to parties where couples are invited		
Assertive erg	To increase salary and status	36	
	To excel fellows in chosen pursuits	40	
	To dress smartly and command respect	40	20
	To maintain good reputation	33	34
	To read more comics		39
	To see that my team wins		
Protective erg	Proud parents who do not lack needs	47	
	To insure that children get good education	40	
	To help distressed adults and children	40	
	To help spouse avoid drudgeries	33	
	To take care of pet		38
	Siblings to mind me		38

Table 5.1 (cont'd)

Sensuality erg (also called narcism)	To enjoy drinking and smoking	38	
	To enjoy fine foods, desserts, delicacies	41	
	To sleep late, take it easy	31	
	To enjoy own company	37	
	To eat well		32
	To have more holidays		41
Curosity erg	To listen to music	37	
	To know more science	29	
	To enjoy graphic arts and theater	40	37
	To make my pictures beautiful		29
Gregarious erg (sports sentiment)	To actively participate in sports	50	
	To follow team and be a rooter	48	
	To spend time in companionship with others	23	28
	To play games with friends		36
	To go to parties where couples are invited		38
Pugnacity erg	To destroy powers that threaten our nation	42	
	To see violence in movies and TV shows	20	37
	To get even with others		
Appeal erg	To heed parents and turn to them in need	39	37
Parental-religious sentiment	To feel in touch with God or similar principle	55	
	Proud parents who do not lack needs	47	
	Influence of religion to increase	60	
Construction erg	Take things apart, see how they work		38
	To make projects in school		33
Narcissism erg	To have attractive face and figure		32
	Nice clothes to wear		31
Self-sentiment	To control impulses and mental processes	40	32
	Never to damage self respect	35	27

Sentiment / Item		
To excel in my line of work	38	
To maintain good reputation	37	34
Never to become insane	39	
To be responsible, in charge of things	31	
To know about science, art, literature	31	
To know more about myself	33	
To grow up normally		28
Superego sentiment		
To satisfy sense of duty to church, parents, etc.	41	
Never to be selfish in my acts	41	
To avoid sinful expression of sex needs	33	
To avoid drinking, gambling—i.e., "vice"	21	31
To maintain good self control	28	28
To admire and respect father		34
Religious sentiment		
To worship God		33
To go to church		
Career sentiment		
To learn skills required for job	34	
To continue with present career plans	33	
To increase salary and status	27	
Sweetheart Sentiment		
To bring gifts to sweetheart	51	
To spend time with sweetheart	41	

The Study of Needs

Cattell has developed a model which he refers to as the *dynamic lattice* (see Figure 5.1) to interrelate attitudes (organized into broader categories referred to as sentiments) and ergs (which are commonly known as needs and drives). The model should be read from left to right; attitudes are subsidiary to sentiments, which in turn are subsidiary to ergs. By subsidiary it is meant that certain elements serve as means to the ends of others. Interests are not explicitly a part of the model, but attitudes involve the more overt, action-oriented expressions of interests. Using the M.A.T. (motivation analysis test), Cattell has been able to assess the major ergs and sentiments by the questionnaire method. A more complete list of ergs and sentiments found in adults and children is derived from Horn (1966) (see Table 5.1).

The study of needs, of course, has a history which dates back long before Cattell. Freud, for example, based psychoanalytic theory on motivation. It can be said that one of the major shortcomings of the Freudian theory was that it tried to derive too many behavioral functions from too few drives (eros and thanatos or life instinct and death instinct). Freud's contem-

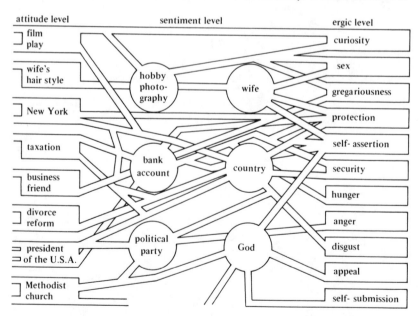

Figure 5.1 A portion of the dynamic lattice, showing the relationship between ergs, attitudes, and sentiments (from Cattell, 1965).

poraries attempted to correct this shortcoming. Thus McDougall developed his inventory of instincts which came under considerable unjustified criticism because of the term itself, connoting the rigid, unlearned behavioral patterns of lower animals. Murray developed a list of needs from clinical observation which is still widely used today and finds expression in major questionnaire types of tests such as Jackson's Personality Research Form or P.R.F. (see Table 5.2).

Table 5.2
Brief Description of Needs Assessed by
Jackson's Personality Research Form
(from Jackson, 1967)

Scale	Description of High Scorer
Abasement	Shows a high degree of humility; accepts blame and criticism even when not deserved; exposes himself to situations where he is in an inferior position; tends to be self-effacing.
Achievement	Aspires to accomplish difficult tasks; maintains high standards and is willing to work toward distant goals; responds positively to competition; willing to put forth effort to attain excellence.
Affiliation	Enjoys being with friends and people in general; accepts people readily, makes efforts to win friendships and maintain associations with people.
Aggression	Enjoys combat and argument; easily annoyed; sometimes willing to hurt people to get his way; may seek to "get even" with people whom he perceives as having harmed him.
Autonomy	Tries to break away from restraints, confinement, or restrictions of any kind; enjoys being unattached, free, not tied to people, places, or obligations; may be rebellious when faced with restraints.
Change	Likes new and different experiences; dislikes routine and avoids it; may readily change opinions or values in different circumstances; adapts readily to changes in environment.
Cognitive structure	Does not like ambiguity or uncertainty in information; wants all questions answered completely; desires to make decisions based on definite knowledge, rather than on guesses or probabilities.
Defendence	Readily suspects that people mean him harm or are against him; ready to defend himself at all times; takes offense easily; does not accept criticism readily.

Table 5.2 (cont'd)

Dominance	Attempts to control his environment, and to influence or direct other people; expresses opinions forcefully; enjoys the role of leader and may assume it spontaneously.
Endurance	Willing to work long hours; doesn't give up quickly on a problem; persevering, even in the face of great difficulty; patient and unrelenting in his work habits.
Exhibition	Wants to be the center of attention; enjoys having an audience; engages in behavior which wins the notice of others; may enjoy being dramatic or witty.
Harmavoidance	Does not enjoy exciting activities, especially if danger is involved; avoids risk of bodily harm; seeks to maximize personal safety.
Impulsivity	Tends to act on the "spur of the moment" and without deliberation; gives vent readily to feelings and wishes; speaks freely; may be volatile in emotional expression.
Nurturance	Gives sympathy and comfort; assists others whenever possible, interested in caring for children, the disabled, or the infirm; offers a "helping hand" to those in need; readily performs favors for others.
Order	Concerned with keeping personal effects and surroundings neat and organized; dislikes clutter, confusion, lack of organization; interested in developing methods for keeping materials methodically organized.
Play	Does many things "just for fun," spends a good deal of time participating in games, sports, social activities, and other amusements; enjoys jokes and funny stories; maintains a light-hearted, easy-going attitude toward life.
Sentience	Notices smells, sounds, sights, tastes, and the way things feel; remembers these sensations and believes that they are an important part of life; is sensitive to many forms of experience; may maintain an essentially hedonistic or aesthetic view of life.
Social recognition	Desires to be held in high esteem by acquaintances; concerned about reputation and what other people think of him; works for the approval and recognition of others.
Succorance	Frequently seeks the sympathy, protection, love, advice, and reassurance of other people; may feel insecure or helpless without such support; confides difficulties readily to a receptive person.
Understanding	Wants to understand many areas of knowledge; values synthesis of ideas, verifiable generalization, logical thought, particularly when directed at satisfying intellectual curiosity.

In spite of the fact that observers such as Murray have been able to compile meaningful lists of human needs from clinical observation (see Table 5.3), we still need factor analysis. Factor analysis enables us to determine the number of needs and the nature of these needs. For example, the P.R.F. questionnaire (Table 5.2) does not yield separate estimates for all the needs hypothesized by Murray. It is evident that some of these needs simply collapse into others, and factor analysis has again served its function of avoiding needless redundancy. Thus the trait of deference can be accounted for by other factors such as succorance and harmavoidance; rejection can be accounted for by autonomy and aggression. It is difficult to imagine a semantic analysis of Murray's inventory that would be capable of determining which traits were, in fact, redundant.

Motivation Component Research

One of the major contributions of Cattell and co-workers is their motivation component research. This approach to the study of motivation has not been systematically developed by investigators other than Cattell and his colleagues. Motivation component research assumes that a motive (need, drive, erg, etc.), whether of major or minor importance, can be expressed in a variety of ways. That is, it has a number of outlets or vehicles of expression. These vehicles can be assessed through various objective test devices.

Five of the major motivational components are presented in Table 5.4, as outlined by Horn (1966b). The parallel between these and Freudian concepts is quite striking. The alpha component is referred to as conscious id. Although seemingly a contradiction, because the Freudian id was assumed to be unconscious, the term actually denotes the conscious expression of wishes and desires. It is the latter to which the concept of id applies. The conscious aspect of this factor is seen clearly in the first loading, preferences. This measure involves readiness to admit preferences for a certain course of action in pursuit of the goals implied by a motive. The wish-fulfillment aspect of id functioning can be seen in reasoning distortion. This involves a tendency to see inept planning toward a goal as truly effective. The beta component is analogous to Freudian ego expression. It is indicative of reality-oriented striving to satisfy the wishes of the id. Thus a person with a high score on this factor will be resistant to auditory distractions when he is attending to interest-related material (Table 5.4). He will also tend to be relatively well informed concerning a required course of action to attain his goals,

TABLE 5.3
Major Needs Proposed by Murray and Used in
Subsequent Questionnaire Development
(from Goldberg, 1970)

Major Manifest Needs (20)	Trait Descriptive Terms	Original Items	EPPS	ACL	CPI (Hase)	AI	PRF
Abasement	Submissive, acquiescent, passive	10	X	X		X	X
Achievement	Ambitious, competitive, aspiring	10	X	X	X	X	X
Affiliation	Friendly, sociable, good-natured	20	X	X	X	X	X
Aggression	Argumentative, critical, severe	15	X	X		X	X
Autonomy	Independent, defiant, stubborn	10	X	X	X	X	X
Counteraction	Resolute, determined, adventurous	20				X	
Deference	Deferent, respectful, compliant	10	X	X	X	X	
Defendance	Self-defensive, self-vindictive	10				X	X
Dominance	Assertive, forceful, decisive	10	X	X	X	X	X
Exhibition	Dramatic, conspicuous	20	X	X	X	X	X
Harmavoidance	Fearful, timid, cautious, careful	10			X	X	X
Infavoidance	Sensitive, shy, nervous	20				X	
Nurturance	Sympathetic, gentle, protective	20	X	X	X	X	X
Order	Organized, clean, neat, precise		X	X	X	X	X
Play	Playful, easygoing, jolly	10			X	X	X
Rejection	Exclusive, aloof, discriminating	20					
Sentience	Sensuous, sensitive, aesthetic	20				X	X
Sex	Erotic, sensual, seductive	10	X	X		X	X
Succorance	Dependent, helpless, forlorn	20	X	X		X	X
Understanding	Intellectual, curious, logical	20			X	X	X

and he will learn new material to serve this end quite readily. The gamma component represents superego functioning, that is, how goals "ought" to be pursued. "Superego projection" consists of the misperception of others having one's own righteous beliefs or values pertaining to the gratification of goals. This vehicle is certainly directly related to the concept of superego. Others fit the concept, although not as directly. For example, availability: association vehicles refer to a readiness to make verbal associations with interest-related material, whether guided by a cue or not (oriented versus unoriented). Perseveration refers to pursuit of a goal even if this behavior is maladaptive.

The remaining motivational components include: the delta component, representing the physiological need expression as a result of present deviation of physiological state from homeostasis; the epsilon component, referring to expression associated with unconscious memories; the zeta component, involving unconscious id expression; and the eta component, referring to stimulation level from surrounding incentives. The general finding of positive manifold among devices led to the search for possible higher-order motivational components. Three second-order component factors have been identified. These include: general integrated expression, marked by beta and gamma components and involving interest in reality-oriented striving which is largely learned; general unorganized id, marked by alpha, epsilon, and delta components and referring to unintegrated and unconscious expression; and a less clearly defined factor called general physiological autonomic involvement.

Motivation components can be conceptualized in two ways. They can be thought of as *general* attributes of the person, expressing how he generally approaches the problem of gratification of goals. Thus some persons, for example, may be more oriented toward wish-fulfillment in a relatively maladaptive manner (alpha), others may be oriented toward concerns with how goals ought to be realized (gamma), and still others may be realistically oriented toward satisfaction of motives (beta). Motivation components could also be thought of as applying to the expression of any *specific* motive. A given goal could be pursued by any one (or a combination) of the sets of vehicles or motivational components.

Table 5.4
The Primary Motivational Components Discovered by Cattell and Co-workers (from Horn, 1966b)

	Alpha	Beta	Gamma	Delta	Epsilon	Zeta	Eta
Preferences	43		49				
Autism	37		30				
Reasoning distortion: means-ends, ends-means	49						
Fantasy: choice to explain and read	45		30				
Identification preference	51						
Defensive reticence	31						
Defensive fluency	27						
Naïve projection	37						
Guilt sensitivity	32						
Utilities choice	45						
Persistence: motor activity	32						
Id projection	38						
Perceptual closure	37						
Attention: auditory distraction	41	40					
Information		26					
Learning		37					
Memory for rewards		35					
Warm-up in learning		31					
Fantasy: time ruminating		39					
Control		21					
Warm-up in learning		31					
Fantasy time ruminating		39					
Control		21					
Availability: unoriented association	31		47				
Availability: oriented association			51				
Reasoning distortion: analogies			38				
Selective perception			38				
Expectancy: effort to be expended			23				
Perseveration: low perceptual integration			32				
Fantasy sentence completion			38				
Superego projection			38				
Availability: unoriented association	31		47				
Availability: oriented association			51				
Reasoning distortion: analogies			38				
Selective perception			38				
Expectancy: effort to be expended			23				
Perseveration: low perceptual integration			32				
Fantasy: sentence completion			38				
Superego projection			38				
Threat reactivity: cardiovascular				43			
Threat reactivity: psychogalvanic				51			
Conflict involvement: slow decisions				42			
Reminiscence					54		
Defense against recall					40		
Availability: speed association					35		
Impulsiveness: decision speed						38	
Impulsiveness: agreement speed						48	
Decision strength						52	
Fluency on cues							33
Persistence: perceptual task							43

Adjustment Process Analysis Chart

Aside from determining structure in the area of motivation, as in the dynamic lattice and motivation components, we can also consider the role of motivational factors (particularly ergs) in overall

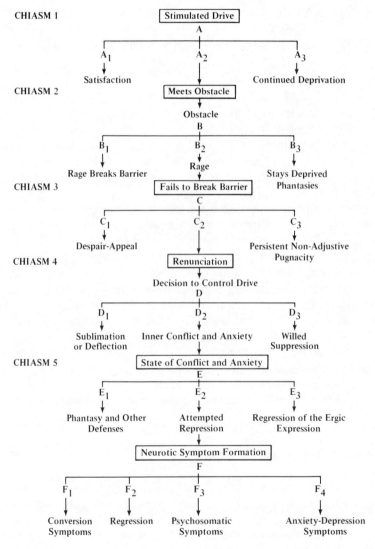

Figure 5.2 A simplified model of the adjustment process analysis chart (from Cattell, 1965).

adjustment to the environment. Cattell's model representing this situation is referred to as the adjustment process analysis chart (Figure 5.2). The model tends to parallel clinical and psychoanalytic thinking in this area, and it points to the history of expression for a given drive or what its path of expression might be as a result of various encounters with the environment. Thus, satisfaction of the drive is the desired goal, but obstacles can lead to displaced energy expressed in behavior ranging from "normal" expressions, such as phantasy or rage, through to neurotic symptom formation.

Future Motivation Research

The area of motivation research, from a factor-analytic perspective, is fairly recent and has received little attention aside from the research of Cattell and his co-workers. Thus it lags behind the study of both temperament and mental abilities in terms of the development of the structural models and theory. Various aspects of this area are in need of further development. In particular, we need to know the mechanism by which the biological energy of ergs is transformed into various interests and attitudes (sentiments). This may require further research into developmental processes, such as identification, which are involved in socialization of the child. Questions arise here such as whether the success of the socialization processes (in creating interests and attitudes) is in turn dependent on early individual differences in temperament or the strength of ergs. We also need to know the mechanism by which motivation components (alpha, beta, gamma, etc.) are formed. Although the present state of motivation research cannot answer these questions, it has provided a framework of concepts necessary for further investigations. Moreover, it has provided us with questionnaires (e.g., Cattell's M.A.T. and Jackson's P.R.F.) that are of applied value in clinical and counselling settings.

Individual Differences in Values

Much has been written on values from sociological, anthropological, philosophical, and religious perspectives. Although there exists within psychology considerable research effort geared toward greater understanding of the nature and role of human values, this interest in values is relatively small when compared to such related topics as attitudes. Thus Rokeach (1973) has noted that between the years 1961 and 1965, for every study on values indexed in *Psychological Abstracts* there were five or six studies on attitudes. This situation seems rather incongruous with Rokeach's belief that values are much more important than attitudes in terms of being relatively broad and pervasive psychological constructs that affect a wide range of behaviors.

The study of values from a measurement perspective goes back to 1931 when Allport and Vernon (1931) constructed a test to measure six basic values originally postulated by the German philosopher Spranger (1928). The six values were:

Theoretical—interest in the pursuit of truth by intellectual means.

Economic—interest in the useful, practical things.

Aesthetic—interest in beauty and art.

Social—interest in helping people.

Political—interest in power or influence over people.

Religious—interest in mystical experience.

In the Allport-Vernon study of values the dimensions were arrived at in a rational way, that is, there was no attempt to comprehensively sample the value domain and then employ factor analysis as a means of identifying the major nonoverlapping constructs. In an early study Lurie (1937) factor analyzed a 144-item test that was based on Spranger's original six values. He found four basic factors: social (interest in human relations), philistine (interest in utility and power), theoretical (interest in truth and cognitive values), and religious (interest in the spiritual side of life); as well as three lesser factors: openmindedness (interest in theoretical and social values), practicality (interest in economic, political, and social values), and esthetic (interest in people as spectators rather than as participants).

Several investigators have factored the original Allport-Vernon value scales, and results indicate that this scale could be reduced to a smaller number of more basic values; in other words, the original six scales are overlapping. Thus Duffy and Crissy (1940) found three factors (philistine, interest-in-people, and theoretical); Ferguson, Humphreys, and Strong (1941) found four factors (esthetic, theoretical, religious-social, and political); and, more recently, Sciortino (1970) found three factors (esthetic, social, and religious). In the Sciortino study, 77% of the total variance is accounted for by three factors, and each one contributes approximately in equal amount to the common variance. We can conclude from these findings that the Allport-Vernon value scales are measuring at the most only three or four value factors.

TABLE 5.5
Rokeach's Terminal and Instrumental Values with Test-Retest
Reliabilities Indicated (from Rokeach, 1973)

Terminal Value	r	Instrumental Value	r
A comfortable life (a prosperous life)	.70	Ambitious (hard-working, aspiring)	.70
An exciting life (a stimulating, active life)	.73	Broadminded (open-minded)	.57
A sense of accomplishment (lasting contribution)	.51	Capable (competent, effective)	.51
A world at peace (free of war and conflict)	.67	Cheerful (lighthearted, joyful)	.65
A world of beauty (beauty of nature and the arts)	.66	Clean (neat, tidy)	.66
Equality (brotherhood, equal opportunity for all)	.71	Courageous (standing up for your beliefs)	.52
Family security (taking care of loved ones)	.64	Forgiving (willing to pardon others)	.62
Freedom (independence, free choice)	.61	Helpful (working for the welfare of others)	.66
Happiness (contentedness)	.62	Honest (sincere, truthful)	.62
Inner harmony (freedom from inner conflict)	.65	Imaginative (daring, creative)	.69
Mature love (sexual and spiritual intimacy)	.68	Independent (self-reliant, self-sufficient)	.60
National security (protection from attack)	.67	Intellectual (intelligent, reflective)	.67
Pleasure (an enjoyable, leisurely life)	.57	Logical (consistent, rational)	.57
Salvation (saved, eternal life)	.88	Loving (affectionate, tender)	.65
Self-respect (self-esteem)	.58	Obedient (dutiful, respectful)	.53
Social recognition (respect, admiration)	.65	Polite (courteous, well-mannered)	.53
True friendship (close companionship)	.59	Responsible (dependable, reliable)	.45
Wisdom (a mature understanding of life)	.60	Self-controlled (restrained, self-disciplined)	.52

A comprehensive research program on the nature of human values is reflected by Rokeach's (1968, 1973) work. Rokeach considers the concept of value as one of the most important within psychology—deserving far more attention by psychologists than has been the case. According to Rokeach (1973), a value is "an enduring belief that a specific mode of conduct or end-state of existence is personally or socially preferable to an opposite or converse mode of conduct or end-state of existence" (p. 5). An important distinction to note here is that a value may refer to a mode of conduct or an end-state of existence; that is, there are instrumental and terminal values, respectively. The Allport-Vernon values deal mainly with terminal values. Rokeach has devised an inventory of 18 values of each type, illustrated in Table 5.5. This set of 36 values has been factor analyzed, resulting in seven factors (see Table 5.6).

The seven value factors reported by Rokeach (1973) have been found in both black and white subpopulations, as well as in male and female groups. The total amount of variance accounted for by these seven factors is around 40%—indicating that much of the variance cannot be accounted for by the major factors. This finding leads Rokeach to conclude that "the 36 terminal and instrumental values are not readily reducible to some smaller number" (p. 48). Although this is true, the next step in such a research program, a step which

TABLE 5.6
Factor-Analytic Structure of Values (from Rokeach, 1973)

Factor	Highest Positive Loadings		Highest Negative Loadings		Percent of Variance
1. Immediate versus delayed gratification	A comfortable life	(.69)	Wisdom	(−.56)	
	Pleasure	(.62)	Inner harmony	(−.41)	
	Clean	(.47)	Logical	(−.34)	8.2
	An exciting life	(.41)	Self-controlled	(−.33)	
2. Competence versus religious morality	Logical	(.53)	Forgiving	(−.64)	
	Imaginative	(.45)	Salvation	(−.56)	
	Intellectual	(.44)	Helpful	(−.39)	7.8
	Independent	(.43)	Clean	(−.34)	
3. Self-constriction versus self-expansion	Obedient	(.52)	Broadminded	(−.56)	
	Polite	(.50)	Capable	(−.51)	5.5
	Self-controlled	(.37)			
	Honest	(.34)			
4. Social versus personal orientation	A world at peace	(.61)	True friendship	(−.49)	
	National security	(.58)	Self-respect	(−.48)	5.4
	Equality	(.43)			
	Freedom	(.40)			
5. Societal versus family security	A world of beauty	(.58)	Family security	(−.50)	
	Equality	(.39)	Ambitious	(−.43)	
	Helpful	(.36)	Responsible	(−.33)	5.0
	Imaginative	(.30)	Capable	(−.32)	
6. Respect versus love	Social recognition	(.49)	Mature love	(−.68)	
	Self-respect	(.32)	Loving	(−.60)	4.9
7. Inner- versus other-directed	Polite	(.34)	Courageous	(−.70)	
			Independent	(−.33)	4.0

Rokeach does not take, would be to go back and construct scales that could account for a greater proportion of the total variance. Recalling from Chapter 2 that the total variance is equal to the common, specific, and error variance, a useful strategy is to attempt to "convert" some of the specific and error variance into common variance by a reworking of the original variables that went into the factor analysis.

Values and Political Ideologies

The use of factor analysis in gaining a better understanding of values and political ideologies is reflected in Eysenck's (1954) work on psychology and politics. Eysenck carried out a factor analysis of various temperament measures and political values and came up with a two-dimensional model (see Figure 5.3) consisting of tough-minded versus tender-minded (T) and radicalism-conservatism (R). The T factor was hypothesized to consist of a projection of the higher-order factor of extroversion and introversion in the area of social attitudes, in which the extrovert corresponds to the tough-minded type and the introvert to the tender-minded type. The R factor was interpreted as being defined by radical attitudes (e.g., communist leanings, favoring easy divorce, birth control, and evolution) as opposed to conservative attitudes (e.g., patriotic, favoring religion, capital punishment, law and order). Eysenck has developed a social attitude inventory for measuring both T and R factors and has been able to locate empirically communist, fascist, socialist, convervative, and liberal groups within his two-coordinate model. Each of these ideologies may in turn be viewed as higher-order constructs that subsume lower-level attitudes which in turn subsume opinions. The latter view of the structure of attitudes is represented in Figure 5.4, in which conservativism as an ideology is represented.

A recent two-value theory of political ideology has been offered by Rokeach (1973) which grew out of a growing dissatisfaction of the liberalism-conservativism continuum as a basis for locating differing political ideologies. The major problem with the liberalism-conservativism dimension is whether it is sufficiently unambiguous to distinguish adequately between major political ideologies. For example, is communism more liberal than socialism? Is fascism more conservative than capitalism? Clearly, these questions cannot be answered in an unequivocal way unless we agree on what we mean by liberalism and conservativism. To avoid needless arguments stemming

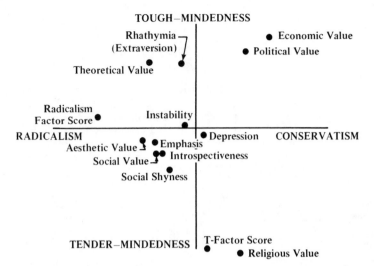

Figure 5.3 Relationship between radicalism, tough-mindedness, social values, and extraversion (from Eysenck, 1954).

from the meaning of liberalism and conservativism, Rokeach has offered a useful conceptual model that cuts across this morass. Essentially, Rokeach believes that it is much more useful to classify political ideologies on the basis of variation in two underlying orthogonal value dimensions—equality and freedom. Because each of these values may be high or low, the resulting model is a four-quadrant scheme for locating different political ideologies (see Figure 5.5).

Communism is the high-equality–low-freedom quadrant of Figure 5.5; the high-equality–high-freedom quadrant yields socialism; the low-equality–high-freedom underlies capitalism, and the low-equality–low-freedom values are inherent in fascism. Rokeach has empirically confirmed this model using a variety of techniques. For example, he had judges conduct a content analysis on the writings of socialists, Hitler, Goldwater, and Lenin (the three specific authors were representative of fascist, capitalistic, and communistic political ideologies, respectively). What the judges did was to rate each sample of writing on various values; freedom and equality accounted for 45% of the various values mentioned and were thus most important in distinguishing between the four political ideologies. These findings, as well as others, bear out Rokeach's two-value model of political ideologies.

One criticism one could make of Rokeach's model is that his terminology confounds both economic systems and political systems.

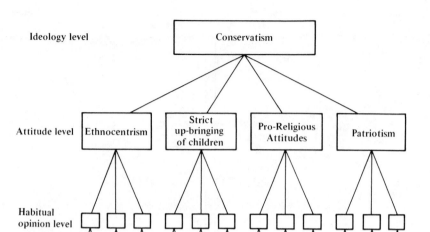

Figure 5.4 The hierarchical structure of the attitude conservativism (from Eysenck, 1954).

Thus although fascism refers to a political philosophy, communism and capitalism refer to economic systems. Democracy, which is a political philosophy, is excluded in Rokeach's system, and it cannot be included by simply equating it with capitalism, because socialism may also be democratically oriented. Part of the problem here is the meaning of the values of freedom and equality. For example, equality can refer to political equality, that is, equal rights before the courts, or, on the other hand, equal distribution of the goods and services of a nation. Further clarification of Rokeach's values underlying the various political ideologies is required to more adequately distinguish between them.

An interesting application of factor analysis to the area of values and ideology has been carried out by Eckhardt and Alcock (1970). Working out of the Canadian Peace Research Institute (CPRI) in Oakville, Ontario, Canada, these researchers have in part been actively trying to gain a greater understanding of the psychological aspects of war. The breadth of this work is impressive and beyond the scope of the present discussion; we confine our attention to the Eckhardt and Alcock (1970) study as representative of CPRI. In this study, factor analysis was employed as a means of testing the idea that there is a significant relationship between personality or temperament and values or ideologies. After arriving at eleven primary

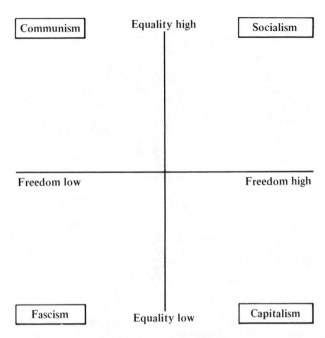

Figure 5.5 A freedom-equality model of political variations (from Rokeach, 1973).

personality factors and seven primary ideological factors, these were in turn factor analyzed, yielding five second-order factors. Of particular interest to the authors were the first two second-order factors, punitiveness and responsibility, since these were most closely related to war/peace attitudes (see Figure 5.6) First-order factors loading punitiveness included the ideological factors of militarism, religiosity, conservativism, nationalism, and less knowledge of foreign affairs; as well as the personality or temperament factors of extraversion, misanthropy, and strict childhood discipline. This second-order factor was labeled punitiveness because of the apparent punitive attitudes expressed in relation to other people. The second-order factor of responsibility was marked by the ideological factors of political and international responsibility, as well as the personality factors of lack of neuroticism, lack of misanthropy, permissive childhood discipline (as recalled), social responsibility, and empathy. Expressions of a sense of responsibility in relation to other people seemed to be the underlying common element in these factors.

These second-order "ideo-affective" factors give support to the hypothesis that personality and ideology are intimately related at

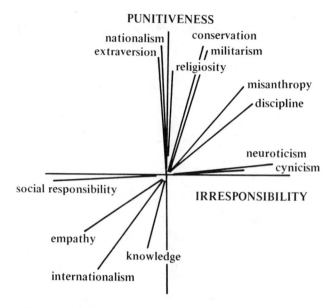

Figure 5.6   Relationship between primary factors and second-order factors of punitiveness and irresponsibility (from Eckardt & Alcock, 1970).

higher levels of analysis. Because they thought that factoring the five second-order factors would yield additional insights, Eckardt and Alcock found a third-order factor marked by punitiveness and responsibility which they called compassion-compulsion—a higher order value dimension. This factor was interpreted as follows:

> The *general value of compulsion is a function of an arbitrary, dogmatic, hypocritical, and/or unduly restrictive culture. Conversely, the general value of compassion would be hypothesized to be a function and expression of a more permissive and more rational culture* (p. 112, original emphasis).

The work of Eckardt and Alcock is important because it exemplifies a continuing research program that has made extensive use of the factor analytic methodology in undertaking peace research.

FURTHER READING:

Cattell, R. B., & Child, D. *Motivation and dynamic structure.* New York: Halsted Press, 1975.

Eysenck, H. J. (Ed.). *Experiments in motivation.* Oxford: Pergamon Press, 1964.

Chapter 6

DEVELOPMENT OF DIMENSIONS OF INDIVIDUAL DIFFERENCES

In this chapter, we are concerned with ontogenetic, or age-related changes in dimensions of individual differences (or traits or factors). Early approaches to considering developmental questions focused on obtaining age *differences* on psychological variables. This view was largely concerned with observing people of different ages at one point in time and noting significant differences on the traits of interest. More recently, researchers have come to realize that to study developmental phenomena adequately, it is necessary to observe the same people (or at least those born at the same point in historical time) at various subsequent points in time or at various ages. This strategy enables the developmental researcher to focus explicitly on age-related change in traits, which should, after all, constitute the very heart of any developmental study. In other words, questions of development must be framed as questions of change, for the very word development carries with it the notion of change (e.g., changes in physical dimensions such as height and weight, and changes in psychological dimensions such as abilities and temperament). Each of these two approaches to developmental questions have been closely identified with the two main research designs in this area. Thus obtaining measures on psychological variables at the same time for different persons at different ages is known as the cross-sectional design. Here one is concerned with age differences. The longitudinal design typically involves obtaining measures of the same people at various points in time, and therefore at different ages. Here one is concerned with age changes. The advantages and disadvantages of each of these research strategies is examined in a subsequent section of this chapter.

In considering age-related change of traits, it should be noted that much of the present research is descriptive rather than explanatory. That is to say, noting changes in traits as a function of age, and then "explaining" such changes as being due to age, does not suffice as an adequate explanation of such changes. What is necessary for an adequate explanation of developmental or age-related change is to consider the relationship of change to influences such as learning-experiential-environmental variables and genetic-biological-maturational variables. Each of these broad explanatory influences is considered in subsequent chapters. Although the ultimate aim of any scientific investigation should be to "explain" a given phenomena, obtaining reliable descriptive data is a necessary prerequisite. In other words, a concern with obtaining an adequate description of age-related change is an important first step toward explaining such change, because one must first have a consistent phenomena before attempting an explanation. Thus the importance of descriptive studies of development should not be underestimated.

In considering the descriptive study of age-related change in traits, we can discriminate whether the changes are qualitative or quantitative in nature. By qualitative change, we mean a change brought about by a reorganization of the traits such that the number of factors in a given domain has changed and/or that the nature or meaning of them has changed. In other words, qualitative change involves structural changes of factors such that the factors at time t_1 are not the same as the factors at time t_2. Indices for qualitative change include changes in factor loadings and/or changes in the interfactor correlations. By quantitative change, we mean a change in the level or amount of a factor, the nature or meaning of which is assumed to remain invariant or constant across time. In other words, quantitative changes in factors involve an increase or decrease in the factor scores, where the essential meaning of the factor, as given by the factor loadings, remains unaltered. Establishing that a factor has essentially the same meaning across different ages introduces some rather complex methodological issues that are technically too demanding to be considered here.

The distinction between qualitative (or structural) and quantitative changes in traits conveniently sets out two broad types of changes that have been extensively investigated. Thus qualitative or structure changes in traits are broadly concerned with how traits emerge and come to be organized, change in their meaning (expression), as well as change in the number required to adequately represent a given domain. Quantitative changes in traits concern such matters as changes in their level as revealed by the factor scores, in which the intrinsic meaning of the trait is assumed to remain invariant across time. Let us now take a closer look at these two broad types of trait changes.

QUALITATIVE OR STRUCTURAL CHANGES IN TRAITS

The Organization and Emergence of Traits

In the end, the question of how traits develop to form a specific pattern of interrelationships, or become organized into a structure, involves understanding how traits become correlated. Thompson (1957, 1966) has outlined four possible ways in which traits become correlated in a given population. The first one involves environmental considerations; the last three resort to genetic interpretations. In the environmental commonality case, traits become correlated if they are subject to common environmental pressures or influences that systematically affect them. An example here would be adequate pre- and postnatal nutrition, which would enhance the level of, say, two ability factors. Such abilities would tend to become correlated during development, because, other things being equal, those individuals with a history of adequate nutrition would tend to score relatively higher on the relevant ability factors than those individuals with an inadequate nutritional history.

In the gamete commonality case, two traits become correlated even though they originally depended on different genes. This situation arises during assortive mating, in which individuals tend to marry within their own socioeconomic and educational level, although they may be superior on different traits. For example, males who are high in numerical reasoning may tend to marry women who are high in verbal fluency. Such couples tend to produce gametes that prove to be medium-high in both numerical reasoning and verbal fluency (and therefore correlated), because superior genes for both of these traits will be equally represented. Figure 6.1 illustrates this case, in which the parents are each high in one trait and average on the other, although the traits are reversed for each parent.

In the chromosomal commonality case, two traits become correlated because they are affected by genes on the same chromosome or chromosomes. This phenomena is known as genetic linkage (see Chapter 9), because at the genetic level, the two traits are "linked"

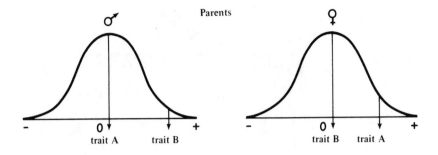

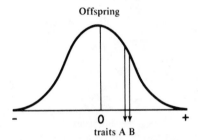

DISTRIBUTION OF ABILITY

Figure 6.1   A simple case of selection communality. *A* and *B* are uncorrelated ability traits. Thus an individual high in *B* may be low, medium, or high in *A*, on the average, however, he will be medium. The same applies to trait *B* with respect to *A*. If inheritance is polygenic and involves equal and additive genes, the $F1$ will be about halfway between the parents in both traits. This means that the traits will coincide or correlate in the offspring (from Thompson, 1957).

by virtue of depending on the same chromosome, and thus the genes for each trait tend to sort together. Figure 6.2 illustrates the simple case of chromosomal commonality, in which two traits at the genetic level share a common chromosome.

The final case outlined by Thompson is gene commonality. In this situation, two traits become correlated if there are one or more genes common to both traits. Figure 6.3 illustrates this case. This phenomena (known technically as genetic pleiotropy) is discussed in greater detail in Chapter 9.

An additional, important, nongenetic source producing correlations between traits should be mentioned at this point. This process involves the overlap of psychological components. In other words,

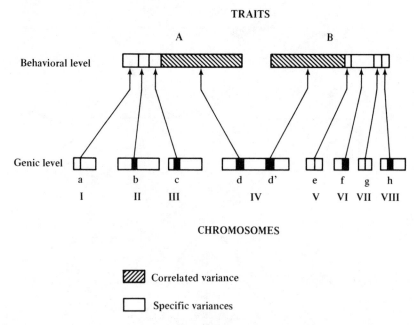

Figure 6.2 A case of chromosomal communality. It is assumed that traits *A* and *B* are made up of variances specific to each and a variance common to both. The specificity arises from genes *a, b, c, e, f, g, h* lying on different chromosomes; I–III in the case of trait *A*; V–VIII in the case of trait *B*. The covariance arises from the fact that genes *d* and *d'* both lie on chromosome IV and tend to assort together. Consequently, the traits vary together in magnitude in the same individual to the degree that the genes *d* and *d'* are linked (from Thompson, 1957).

two traits may become correlated to the extent that they tap psychological components that are conceptually similar, that is, are from a similar conceptual component universe. Tryon (1935) considered this process for producing correlations as the most potent. Tryon was actually concerned with accounting for the *specific* psychological components that become correlated and in turn provide for abstracting a more general factor or trait. This observation allows us to consider at two distinct levels the five ways correlations may come about. First, consistent with Tryon, all five of these cases can provide the means for specific psychological variables or components becoming correlated, thus permitting the inference of a specific factor. The second level at which these five processes can be considered is at the trait level, where one is concerned with the intertrait relationships or organization. For example, all traits in the abilities domain are typically found to be positively correlated, which may be explained

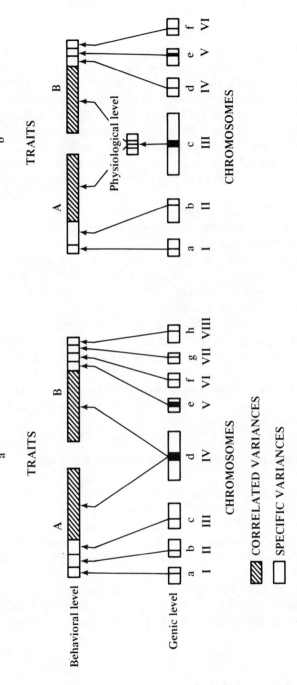

Figure 6.3 A case of gene communality. In 6.3*a* the pleiotropic gene (*d*) results in covariation in two traits *A* and *B*. In 6.3*b* a physiological effect arising from one or a few genes (*c*) has correlated effects on both trait *A* and trait *B* (from Thompson, 1957).

by alluding to the various ways that correlations come about.

Although the ways correlations come about may be applied at both the specific psychological component or variable level and at the trait level, it should be quickly added that some of these cases may be more appropriate at each level. Thus in considering the formation of a given trait, the specific defining variables probably become correlated mainly because of the conceptual overlap of psychological components, as well as genetic commonality. To the extent that the cases outlined by Thompson are operative at this level, this may be viewed as introducing correlated psychological components that obscure the strictly psychological interpretation of traits as functional unities. That is to say, if a numerical psychological component and a verbal psychological component become correlated because of chromosomal, gamete, and/or environmental commonality, a trait will arise that will be difficult to interpret psychologically as a clear functional unity. In considering the formation of correlations between traits, it seems that all five cases considered here may operate, although Thompson considered environmental commonality as the most potent source. To the extent that this is the case, the strict psychological interpretation of higher-order factors (see Chapter 2) as distinct functional unities will become obscured, since higher-order factors are obtained by factoring the primary traits. In any case, the important point of this section is that the formation of traits and their organization may come about because of several distinct types of mechanisms.

Major Types of Qualitative or Structural Changes in Traits

It is possible to make some finer discriminations on the types of qualitative or structural changes that occur. Coan (1966, 1972) has provided a useful inventory of the logical possibilities in this regard. By factor metamorphosis is meant the process whereby a factor gradually changes its basic nature or meaning. In other words, a factor at an early age may gradually undergo a transformation such that at a later age a different factor comes into existence, even though the two factors represent a single historical continuity. Coan draws on the temperament domain to illustrate this process, stating:

> . . . it is well known that certain features of behavior tend to become "internalized" in the course of development. Gesell notes that young children become increasingly

more "self-contained," and students of thinking have
commonly explained the emergence of mental processes in
terms of the inhibition of direct or outward action. It is
hardly surprising, then to find that the expression of many
factors assumes an increasingly covert form with advancing age. A factor manifested in emotional outbursts in the
early years, for example, will be expressed later in a dis-
turbed feeling state that may not be obvious to others
(Coan, 1966, p. 746).

and further

> Another obvious facet of behavioral development in
> general is the process of socialization. Both the positive
> and the negative expressions of all personality factors
> seem to tend toward an increase in socially patterned and
> socially acceptable forms of activity. The assertiveness of
> the Dominance factor thus tends to shift from merely
> aggressive activity to successful dominance, while the
> emotional sensitivity of the Premsia factor may be mani-
> fested early in a self-preoccupation and later in a genuine
> concern for the feelings of others. In some cases, then, we
> may see what looks like a reversal in the direction of
> expression (Coan, 1966, p. 746).

Other possibilities that Coan considers include factor emergence, whereby a factor comes into existence because of an increase
in the correlation between psychological components. Factor con-
vergence occurs when two or more factors at an early age converge
or become correlated to such an extent that only a single factor is
present at a later age. A decrease in the correlation of psychological
components defining a factor results in factor disintegration. If a
factor splits into two distinct factors across time, this is known as
factor divergence. The latter phenomena of the differentiation of
factors has been extensively studied in the abilities domain, and is
considered in greater detail below. The final type of structural change
Coan considers is factor component interchange, in which changes
in correlations of the various psychological components that initially
define a factor results in a recombination of the defining variables.
For a recent extension of Coan's distinctions see Buss and Royce
(1975b).

It should be stressed at this point that all the conceptual distinctions Coan has made in regard to the types of structural change factors undergo must ultimately rest on much more sophisticated measurement and scaling techniques than are presently available. Thus it must be possible to detect "real" structural changes as opposed to spurious changes; the latter may come about because of changes in population distributions across time, inadequate or inappropriate sampling of test items or psychological components at various ages, as well as other sources too complex to consider here. However, Coan's inventory is a useful guide for directing future research, and it will be most valuable once the measurement and scaling problems have been overcome. In the following section, factor divergence, one of Coan's types of structural change, is singled out for special consideration, because this process is part of a much more general developmental process.

The Differentiation Hypothesis

One of the most deeply entrenched views of development involves the idea that later structures differentiate out of a smaller number of earlier structures. Increased differentiation through development is a well-established phenomenon in biological science (known as epigenesis). Phylogenetic as well as ontogenetic evidence points to increasing elaboration of physical structures. Thus it is a reasonable hypothesis to suggest that psychological processes of development should operate in a similar manner as these biological changes. Psychologically, this process holds that in the course of development new behavioral forms emerge that have properties not reducible to earlier forms. In the context of trait theory, differentiation would mean that with an increase in age, there is an increase in the number of factors required for characterizing a given domain. This implies that there is a decrease in the interfactor correlations, as well as the possibility that two or more factors may be necessary at a later age, whereas before only one was required. In other words, factors undergo structural transformations necessitating that factors at a later age have different properties (i.e., re their basic nature or meaning) not reducible to the earlier factors.

The differentiation hypothesis could be applied to any area of individual differences, but has generated the most research in the study of intelligence (e.g., Burt, 1954; Garrett, 1938, 1946). A number of studies have been conducted in attempting to test the hypothesis that intelligence will become increasingly differentiated through childhood and adolescence (the age-differentiation hypothesis) and that intelligence will also be more highly differentiated with higher levels of mental ability, for example normals versus mentally retarded (the ability-differentiation hypothesis). Reinert (1970) has combined these ideas in stating a more general performance-differentiation hypothesis. This hypothesis states that the degree of differentiation of the factor structure of intelligence depends on the absolute level of performance. Thus we would predict that from birth through childhood and adolescence, intelligence should become more highly differentiated. The hypothesis would further predict that a decline in performance (ability level) through later life would be matched by decreasing differentiation of abilities, or integration. In fact, empirical evidence tends to support an integration—differentiation—integration sequence, which is parallelled by early childhood, childhood and adolescence, and adulthood and old age, respectively.

On theoretical grounds a differentiation approach to the development of abilities would be favored by Cattell (who argues that Gf and Gc both originate in G) and opposed by Guilford (who disavows any notion of G). In fact, Cattell's factor rotational procedures (oblique rotation) allows factors to assume different interfactor correlations, which is a necessary condition for detecting differentiation. In this respect Cattell's system has a distinct advantage over Guilford's, because the latter has opted for orthogonal rotation procedures, thereby precluding the possibility that factors may change in number or in their intercorrelations. For Guilford, his 120 structure of intellect factors must be fixed for all ages, that is, constant in number as well as all mutually orthogonal or uncorrelated.

The differentiation hypothesis has generated a great deal of research, but empirical findings are in an extremely confused state, with evidence appearing both for and against differentiation (for a review, see Reinert, 1970.) Methodological difficulties are probably the primary source of the confusion in this area. Some of these methodological problems include the preponderance of cross-sectional designs which confound generational and age-related effects. This issue is extensively examined subsequently. Differences in the homogeneity of samples with regard to variables relevant to intelligence can also produce spurious differences in the number of factors, because groups more homogeneous with respect to such variables as general intellectual level or socioeconomic status yield more factors than heterogeneous groups. Problems associated with measurement instruments such as uni- or multidimensional tests, as well as providing comparable "floor" and "ceiling" levels of difficulty across ages, affect the variability, which in turn affects the number of factors extracted for each age group. Discrepancies in factor-analytic techniques is another contaminating source, because the criteria for how many factors to extract, for example, will mask genuine age changes in the number of factors.

Bracketing the methodological issues mentioned previously, there are still problems of interpreting the process of differentiation, assuming that this phenomena has been reliably demonstrated as associated with genuine age-related changes. Two broad classes of influences operate to produce differentiation: biological-maturation and environmental conditions. Moreover, they interact with one another. Thus it is possible to find increased differentiation as a function of maturation in one set of environmental conditions, but not in a different set of environmental conditions. These interpretation problems, however, do not enter into the descriptive problem of detecting uncontaminated age-related changes in the number of factors, and such interpretative problems are further considered in the next two chapters. At present we can expect on a priori grounds to find some support for the differentiation hypothesis. At least through childhood to adolescence and adulthood, we might expect both maturation and environment to promulgate increased behavioral complexity. In this regard, Reinert (1970) has commented:

> If one considers only those studies that reported differences in factor structure, then the majority give evidence for a trend toward increasing differentiation of the factor structure going from lower to high developmental stages. This process seems to parallel the increase and/or decrease of the average test-scores in the sense of the performance-differentiation hypothesis discussed above (p. 482).

QUANTITATIVE CHANGES IN TRAITS

In this section we are concerned with changes in the level of traits whose essential nature is presumed to remain fairly constant, although the expression of a particular trait may change from age to age. Abilities are considered first, followed by temperament factors. A missing section here on changes in motivational factors reflects the early stage of research that characterizes this domain.

Life-Span Development of Abilities

Figure 6.4, from Horn (1970), illustrates the general theory of Gf and Gc in relation to life-span developmental change. This model focuses on the growth and decline of abilities. It should be noted that *Gf* is expected to reach its peak of performance relatively early (in the teenage years), and to decline progressively thereafter. *Gc* follows *Gf*s rapid increase in childhood years, but then exhibits a more gradual increase through adulthood. The basic theory of *Gf* and *Gc* involves a consideration of the influences expected to act on the individual through the life span. The physiological maturation of the brain through childhood is reflected in the growth of *Gf* and *Gc*. *Gf* is expected to decline after childhood, however, because of a maturational decline as well as the accumulation of accidental inquiries incurred. Horn (1970) points to the parallels between maturational decline (aging) and brain injury itself in terms of gross Central Nervous System (CNS) changes. For example, overall weight of the brain tends to decline during adulthood, as it would from accidental injury. On the other hand, *Gc* is defined by its dependence on learned "aids," and as a consequence, *Gc* will be expected to increase as educational exposure increases.

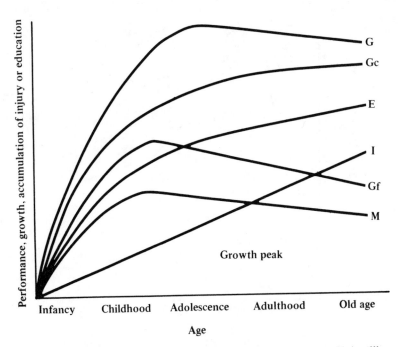

Figure 6.4 Development of fluid intelligence (*Gf*) and crystallized intelligence (*Gc*) in relation to maturational growth and decline of neural strutures (*M*), accumulation of injury to neutral structures (*I*), accumulation of educational exposures (*E*), and overall ability (*G*) (from Horn, 1970).

Horn (1970) has also summarized the empirical support for the theory of fluid and crystallized intelligence. In connection with *Gc* he points out:

> There are no less than 20 studies, cross-sectional as well as longitudinal, showing that for subtests such as Vocabulary, General Information, Similarities, and Judgement the average score for older adults (up to an age of about 60) are either no lower, or else are higher, than the average scores for younger adults (p. 453).

Horn also offers evidence that primary factors that define *Gf* such as reasoning and memory abilities (short-term, not long-term memory) will decline with age.

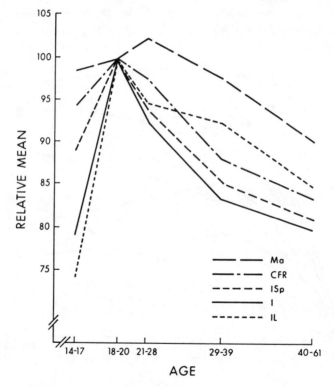

Figure 6.5 Performance as a function of age. Fluid abilities: associative memory (MA), figural relations (CFR), intellectual speed (ISp), induction (I), and intellectual level (IL) (from Horn and Cattell, 1966).

A study by Horn and Cattell (1966), illustrates research on this issue. The cross-sectional method was used, testing subjects between 14 and 61 years of age. One of the more striking results of the study was the difference in age plots for *Gf* and *Gc* (Figures 6.5 and 6.6). Fluid intelligence yields a rather sharp decline after 18 to 20 years of age, whereas crystallized intelligence tends to increase gradually throughout the age span studied. Visualization functions, which are not illustrated here, were also found to decline after 21 to 28 years of age at a rate close to that for fluid abilities.

Abilities Early and Late in Life

In the immediate preschool years, a child's mental ability may be assessed in terms of dimensions that can be very similar to those of later childhood and adulthood. Thus correlations between IQ at ages 3 to 5 years and those at maturity are generally statistically significant (Bloom, 1964). "Mental development" tests given at ear-

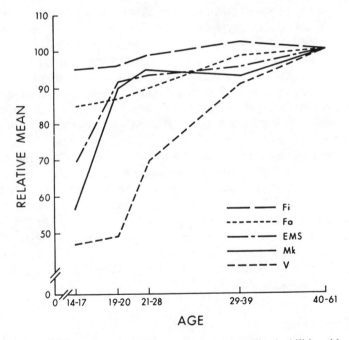

Figure 6.6 Performance as a function of age. Crystallized abilities: ideational fluency (Fi), associational fluency (Fa), experiential evaluation (EMS), mechanical knowledge (Mk), and verbal comprehension (V) (from Horn and Cattell, 1966).

lier ages, particularly within the first 2 years of life, are of negligible value in predicting later IQ. Bayley (1943), for example, claimed that scores on these tests from the first 18 months of life were completely useless in predicting Stanford-Binet IQ at ages 6 to 7. The infant tests consist of items that are primarily sensorimotor in nature. Bayley's Scale of Mental Development (Bayley, 1968), for example, contains items such as block building, word imitation, and placing round and square blocks in a form board. This lack of relationship between semsorimotor tests and later IQ should not, of course, discourage research on infant intelligence. Future research should follow up Vandenberg's (1973) suggestion that the use of multifactor tests of ability rather than general IQ tests might bring out existing relationships more effectively. The value of this approach is certainly indicated by the data of Table 6.1. If we were to use factored tests in this kind of research as early predictors as well as later criteria of performance, the relationships might even be stronger. However, there are little available data on preschool mental abilities taking a factor-analytic approach.

An often-reported finding in the literature concerns the sudden decline of mental ability late in life. Because of the confounding inherent in the cross-sectional method which is typically used as a basis for this conclusion, and because of the social importance of the conclusion, a closer examination is warranted. First of all, we must acknowledge the observation that data often indicate a sudden very sharp decline of abilities in the 60's and 70's. However, we must again make the distinction between fluid and crystallized abilities. Moreover, the cross-sectional approach is particularly disadvantageous for this research, because a sharp decline may be indicative primarily of impending mortality in some members of the group (for a discussion of these methodological problems, see below). Thus Jarvik, Blum, and Varman (1972) used a longitudinal approach and found that between the ages of approximately 64 (tested in 1947) and 84 years (tested in 1967), the more "crystallized" subtests of the WAIS (e.g., vocabulary) showed little or no decline, whereas the more "fluid" and speeded subtests such as digit symbol substitution did exhibit considerable decline.

Life-Span Development of Personality

In the study of personality, research methods and findings have not progressed to the same stage as they have for abilities. Research

Table 6.1

Correlations between Six Abilities Measured at Age 3 with the Pacific Multifactor Test (PMT) and the Score on the Bayley Scale of Mental Development Administered at Six Different Ages (the number of cases are in parentheses) (from Vandenberg, 1973).

PMT Ability at Age 3 Years	Bayley Scale of Mental Development Administered at					
	3 Months	6 Months	9 Months	12 Months	18 Months	24 Months
Motor	08 (36)	17 (103)	22 (105)	25** (113)	17 (100)	19 (95)
Perception	09 (64)	08 (76)	21 (80)	21 (84)	30** (75)	43** (72)
Language	−18 (79)	03 (96)	28** (101)	19 (104)	43** (93)	45** (89)
Reasoning	01 (82)	24** (100)	25 (102)	17 (108)	36** (98)	43** (94)
Memory	−24 (68)	21 (85)	36** (86)	20 (90)	58** (80)	37** (77)
Number	−33 (31)	02 (36)	33 (39)	34 (39)	57** (35)	36 (37)

** p < .01; decimals omitted.

available to date is primarily cross-sectional, although the findings are interesting and suggest further work which might be done.

Table 6.2 from Cattell (1957) shows cross-sectional age differences in 16 PF scores from adolescence (16 years) to middle age (34 years), and from middle age to 60 years. The first point of interest is that age differences through the two blocks of time tend to be consistent. That is, we do not find a decline in scores over the first period offset by a rise over the second period (or vice versa). This kind of result is consistent with the findings on mental abilities. Generally, there is a strong tendency for traits related to emotional instability to decline over the life span. This is most noticeable for factor O (guilt proneness), factor L (protension), factor $q4$ (ergic tension), factor H (threat sensitivity) and factor C (ego strength). We

Table 6.2
Age Trends in Q data Factors from 16 to 60 yr (from Cattell, 1957)

	Factor	Rate of Change per Year in S.T. Score $\times$ 100		Verbal Summary
		Age 16–34 years	*Age 34–60 years*	
A	Cyclothymia	0	0	No change
B	Intelligence	0	−5	Slight late fall
C	Ego strength	+3	0	Slight early rise
E	Dominance	0	0	No change
F	Surgency	−3	−2.5	Continuous fall
G	Super ego	0	0	No change
H	Parmia	+5	+3.5	Continuous rise
I	Premsia	+8	+3	Marked early rise
L	Protension	−9	−3	Marked early fall
M	Autia	0	0	No change
N	Shrewdness	0	0	No change
O	Guilt proneness	−9	−5	Marked fall
Q_1	Radicalism	0	−1	Very slight late fall
Q_2	Self-sufficiency	0	0	No change
Q_3	Will control	+4	+4	Continuous rise
Q_4	Id pressure (ergic tension)	−8	−4	Marked fall

also find a decline of extraversion, but this appears to be primarily limited to the case in which a strong motor component is involved (factor *F,* surgency). In addition, individuals tend to become more tenderminded (factor *I,* premsia) and develop better self-concept control (*q*3).

Personality: Ages 11 to 25

Figure 6.7 is taken from Coan (1966), who has assembled several studies to show changes in *Q* data for Cattell factors between the ages of 11 and 25. *Factor A* (warmth versus aloofness) yields the expected sex difference, with females higher on warmth *(A)* at all age levels. There is also a tendency in both sexes toward increased *A* scores in the latter part of the period studied. *Factor B* (intelligence) shows the expected rise to asymptote through this period. *Factor C* (ego strength) tends to increase over this age period. *Factor E* (dominance versus submissiveness) shows the expected sex difference, with a suggested rise in both sexes to approximately age 23, and then a divergence (possibly due to marriage), with male scores increasing and female scores decreasing. *Factor F* (surgency) gives the expected rise during adolescence, followed by decline in the early 20's. *Factor G* (superego strength) gradually rises between the ages of 11 and 25. The increased "conscientiousness" over this period may be more a function of increased responsibilities (through formal education and employment) than the incorporation of social mores, because it would seem the latter are fairly well established by age 11. *Factor H* (adventurous versus threat sensitive) tends to show increased adventurousness through later adolescence, followed by a decline in the early 20's. The latter, however, may be short term and situational, perhaps related to the responsibilities of marriage, work, and child rearing which typically come during this period. A more long-term increase in scores (i.e., reduced threat sensitivity) is indicated by Cattell's (1957) data. *Factor I* (tendermindedness) gives females much higher scores, but does not show much of a relationship to age. *Factor L* (protension) yields higher score for males and a tendency for both sexes to become less extrapunitive with age. *Factor M* (imaginativeness) gives females a higher score to age 23, at which time a reversal takes place, with male scores rising and female scores falling. Again, this may be related to the effect of marriage on personality. Both sexes tend to develop increased "shrewdness" with age, as indicated by *Factor N.* This, too, is probably related to the external demands of functioning independently in a world outside the family.

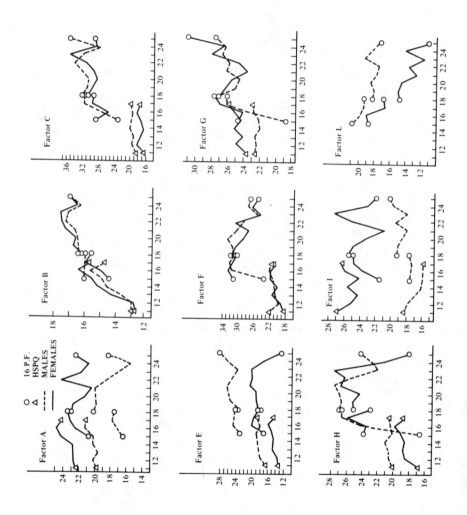

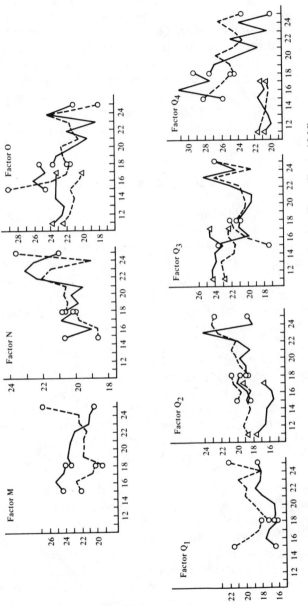

Figure 6.7   Age trends from 11 to 25 years of age on Cattell's personality primaries (from Coan, 1966).

Factor O (guilt proneness) gives us the decline for both sexes during the 20's, which appears to continue over the life-span. *Factor Q_1,* (radicalism) and *Factor Q_2* (self-sufficiency) suggest as light rise in scores through this age period. For *Factor Q_2,* it appears that the lower self-sufficiency of females in early adolescence disappears in later adolescence, but then returns after age 23—possibly due to marriage. *Factor Q_3* (self-concept control) shows little relationship to age or sex. *Factor Q_4* (ergic tension) gives us an increase in early adolescence, followed by a decline which also continues over most of the life-span.

Temperament in Early Childhood and Infancy

Much additional research is needed to complete our understanding of individual differences in temperament during the preschool years. Nevertheless, we do have support for the following major conclusions: (a) It is possible to measure temperament during the preschool years reliably, but we must place less reliance on self-report and more on behavioral ratings. (b) The broader traits (emotional stability and introversion-extroversion) can be assessed within the first 2 years of life, and most of Cattell's primaries can be assessed a couple of years later. (c) Finally, temperament is certainly influenced by environmental factors such as parental care, but to a large extent it also develops "spontaneously" by genetic-maturational influences.

A major study of the relationship between temperament in infancy and early childhood and the subsequent development of behavioral disorders has been reported by Thomas, Chess, and Birch (1968). This research is important both for its findings on the early measurement of temperament and for its study of the relationship between temperament and behavioral disorders in interaction with parental behaviors. A major source of information on the developing child was obtained from parental interviews, beginning at an average age of 3.3 months. Children were rated according to nine categories derived from the parental interviews: (1) *Activity level* ". . . describes the level, tempo and frequency with which a motor component is present in the child's functioning" (p. 20). (2) *Rhythmicity* ". . . was based upon the degree of rhythmicity in regularity of repetitive biological functions. Information concerning rest and activity, sleeping and waking, eating and appetite, and bowel and bladder function was utilized in the scoring" (p. 20). (3) *Approach versus withdrawal*

". . . describes the child's initial reaction to any new stimulus, be it food, people, places, toys or procedures" (p. 21). (4) *Adaptability* is concerned not with the initial reaction to a novel stimulus, but whether the child is able to adapt over time. (5) *Intensity* does not deal with negative responses alone: it is based on the intensity of reaction, whether positive or negative. (6) *Threshold* describes the level of external stimulation required to evoke a discernible response. Once again the stimulation may be either positive or negative. (7) *Mood* ". . . describes the amount of pleasant, joyful, friendly behaviour as contrasted with unpleasant, crying, unfriendly behaviour" (p. 23). (8) *Distractibility* ". . . refers to the effectiveness of extraneous environmental stimuli in interfering with, or in altering the direction of, the ongoing behavior" (p. 23). (9) *Persistence* combines attention span or duration of pursuing a given activity with perseverance in the face of difficulties.

A total of 136 children were studied. Forty-two of these children developed behavioral disturbances as they were observed through the first 10 years of life. This diagnosis of disturbance was based jointly on whether a referral was made by a parent or teacher and the following psychiatric diagnosis. The design of the study had the advantage of having assessed temperament in infancy—a time at which we can hypothesize that individual differences would be largely due to hereditary and constitutional factors. Thus later behavioral changes, particularly behavioral disturbances, could be considered as an interaction between the biologically given temperament and environmental conditions. The most common *reported* behavioral problems involve peer relationships, discipline, learning difficulties, and negative mood. Because of the relatively permissive attitudes in the largely upper-middle-class families studied, behaviors related to feeding habits, toilet training and masturbation were generally not reported as problems—illustrating the relationship between behavioral problems and social values. Uncooperativeness in accepting household routines (e.g., going to bed), or aggressiveness toward siblings and peers, however, is likely be considered a behavioral problem regardless of social class.

The discussion presented by Thomas, Chess, and Birch (1968) is largely in terms of the relationship between the nine categories of temperament and the development of behavioral problems. This discussion, however, attempts to examine the relationship between temperament and behavioral disorders by extrapolating from a factor analysis conducted by the foregoing authors to an Eysenckian framework. In Table 6.3 there are two factors *(A* and *B)* that corre-

Table 6.3
Factors *A* and *B* (from Thomas, Chess and Birch, 1968)

Category	Year	Factor *A*	Factor *B*
Approach/withdrawal	1	.67	—
	2	.42	—
	3	.59	—
	4	—	.25
	5	.71	—
Mood	1	.61	—
	2	.77	—
	3	.74	—
	4	.46	.29
	5	.62	.22
Adaptability	1	.57	.33
	2	.62	.29
	3	.34	.32
	4	.52	.56
	5	.54	.21
Intensity	1	−.41	−.32
	2	−.45	−.28
	3	−.35	—
	4	−.71	−.23
	5	−.35	−.77
Rhythmicity	1	—	.22
	2	—	.64
	3	—	.71
	4	—	.71
	5	—	—
Threshold	1	—	.76
	2	—	.49
	3	—	.27
	4	.59	.06
	5	—	.37
Activity	1	—	−.27
	2	—	−.22
	3	—	—
	4	—	−.24
	5	—	−.51
Distractibility	1	—	—
	2	.22	—
	3	—	—
	4	.58	—
	5	.33	—
Persistence	1	—	—
	2	—	—
	3	−.25	—
	4	−.45	—
	5	—	−.46

Table 6.4
Ratings Used to Determine Personality Factors in Nursery-School Children
(from Peterson and Cattell, 1958)

1. Prefers younger playmates	*vs.*	Prefers older playmates
2. Not destructive	*vs.*	Destructive
3. Selfish	*vs.*	Generous
4. Fearful	*vs.*	Fearless
5. Taciturn	*vs.*	Talkative
6. Active	*vs.*	Inactive, Bored
7. Inquisitive about sex	*vs.*	Not inquisitive about sex
8. Seldom cries	*vs.*	Often cries
9. Seldom complains	*vs.*	Often complains
10. Dislikes school	*vs.*	Likes school
11. Quiet in speech	*vs.*	Loud in speech
12. Often uses forbidden words	*vs.*	Seldom uses forbidden words
13. Seldom sulks or pouts	*vs.*	Often sulks or pouts
14. Has many accidents	*vs.*	Has few accidents
15. Has little physical endurance	*vs.*	Has great physical endurance
16. Speaks fluently	*vs.*	Stutters
17. Articulates well	*vs.*	Articulates poorly
18. Resists going to bed	*vs.*	Eager to go to bed
19. Under-achieves in school	*vs.*	Over-achieves in school
20. Never runs away from home	*vs.*	Often runs away from home
21. Often tells lies	*vs.*	Never tells lies
22. Never steals	*vs.*	Steals
23. Afraid of animals	*vs.*	Unafraid of animals
24. Unafraid of strangers	*vs.*	Afraid of strangers
25. Afraid of the dark	*vs.*	Unafraid of the dark
26. Never bites fingernails	*vs.*	Bites fingernails
27. Sucks thumb	*vs.*	Never sucks thumb
28. Never masturbates	*vs.*	Masturbates
29. Has frequent stomach upsets	*vs.*	Seldom has stomach upsets
30. Has frequent eliminative disturbances	*vs.*	Seldom has eliminative disturbances
31. Seldom has colds	*vs.*	Frequently has colds
32. Seldom has headaches	*vs.*	Frequently has headaches
33. Has frequent temper tantrums	*vs.*	Seldom has temper tantrums
34. Talked early	*vs.*	Talked late
35. Domineering	*vs.*	Not domineering
36. Toilet trained early	*vs.*	Toilet trained late
37. Solemn	*vs.*	Cheerful
38. "Shows off"	*vs.*	Seldom "shows off"
39. Complaint	*vs.*	Not compliant
40. Seldom daydreams	*vs.*	Daydreams excessively
41. Unhappy unless with others	*vs.*	Prefers to be alone
42. Shows little affection	*vs.*	Affectionate
43. Refuses to eat certain foods	*vs.*	Eats anything served
44. Not enuretic	*vs.*	Enuretic

spond to a substantial degree with Eysenck's neuroticism *(A)* and introversion *(B)*, although these factors have not been identified as such by the authors of the original study.

Factor *A* has highest loadings from assessments of mood through the first 5 years of life, which would appear to be highly related to an anxiety-neuroticism dimension. Factor *B*, on the other hand, has highest loadings from rhythmicity and threshold of response. Activity also loads on this factor, leading to its identification as introversion-extraversion. Of particular interest here is the fact that both dimensions have major loadings from the first year of life.

It is impossible to say at this stage of research whether we could determine a greater variety of personality factors in the first year of life. We do have empirical evidence, however, that most of the Cattell primaries are appearing by the age of 4 to 5 years. For example, Peterson and Cattell (1958) were able to isolate 14 factors in a study of 80 nursery school children. The 43 variables consisted of parental ratings of the children, whose average age was 4 years, 7 months. It is obvious from Table 6.4 that these variables are not closely aligned with the self-report indices we find in typical *Q* data or behavior ratings (*L* data) in adults. Thus the factor interpretation will inevitably be somewhat obscure. One method of aiding the interpretation of factors, however, has been to correlate the factors with those found in older children (6 to 7 year olds) where factor identification is somewhat clearer.

One example of factor identification in the nursery school children is the ego strength versus weakness factor *(C)*. Emotional instability is identified in 4 year olds by manifestations such as showing off, loudness of speech, fear of animals, poor physical endurance, excessive daydreaming, temper tantrums, and resistance to going to bed. Peterson and Cattell (1959) have described the developmental changes in surface characteristics of this factor as follows: "Proneness to Neuroticism vs. Ego Strength (C−) exhibits a developmental change from uncomplicated emotional instability and sensitivity in early childhood, through predominant expression as conduct disorder in middle childhood, through predominant expression as neurotic symptomatology among adults" (p. 562). Of major importance for the present discussion, however, is the observation that personality appears with considerable complexity in the preschool years and that temperament dimensions can be identified with some degree of accuracy at this age.

RESEARCH DESIGNS FOR LIFE-SPAN
DEVELOPMENTAL CHANGE

An important methodological issue arises in the discussion of life-span developmental change, and this issue has long been a source of controversy and confusion. For many years, psychologists have been aware that *cross-sectional data* usually indicate quite strong declines for most abilities. Cross-sectional data are based on comparisons of a number of different age groups at a given time. *Longitudinal data* on the other hand, are derived from a follow-up of a group of individuals over an extended number of years. These data tend to show less decline than cross-sectional data, and perhaps even indicates an increase in some abilities. How do we reconcile these differences? First of all, we must realize that cross-sectional data confound age changes with generation differences. In other words, if one were to measure several different age groups at the same time and found significant differences, such differences could be associated with either age changes and/or cohort (generation) differences. Any cohort differences would arise because the older age groups are from a generation that would differ in such things as nutritional, educational, and cultural experiences compared with those of the generation from which younger age groups are drawn. To the extent that such generational differences affect the dependent variables (e.g., ability or temperament traits), genuine age-related changes will be contaminated by the cross-sectional design.

Consider again now the observation that, in the abilities domain, cross-sectional studies typically show a decline, whereas longitudinal studies show an increase. Figure 6.8 from Baltes (1968) illustrates how these two paradoxical findings are reconciled in light of the previous comments regarding the effects that different cohorts may have on age-related changes in behavior. In Figure 6.8 several hypothetical growth functions are illustrated for different cohorts. It can be seen that those individuals born at a relatively early point in time are hypothesized to do less well then more recent generations (the dotted lines). Assuming the dependent variable is from the abilities domain, such cohort differences may be due to such contributors as different nutritional and educational experiences. The solid line in Figure 6.8 represents the sampling of various age groups at one time, that is, a typical cross-sectional design. As can be seen, the growth curve based on these groups tends to rise and then decline. Such a growth function is quite different from all the dotted lines, which represent longitudinal data for several different cohorts.

We have here, then, an explanation for reconciling the discrepant findings from longitudinal and cross-sectional designs. The reader may wonder why cross-sectional designs are carried out, given that they confound both age and cohort effects. Expediency is probably the main reason, because cross-sectional data are much less time consuming to obtain than are longitudinal data.

Even if sufficient resources and time were available for carrying out longitudinal designs, it should be noted that they are not without methodological pitfalls. One problem involves *selective sampling,* for it is known that individuals who voluntarily participate in longitudinal studies tend to be higher in both average intelligence and socioeconomic status. This state of affairs limits the generality of such studies. Another problem with longitudinal (and cross-sectional) studies involves the phenomena of selective survival. By this it is meant that a given population will change in its composition because

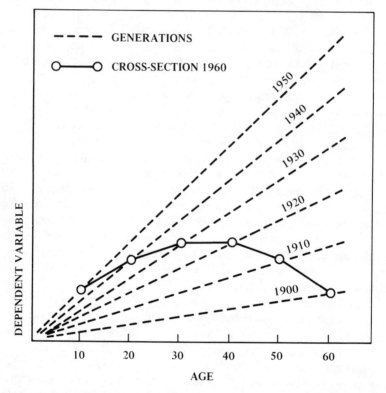

Figure 6.8 A hypothetical example for the effects of generation differences on the results of a cross-sectional study (from Baltes, 1968).

of the death or incapacitation of its members. To the extent that the dependent variable is correlated with survival rate, this will introduce spurious age-related changes, especially at later ages. For example, there is evidence that brighter individuals live longer. When measuring abilities at an advanced age, only the more intelligent members will be participating, thereby introducing spuriously high levels of intelligence. Whereas selective survival applies to the underlying population and may occur in both longitudinal and cross-sectional data, selective drop out is characteristic of only a longitudinal sample, and implies that a given longitudinal sample is heterogeneous across ages. To the extent that the dependent variable is correlated with the drop-out rate, age-related changes become contaminated. Finally, testing effects may adversely affect longitudinal data. When a given sample of individuals is repeatedly subjected to assessment, practice effects and test sophistication affect later measures. This problem can be overcome by the use of control groups, in which a set of samples from one generation is drawn and each sample is randomly assessed at only one age.

There is a similar design used for assessing generational or cohort-related effects. This is the time-lag design, in which different cohorts at the same age are compared. Because earlier generations will reach the age of interest before later generations, this design requires successive measures across time. (Figure 6.9 illustrates these three traditional designs, as well as others to be discussed.)

The inadequacies of the cross-sectional design and the simple longitudinal design (in which only one cohort is sequentially assessed, therefore prohibiting the determination of cohort effects) has led to vigourous attempts to provide more adequate designs. Schaie (1965, 1970, 1973) in particular has outlined a rather complex scheme of descriptive data-gathering strategies. Briefly, it is Schaie's contention that, besides age and cohort, a third variable, time of testing, should be considered in any general developmental model. Effects associated with time of testing are assumed to reflect an environmental treatment effect. These three variables are considered by Schaie two at a time; that is, three separate bifactorial analysis of variance designs are outlined. In each of the three separate bifactorial analysis of variance designs, the dependent variable is confounded with the third variable. In other words, in adopting any of the designs the assumption must be made that the dependent variable is not related to the excluded third variable. The three variables, age, cohort, and time of measurement, are not included in one single trifactorial design because they cannot all be independently varied, which, of course, is necessary for the logic of analysis of variance. These three variables cannot be independently varied because in specifying any two, the third is completely determined. For example, if a cohort was born in 1910 and is to be assessed at age 50, the time of measurement can only occur at one point, namely 1960.

Table 6.5
Developmental Research Methods: What they Measure and Fail to Measure (adapted from Schaie, 1965)

Method	Measures	Confounds Assessment of
Cross-sectional	Age differences	Generation and maturation differences
Longitudinal	Age changes	Maturation and environmental treatment
Time lag	Cultural change	Environmental and generation treatment differences

Table 6.6.
Schaie's Three Sequential Models

Method	Variables Studied	Measures	Variable Confounded
Cohort-sequential	Age Changes Cohort Differences	Maturation Cultural Change	Time of Measurement
Cross-sequential	Time of Measurement Cohort Differences	Environmental Impact Cultural change	Age Changes
Time-sequential	Age Changes Time of Measurement	Maturation Environmental Impact	Cohort Differences

Besides incorporating these three variables for generating different data-gathering strategies, Schaie has entered into the enterpretive realm, identifying age with maturational effects, time of measurement with environmental effects, and cohort with genetic and/or environmental effects. Table 6.5 summarizes Schaie's view on the three traditional developmental designs; Table 6.6 summarizes his three bifactorial designs which attempt to overcome the inadequacies of these traditional developmental designs. The time-sequential method involves sampling two times of measurement with respect to all ages of interest. For example, we might study the ages 20, 30, 40, 50, 60, and 70 in 1950 and compare the results to groups representing the ages 20, 30, 40, 50, 60, and 70 in 1960. The traditional time-lag method, sampling one age group at these two times, would confound environmental treatment with the generation difference between the two groups. Comparing our two sets of age samples, then, we get a direct estimate of the environmental treatment effect (i.e., what effect has the 1950–1960 period had on the population?). If we compare the various ages, we can arrive at age-related changes. Because groups the same age are drawn from *different* generations, this design will give unambiguous results only if there are *no* cohort effects. Schaie's cross-sequential method enables us to estimate effects associated with generational differences and time of measurement. Here we typically study a number of cohorts at various times of measurement. For example, we may be interested in cohorts born in 1920, 1930, and 1940, and the times of measurement may be 1950 and 1960. Because the ages of the groups across the times of measurement will not be the same (for 1950, the age groups, respectively, would be 30, 20, and 10; for 1960 they would be 40, 30 and 20), this design will give unambiguous results only when the dependent variables are unrelated to age. In the cohort-sequential method, two or more cohorts are examined across age. Because the time of measurement for any two cohorts at the same age will be different, this method will give unambiguous results only when the dependent variable is unrelated to time of measurement. A major difficulty in applying Schaie's model is to have sufficient evidence beforehand that the dependent variable is unrelated to one of age, cohort, or time of measurement. One must decide this *before* selecting one of the designs—it does not make conceptual sense to apply more than one design analysis to the same data. If one were to do this by appropriately rearranging the cells for, say, the cross-sequential and cohort-sequential data analysis, it would be tantamount to first assuming that the dependent variable is unrelated to the time of measurement. Clearly, this approach is not permissable.

Recently, a much more simplified developmental model has been offered by Baltes (1968), who has criticized Schaie's formulation on two counts. First, Baltes disagrees with Schaie's functional interpretation of age, cohort, and time of measurement, because these three variables simply classify individuals within the time continuum. To assess environmental and genetic effects, for example, much more elaborate designs are required (see Chapter 9). More directly related to the present discussion is Baltes' belief that only two variables rather than three are required. Baltes' single bifactorial model makes use of age and cohort, dispensing completely with the time of measurement variable. It was Baltes' position that the simple longitudinal (one cohort) and simple time-lag (one age) designs measure pure age and cohort effects, respectively, and that the time of measurement does not confound either the age or cohort variables. Figure 6.9 illustrates Baltes' model. In this figure the longitudinal-sequential data-gathering strategy involves getting measures on two cohorts across age, and the cross-sectional sequential involves measures for two adjacent cross-sectional designs; both of these strategies involve measures on separate occasions. In addition, a third possibility is indicated within this framework, the time-lag sequential (Buss, 1973b), which involves measures at two ages across cohorts. All three of these data-gathering strategies permit the assessment of both age and cohort effects, and the choice between them depends on the time to be spent on data gathering, as well as whether one wishes to sample intensively either ages at specific cohorts (longitudinal sequential) or cohorts at specific ages (time-lag sequential), or extensively both age and cohorts (cross-sectional sequential). The "Schaie-Baltes controversy" has been extensively debated (e.g., see Buss, 1973b, 1975b; Labovie, 1975), although the complexities of this debate involve subtleties which are too demanding for an introductory treatment.

Brief mention should be made of Cattell's (1970b) treatment of developmental methodology. Like Baltes, Cattell adopts an age $\times$ cohort bifactorial. In regard to the functional interpretation of these two variables, both Cattell (1970b) and Buss (1973b) have noted the possibility of partitioning the variance associated with both of these variables into environmental and genetic components. This is possible by noting changes in heritability ratios (the proportion of variance accounted for by genetic factors—see Chapter 9) across both age and cohort. In addition, Cattell has advocated separating developmental curves into genetic and environmental additive curve components. It should be noted, however, that to the extent one is plotting absolute performance scores, it makes no conceptual sense to break down *a* score (as opposed to variances) in terms of genetic and environmental sources. The issues surrounding this point are both subtle and complex, and they are considered further in Chapter 9.

Empirical Findings

Schaie's work has, first of all, confirmed the frequently reported finding that a variety of abilities show a decline from cross-sectional

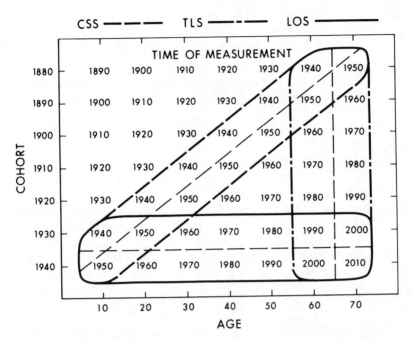

Figure 6.9 A modification of Baltes's age-X cohort bifactorial developmental model in which cell is indexed by time of measurement. The cross-sectional sequential (CSS) is best thought of as a data-gathering strategy, whereas the longitudinal sequential (LOS) and time-lag sequential (TLS) may be best considered as data analysis designs. The actual dates are illustrative only and are not meant to reflect recommended ranges of time intervals (from Buss, 1974b).

data taken at one time (i.e., maturation and generation confounded). In addition, the finer distinctions among developmental determinants tend to support the theory of fluid and crystallized intelligence and its relation to development (Schaie and Strother, 1968a, 1968b). Thus fluid abilities and those related to psychomotor speed tend to show fairly steep longitudinal (maturational) decline, consistent with the cross-sectional data. They also show generational differences, with more recent generations obtaining *higher* scores. However, short-term environmental treatment effects (between the 1956 and 1963 periods studied) tend to reduce these abilities, so that we may expect a leveling-off of the generation effect for fluid abilities. Crystallized abilities do not reflect the developmental-maturational decline, but tend to hold fairly constant. They also show (as predicted) stronger intergeneration improvement. Short-term environmental effects have been found to improve these abilities. Of course, the environmental effects found by Schaie and Strother must be interpreted in the context of the particular period studied. The intergeneration improvement in mental abilities is probably due to both educational improvements and nutritional improvements in this century. Present indications of short-term environmental treatment effects are that this trend may have reached an asymptote for fluid abilities, though not as yet for crystallized abilities.

Baltes' model has been applied to both the abilities and temperament domains. In the temperament domain the results (Baltes and Nesselroade, 1972; Nesselroade and Baltes, 1974; Woodruff and Birren, 1972) are too complex to summarize for each individual factor. It will suffice to say that cohort effects are greater than age effects, suggesting that the particular historical period in which one is born is more influential on temperament than are specific ages for the particular age range sampled (adolescence). In general terms, these results argue against an age-stage model for temperament, where there is a sequential invariant pattern of changes across age. It seems that with adolescents the time at which they are measured (cultural moment) is more influential than their chronological age with respect to scores on temperament traits.

FURTHER READING:

Baltes, P. B. Longitudinal and cross sectional sequences in the study of age and generation effects. *Human Development*, 1968 *11*, 145–171.

Buss, A. R., and Royce, J. R. Ortogenetic changes in cognitive structure from a multivariate perspective. *Developmental Psychology*, 1975b *II*, 87–101.

Coan, R. W. Child personality and developmental psychology. In R. B. Cattell (Ed.), *Handbook of multivariate experimental psychology*. Chicago: Rand McNally, 1966.

Nesselroade, J. R. Application of multivariate strategies to problems of measuring and structuring long-term change. In L. R. Goulet and P. B. Bates (Eds.), Life-span developmental psychology: Research and theory. New York: Academic Press, 1970.

Wohlwill, J. F. *The study of behavioral development*. New York: Academic Press, 1973.

Chapter 7

LEARNING, CULTURE, AND THE ENVIRONMENT

Integrating Learning Concepts and Traits

The idea that there is a significant relationships between learning and intelligence would seem to be a reasonable hypothesis, although the exact nature of this relationship has been argued in the past. Early definitions of general intelligence stressed the idea that intelligence is the ability to learn. It is now generally acknowledged that this definition of intelligence is faulty and inadequate for two major reasons. First, as reviewed in the chapter on abilities, intelligence cannot be considered as a unitary construct; rather, it is composed of many separate functional unities or traits. A second important factor is the finding that the correlations between I.Q. and the amount of gain as a result of training or learning are generally quite low. Related to this idea is the observation that improvement or gain in one learning task is often uncorrelated with improvement or gain in other tasks. Although we have every reason to believe that we cannot define intelligence as the ability to learn, this does not deny the possibility that there may be a significant relationship between the two. In fact, there have been several attempts to explore the relationship between learning and ability (as well as temperament and motivation).

One of the earliest attempts to provide a theoretical integration of learning and abilities is that of Ferguson (1954, 1956). In Ferguson's view, abilities are considered to be attributes that obtain a crude stability or become relatively invariant in level in adulthood through the process of learning. Thus abilities are seen to represent performance at crude limits of learning, whereas the limits of learning are determined by both biological and experiential factors. In this view, the human psychological environment exerts a strong influence on what will be learned and at what age it will be learned. Because of the importance of learning and the environment in determining the nature and level of abilities, one would predict different ability patterns and profiles cross-culturally. In Ferguson's view, the crucial link between learning and ability involves *transfer*. Transfer is defined in terms of the mathematical concept of a *function*. When any two variables are related to each other such that the value of one depends on the value of the other, they are said to be a function of each other. Thus Ferguson's transfer model stated that performance on task y is some unspecified function of performance on task x and the amount of practice on the two tasks (T_x, T_y); that is, $y = \emptyset\ (x, T_x, T_y)$. In the situation in which practice is defined in terms of performance, then, the transfer model simplifies to $y = \emptyset\ (x)$, that is, performance on some task y is some unspecified function of performance on task x. Because an ability factor is defined by the intercorrelations of several tests, these tests are related, or are a function of each other, and may be seen as special instances of the transfer function. In this way a theoretical link is made between learning and ability factors. Some of the implications from Ferguson's theory are explored below.

Another attempt to integrate within one framework the concept of intelligence and learning is that of Whiteman (1964). What Whiteman did was to consider several concepts related to intelligence according to two properties: (1) the intersituational consistency of performance and (2) the hierarchical organization of levels. Of particular interest within the present context is the comparison of an ability factor with both a learning set and Piagetian operation. Thus an ability factor, a learning set, and a Piagetian operation may all be defined in terms of their intersituational consistency; that is, they are all broad theoretical constructs of some generalizability, or, in other words, are transituational in nature. Similar to Ferguson's theorizing, Whiteman postulates that the concept of a learning set may account for the generality as well as the development of an ability factor because of the experiential conditions specified by the learning set. In other words, the greater the range of experiences that define the development of a given learning set, the greater the generality of the accompanying ability factor. In this way one "may specify a possible etiology for the emergence of a general factor" (Whiteman, 1964, p. 300).

In discussing the relationship between ability factors and learning sets in regard to the idea of hierarchical organization, Whiteman postulates that underlying the hierarchical organization of ability factors is a hierarchical organization of learning sets. Adopting Ferguson's position that the general factor evolves partly as a result of reciprocal influences amongst the lower-order factors, Whiteman suggests that learning sets that involve the operation of more than one lower-order factor would facilitate the development of a higher-order general ability factor. In this view, then, different ability factors are seen as having their basis (both developmentally and structurally) in differential learning experiences, as reflected by the concept of learning set.

A recent and comprehensive attempt to integrate the fields of learning and human abilities is that of Guilford (1967). Guilford's structure-of-intellect model has already been reviewed in Chapter 3. The reader may wish to review this model to facilitate understanding of the present treatment. An important concept in Guilford's SI theory is information—which is defined in the broadest possible terms as that which an organism discriminates. More specifically, the four content areas (figural, symbolic, semantic, behavioral) refer to the substantive aspects of information; whereas the six product categories (units, classes, relations, systems, transformations, implications) refer to the formal aspects of information and its differentiation. The collapsing of the third dimension of Guilford's model, that is, the operations, produces a total of 24 intersections (four contents times six products) which together have been called a psychoepistemology. According to Guilford, *what* is learned is in the form of products of information.

In his book Guilford (1967) reviews much of the experimental literature on learning and interprets it within the framework of his SI model. For example, those learning studies that have emphasized the establishment of connections (e.g., human serial learning, paired associate learning) are interpreted by Guilford as involving the formation of *implications*. Research pertaining to the learning of concepts is seen as the learning of *classes*. Learning associated with the Gestalt concept of reorganization and the Piagetian concepts of accommodation are seen as the learning of *transformations*. The learning of the relations and systems products is also considered by Guilford; examples of the latter include the learning of patterns, principles, rules, problem structures, orders, models, and theories—all input systems. Examples of output systems that are learned are motor patterns, plans, strategies, tactics, methods, and programs. The important concept of reinforcement is reinterpreted by Guilford

in terms of *feedback information.* In Guilford's view, feedback information is able to encompass previous interpretations of reinforcement such as need reduction, pleasure-pain, reward and punishment,
confirming reaction, and knowledge of results.

In summary, then, Guilford has attempted to draw traditional
experimental learning research under the umbrella of his structure-
of-intellect model and related information-theoretic concepts. Although Guilford's attempt toward theoretical unification of ability
factors and learning concepts is praiseworthy, thus far it is difficult
to see what consequences this formulation has for future research.
In other words, Guilford's strategy here may be likened to taking one
set of concepts and translating them into another set of concepts in
which it remains to be demonstrated what has in fact been gained
in the process.

In addition to attempts toward integrating learning concepts
and ability factors within a single unifying theoretical framework,
there have been more modest attempts at exploring the relationship
between learning and traits while keeping these two kinds of "things"
conceptually separate. One may detect two general kinds of concerns
in this regard: (1) learning effecting the development of traits, and
(2) the role of traits, and especially ability factors, in learning.

Learning Effecting the Development of Traits

The relationship between learning effecting the development of
traits may focus on several distinct aspects, including learning where
such changes in traits may be in their level, nature, or organization.
These three aspects are reflected by changes in factor scores, factor
loadings, and trait intercorrelations, respectively. Consider first the
abilities domain and the effects of learning in producing changes in
ability factor scores. It has recently been proposed (Buss 1973a) that
the basic experimental learning principles can be reformulated such
that they refer to changes in ability factor scores rather than behavior
per se. These reformulated learning principles are as follows:

> P1. A *reinforcement* is any stimulus event that will
> increase or maintain the score of an ability factor. If rein-
> forcement occurs on a continuous schedule, the maximum
> possible change in the ability factor score is quickly
> reached. If, however, the same maximum change in the
> ability factor score is brought about more slowly by a

schedule of partial reinforcement, the effect of the latter will result in more permanent change over time.

P2. *Extinction* occurs when there is a decrease of an ability factor score caused by failure of reinforcement. Extinction is more rapid when acquisition occurs under a schedule of continuous reinforcement as opposed to a schedule of partial reinforcement.

P3. The involvement of an ability factor under stimulus conditions somewhat different from original learning is called *stimulus generalization.*

P4. *Discrimination* is achieved when an ability factor is operative in one stimulus situation but not in another.

P5. *Drives* provide the impetus for action as well as defining the direction of behavior (goals). In human ability learning, perhaps the most important drive or motive is achieving cognitive proficiency which facilitates adaptation to the environment.

P6. The score of an ability factor is enhanced by an intermediate drive level (inverted U function). However, the more complex the task, the lower is the optimal drive level *(Yerkes-Dodson law).*

P7. Increases in the score of an ability factor is facilitated more by *distributed practice* as opposed to *massed practice.*

P8. *Transfer* occurs when practice on task x has an effect on performance on task y (positive versus negative transfer). Transfer effects have their basis, in part, in changes in underlying factor scores brought about by practice on task x [for a detailed treatment of this learning principle, see Buss, 1973c].

P9. *Overlearning* enhances the stability of the level of an ability factor since skills can be evoked at a low threshold.

P10. Further growth of an ability factor is moderated in the organism by a physiological and psychological *readiness* variable, by which is meant that the individual must be ready for the conditions of the task in the sense that appropriate behavior is in individual's repertoire (Buss, 1973a, pp. 278, 280).

These 10 basic learning principles affect the development of all ability factors. The general view as to how learning principles 1 to 10 are involved in the development of ability factors is as follows. The human organism develops within a biological framework. As such, it is engaged in a process of adaptive behavior to meet the demands of the environment. Control over situational presses leads to the development of cognitive structures (increases in ability-factor scores) through learning. With respect to ability-factor development, the major drive (motive, energy source, and goal) revolves around mastery of the environment. Growth of abilities leads to achieving this goal. Behavior that leads to successful and proficient environment control is enhanced and reinforces the hypothesized constructs (ability factors) giving rise to such behavior. If reinforcement is delivered on a continuous schedule, ability-factor score changes are more rapid than if a partial reinforcement schedule were in effect. The latter, however, would result in more permanent change, that is, be more resistant to extinction effects. Inappropriate or maladaptive behavior becomes extinguished and facilitates the formation and operation of relevant ability factors. Through the dual process of stimulus generalization and discrimination, the organism learns the generality and specificity of appropriate ability factors. The more frequently an organism puts into operation a given ability factor, the more efficient it becomes, thus solidifying it into a functional unity that has a low threshold for implementation (overlearning). Stimulus generalization can be seen as a special instance of transfer, in which competencies and general skills are built up by practicing the underlying ability factors that are common to similar tasks. Distributed practice on a given task leads to better performance and thus to greater reinforcement (environmental mastery). As such, it results in increases in the ability factor that is operative to a greater extent than massed practice, since the latter situation leads to poorer performance, less mastery of the environment, and thus less reinforcement. Throughout this general developmental process, the level that an ability factor can reach is subject to the physiological and psychological readiness of the organism. With respect to psychological readiness, the organism's development is seen as cumulative. Prior learning determines the level later learning can reach.

Several nontrait psychologists have put forth the view that intellectual growth involves cumulative learning (e.g., Gagné, 1965, 1968a, 1968b; Hunt, 1961; Stinchcomb, 1969). Gagné, for example, has proposed that intellectual development involves progressing through seven stages of learning: simple S-R, chaining, verbal association, multiple discrimination, concept, principle, and finally, problem solving. These stages increase in complexity in terms of the type

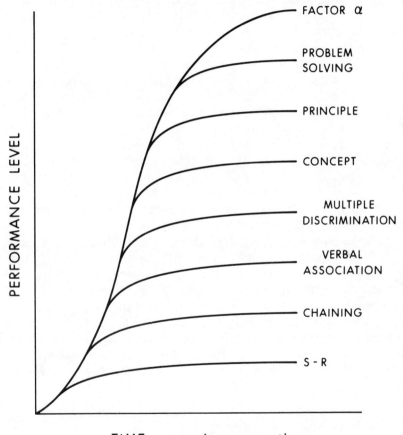

TIME, experience-practice

Figure 7.1 Growth curve of ability factor *a* according to learning stage theory. Learning is cumulative and from simple to more complex. The level achieved on each type of learning sets limits on later types of learning and thus the ultimate level a given factor reaches (from Buss, 1973a).

of learning involved. The hypothesized relationship between Gagné's types of learning and the development of an ability factor is represented in Figure 7.1 (taken from Buss, 1973a). In this model the level of a factor depends on the *learning stage* reached in development. The theoretical growth curve of a factor is S-shaped, consistent with the evidence from Thurstone (1955) who applied his absolute scaling methods to his seven primary mental ability factors. As can be seen, later, complex learning, on which a high performance level of factor *a* depends, is a direct outgrowth of more simple types of learning. Transfer takes place within each of Gagné's types of learning as practice on diverse tasks occurs (learning principle P8). In addition, transfer occurs between lower types of learning to higher types of learning (learning principles P9 and P10). Gagné (1965) refers to each of these types of transfer as lateral and vertical, respectively. Lateral transfer is left unexplained by his theory, whereas vertical transfer is simply accounted for in that learning at a higher level will be made easier when low-level learning has been mastered. Figure 7.1 has certain implications that go beyond this simple statement. It implies that deficits in lower types of learning have more serious consequences on the ultimate performance level of an ability factor than do deficits in later types of learning. This is indicated in Figure 7.1; low-level types of learning branch off the factor performance curve when the latter is *positively accelerating,* whereas high-level types of learning branch off when the factor performance curve is *negatively accelerating.* Therefore, deficits in low-level types of learning will have more serious effects on the ultimate factor performance level than will deficits in high-level types of learning. Such a model is consistent with Hebb's (1949) theory of the importance of early experience for later functioning, as well as Schneirla's (1957) view that gains from experience are likely to be greatest at early stages of ontogeny. That this same relationship holds for negative influences as well, such as brain damage, has also been argued by Hebb (1949), although the evidence here is not conclusive (for a review, see Hayes, 1962).

Formal Representation of Change

Several people (Buss, 1973c, 1974c; Cattell, 1971; Nesselroade, 1970) have attempted to represent in a formal manner the changes in traits brought about through learning. Although differing in specifics, all attempts to formalize these changes involved specifying the basic factor equation at two points in time. Thus one may specify present action performance in terms of:

$$z_{xi} = b_{x1}F_{1i} + b_{x2}F_{2i} + \ldots + b_{xk}F_{ki} \qquad (7.1)$$

where z_{xi} is the common part of individual i's standard performance score on variable x, the bs are the k factor loadings, and the Fs are the k factor scores. Equation 7.1 specifies a person's score on a variable as an additive function of his weighted factor scores. The factor scores are unique for individual i and remain invariant across any variable considered (no variable subscript), whereas the factor loadings are unique for variable x and remain invariant across any individual considered (no-person subscript). The latter statement needs to be qualified by the restriction that it *necessarily* holds only when considering the specification of scores on variables at one point in time, because it is possible that both factor scores and loadings may change over time and thus confound the two invariant relationships just mentioned.

Consider now that Equation 7.1 specifies the performance of a given individual on a given variable at an occasion o_1. It is possible to construct a similar equation for occasion o_2, in which changes on variable x will be a function of either changes in factor scores, factor loadings, or both (Buss, 1973c; Nesselroade, 1970) and where it is assumed that the same factors are involved. Consider first the case for changes in factor scores of Fs. This situation may be represented by

$$z^*_{xi} = b_{x1}F^*_{1i} + b_{x2}F^*_{2i} + \ldots + b_{xk}F^*_{ki} \qquad (7.2)$$

where the symbols are the same as in Equation 7.1 and the * indicates values on occasion o_2 that are different from values on occasion o_1. Equation 7.1 may now be subtracted from Equation 7.2 in the following straightforward manner:

$$z^*_{xi} - z_{xi} = b_{x1}(F^*_{1i} - F_{1i}) \\ + b_{x2}(F^*_{2i} - F_{2i}) + \ldots + b_{xk}(F^*_{ki} - F_{ki}) \qquad (7.3)$$

which represents *quantitative* change in a multidimensional variable. That is to say, the change in performance in variable x from occasion o_1 to occasion o_2 comes about as a result of increases or decreases on factors whose basic natures are assumed to remain invariant, because the factor loadings remain the same. The implication here is that the theoretical underpinnings for quantitative change in a multidimensional variable reside in the factor scores (Fs), and that for a given individual i, such changes in factor scores will yield quantitative changes across multidimensional variables, assuming constant factor loadings for those variables.

Consider now that situation in which a change in performance on variable x from occasion o_1 to occasion o_2 is a result of changes in the factor loadings or bs, which may be interpreted as a change in the factor demands of variable x over time. This situation can be represented in an equation that is similar to Equation 7.3:

$$z^*_{xi} - z_{xi} = (b^*_{x1} - b_{x1})F_{1i} \\ + (b^*_{x2} - b_{x2})F_{2i} + \ldots + (b^*_{xk} - b_{xk})F_{ki} \qquad (7.4)$$

where the only difference from Equation 7.3 is that the change in variable x is now due to changes in factor loadings rather than factor scores. Equation 7.4 represents *structural* change in a multidimensional variable, because such a change comes about as a result of structural changes in the uncerlying factor demands that define variable x. This brings us to the conclusion that the theoretical underpinnings for structural change in a multidimensional variable reside in the task demands (bs), and as such, will occur across persons for that variable, assuming constant Fs for other persons (it should be recalled that the factor loadings have no person subscript.

The third possibility for change in a multidimensional variable involves that situation in which both factor scores and factor loadings change across occasions. It is not possible to represent this subtraction of one specification equation from another in terms of the individual subtraction of both component factor scores and factor loadings, for no simple algebraic solution exists when both of these components change. This third possibility may be represented, however, by

$$z^*_{xi} - z_{xi} = (b^*_{x1}F^*_{2i} + \ldots + b^*_{xk}F^*_{ci}) \\ - (b_{x1}F_{1i} + b_{x2}F_{2i} + \ldots + b_{xk}F_{ki}) \qquad (7.5)$$

which simply involves determining each of the separate values on variable x before the subtraction operation is carried out. Because this type of change in variable x involves both quantitative change (changes in Fs) and structural change (changes in bs), it is referred to as *quantistructural* change. It should be mentioned in passing that detecting quantitative, structural, and quantistructural changes depends on detecting genuine as opposed to spurious changes in factor scores and factor loadings. Factoring covariance as opposed to correlational matrices as developed by Bentler (1973) and Cattell (1970a, 1972a) will meet these requirements, although a discussion of these techniques are beyond the scope of this chapter.

In the foregoing formal representation of change, within the context of learning, one may view the quantitative changes in factor scores as brought about by the previously discussed 10 learning principles. The qualitative or structural changes as reflected in the factor loadings may be seen as reflecting changes in Gagné's types of learning which underlie the growth of an ability factor. Thus, referring back to Figure 7.1, Gagné's types of learning may be viewed as an invariant sequence of learning stages consisting of the different *kinds* of learning. Empirical evidence supporting this view is reviewed by Gagné (1968b), although he does not use the word stage. Quantitative changes in factor scores would occur within any learning stage, and qualitative changes would parallel the transformations from stage to stage. Once the individual reaches the terminal learning stage for a given factor, further changes in factor scores would be quantitative in nature; this is consistent with the views of Flavell (1970) and Kohlberg and Kramer (1969) concerning the kinds of changes in an adult's cognitive structure. It would be expected that the majority of ability factors would progress in harmony through the various learning stages, although possible exceptions would resemble Piaget's (1970) concept of horizontal decalage.

The Role of Traits in Learning

In considering the role of traits in learning situations, ability and psychomotor factors have been singled out for special consideration by researchers. Carrying out some of Ferguson's (1954, 1956) earlier theorizing, Fleishman (1967, 1972) has extensively examined the changing importance of various factors during an on-going learning task. In this view, abilities are seen as exerting their effects differentially during the learning process. Fleishman's typical procedure involves getting measures on a battery of marker tests for known factors as well as trial scores; typically on a psychomotor task. When these measures are all factor analyzed, it is possible to chart the changing factor loadings across trials or time, or, in other words, the relative importance of various factors in accounting for individual differences in the task over time. The typical results are illustrated in Figure 7.2. One may draw the following general conclusions from this line of work: (1) the particular combinations of ability factors influencing individual differences in performance changes as practice continues; (2) these changes increase at first but eventually become stabilized; (3) in psychomotor tasks, the contribution of nonmotor factors such as verbal and spatial relations progressively decreases in importance, although they account for a significant percent of the variance at the beginning of the task; and finally, (4) there is usually an increase in a factor specific to the task itself.

Fleishman's procedure has been questioned on methodological grounds, but the complexities of this controversy are too technical to warrant treatment here. Bracketing for the moment possible criticism of Fleishman's strategy, we can note that this paradigm has been applied to other learning situations besides psychomotor tasks.

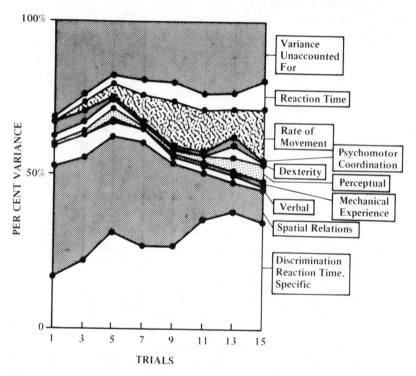

Figure 7.2 Percentage of variance represented by each factor at different stages of practice on the discrimination reaction time task. Percentage of variance is represented by the *area* shaded in for each factor (from Fleishman and Hempel, 1955).

Thus Dunham et al. (1968) charted out the changing role of various Guilford factors in the learning of concepts. In this study some negative factor loadings of various abilities on early trials indicated that those abilities were handicaps near the beginning, but later these same factors became increasingly helpful, as the factor loadings increased in a positive direction. Most important for present purposes is to appreciate the logic of Fleishman's paradigm. That is to say, this research strategy illustrates in a rather nice way that individual differences in ability contribute to individual differences in learning performance, in which different factors are differentially involved at different stages of the learning task. Fleishman's procedure illustrates how factor analysis may be used to represent the dynamics of an on-going process. Critics of factor analysis tend to stress its static quality, although the work of Fleishman and others serves to emphasize that the factor analytic methodology is not limited to answering structural questions of a static nature.

Another approach toward gaining some understanding of the role of ability factors in learning situations has been offered by Merrifield (1966). What Merrifield has done is to adopt Gagné's different types of learning and has hypothesized which ability factors from Guilford's structure-of-intellect model would be most important. In this view, then, individual differences in learning are partly a consequence of individual differences in ability factors. The hypothesized relations between Gagné's types of learning and Guilford's ability factors are represented in Table 7.1. The information in this table is indeed complex and is not subject to easy interpretation. Signal learning or classical conditioning is thought to involve individual differences in implication, memory, and evaluation. Stimulus response learning is thought to require more evaluation than signal learning because of the greater emphasis on discrimination. Chaining is the acquisition of a system in which both cognition and convergent productive thinking is involved. Verbal association depends on transformation, for example, learning foreign languages. Memory and divergent productive thinking are also probably important in this type of learning. Multiple discrimination involves thinking about class properties as well as systems. Concept learning is heavily dependent on semantic material and involves the naming of a class of objects. Principle learning involves classes, relations, or systems, in which the dominant operation would seem to be cognition. Problem solving depends on evaluative, cognitive, and divergent productive thinking, where the products are either units, implications, or transformations. As mentioned previously, the complexity of this model

Table 7.1

Hypothesized Relations among Types of Learning and Parameters of Ability
(from Merrifield, 1966)

Structure-of-intellect parameters	Gagné's types of learning							
	Signal (1)	S-R (2)	Chain (3)	Verbal association (4)	Multiple discrimination (5)	Concept (6)	Principle (7)	Problem solving (8)
Operations								
Cognitive (C)	X							
Memorative (M)			X	X	X	X	X	X
Productive								
Divergent (D)		X	X	X				X
Convergent (N)		X		X		X		X
Evaluative (E)	X				X	X		X
Contents								
Figural (F)	X	X	X	X	X			X
Symbolic (S)			X	X	X		X	X
Semantic (M)		X	X	X	X	X	X	X
Behavioral (B)					X			
Products								
System (S)			X		X	X	X	X
Class (C)					X	X		
Unit (U)	X			X				
Relation (R)		X		X			X	X
Transformation (T)				X	X	X	X	X
Implication (I)	X	X					X	X
Selected Abilities Potential covariants in learning studies	MFI EFI MFU EFU	NFR NFI NMR NMI EFR EFI EMR EMI	CFS CSS CMS NFS NSS NMS	MMR MSR DMR DMT NFU EFR EMR	MSR EFC EFR EMR EMR EMS EBC	CMC CMR CMS NMC NMR NMS EMS	CSI CMS CMU CMI CMR	CMT DMT NMT CMI EMI NMI DFT

defies a simple summary. The reader may appreciate that individual differences in learning as a function of ability factors may indeed be a complex field of enquiry.

Thus far in this chapter we have considered the relationship between learning and ability factors. That this relationship is an important one for both theoretical and practical purposes has been commented on by several investigators of individual differences. Perhaps the following quote from Jensen (1967) sums up the general feeling of this topic:

> One of the major tasks of differential and experimental psychology is the theoretical integration if ID's [individual differences] in learning and the structure of mental abilities as represented by tests like the *Primary Mental Abilities*. I see mental abilities measured on this level as less basic and more descriptive than the dimensions of individual differences in learning which I have suggested. Therefore, I would not expect to understand individual differences in learning in any fundamental sense, in terms of psychometric tests. (pp. 131–132)

In addition to stressing the importance of a theoretical integration of learning and ability factors, we can see from the above quote that Jensen believes that learning processes are more basic and should be employed in explaining individual differences in abilities. Thus Jensen would probably not advocate explaining individual differences in learning in terms of ability factors as has Fleishman. More recently, Jensen has identified two broad abilities linked to two different kinds of learning, although since this view is intimately tied up to the notion of socio-economic differences in abilities, we will discuss this aspect of Jensen's work in Chapter 9.

Dimensionalizing the Environment

Recently, there have been several investigators drawing attention to the problem of how to conceptualize and assess situations (e.g., Barker, 1968; Craik, 1971, 1972; Frederiksen, 1973; Sells, 1963). One line of inquiry into this problem has stressed the importance of the physical environment (e.g., Wohlwill, 1970b). Wohlwill has reviewed the effects of the physical environment as a source of stress affecting development and psychological health, and he has offered several major dimensions of sensory deprivation and over-stimulation (e.g., level, diversity, patterning, instability, and meaningfulness). Another approach to conceptualizing human psychological environments has been given by Moos (1973), who reviewed six major categories of environmental dimensions that are nonexclusive, overlapping, and mutually interrelated: ecological dimensions, dimensions of organization structure, personal characteristics of milieu inhabitants, behavior settings, functional or reinforcement properties of environments, and finally, psychosocial characteristics and organizational climate.

The value of Moos' (1973) approach is that it attempts to consider both the ecological or physical aspects of the environment as well as the behavioral and social components. In a recent follow-up article (Insel and Moos, 1974), the authors provide an additional elaboration of dimensions relating to psychosocial characteristics and organizational climate. The dimensions in this major category are in turn broken down into three subcategories: relationship dimensions, personal development or goal orientation dimensions, and system maintenance and change dimensions. In reviewing the literature in this area the authors conclude that there is considerable agreement in conceptualizing the psychosocial characteristics and organizational climate in terms of these three subcategories. Especially noteworthy in the present context is Stern's (1970) factor analysis of the *Organizational Climate Index,* which is an instrument for measuring institutional environments such as college atmosphere. Stern identified six first-order environmental factors: intellectual climate, personal dignity, closeness, achievement standards, orderliness, and impulse control. A higher-order factor analysis revealed two factors: one facilitating growth and self-enhancement, and the other reflecting organizational stability and bureaucratic self-maintenance.

Studies in the domain of parental behavior have also indicated that it is possible to apply factor analytic techniques to what is essentially an important aspect of the environment from the child's perspective. Two major factors of parental behavior have been replicated in a number of studies. These are the factors of love-hostility and autonomy-control. Figure 7.3, from Bayley (1964), describes these factors from ratings of maternal behavior, at ages of 0 to 3 years and 9 to 14 years. Ratings in the 0-to-3-year period were based on observations during the mothers' visits to the institute, whereas the 9-to-14-year ratings were based on one or two interviews in the home.

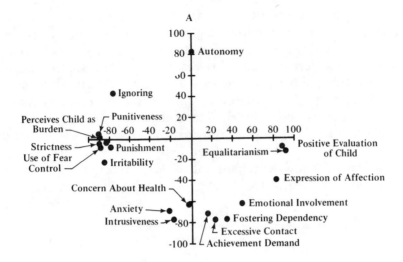

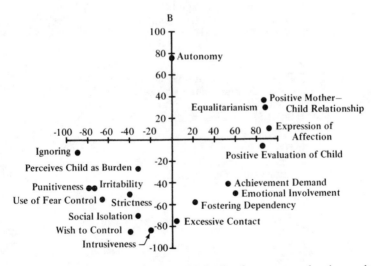

Figure 7.3 Major dimensions of parental behavior from maternal ratings, where (A) is birth to 3 years, and (B) is 9 to 14 years (from Bayley, 1964).

These dimensions have also been replicated in fathers (Becker, 1960), and have been related to various behavioral problems in children (Becker, Peterson, Luria, Shoemaker, and Hellmer, 1962). Table 7.2 shows these relationships for both dimensions and both parents (as well as several other less frequently replicated factors). In general, it appears that hostility and restrictiveness are predictive of problem behavior in children as rated by their nursery school teachers. Of course, further studies are required to determine the extent to which parental behavior causes the child behavior or vice-versa.

In summary, some progress has indeed been made in dimensionalizing human psychological environments, although there has been, as yet, little if any attempt to systematically relate an adequate set of environmental differences dimensions to individual differences dimensions within a developmental context. A noteworthy partial exception to this evaluative statement is Wolf's (1966) highly stimu-

Table 7.2
Dimensions of Parental Behavior Common to Both Parents*
(Adapted from Becker, 1960)

		Factor Loading
Factor 1:	*Warmth vs. hostility*	
	1. Non-acceptance of child	.79
	2. Non-readiness of explanation	.76
	3. Not child centered	.73
	4. Hostile relationship with child	.68
Factor 2:	*Permissiveness vs. restrictiveness (on routines)*	
	1. Pressure for conformity—neatness, orderliness	.72
	2. Restrictiveness—care of house and furniture	.70
	3. High standards—neatness and orderliness	.68
	4. Strict in requiring obedience	.59
Factor 3:	*Child-rearing anxiety vs. unsolicitousness*	
	1. High child-rearing anxiety	−.75
	2. Unsolicitousness for child's welfare	.71
	3. Little disciplinary friction	.59
	4. Maladjustment of mother	−.59
Factor 4:	*Low vs. high sex anxiety*	
	1. Permissiveness for sex play among children	−.73
	2. High sex anxiety	.71
	3. Permissiveness for masturbation	−.71
	4. Nonprotectiveness	−.52
Factor 5:	*High vs. low physical punishment*	
	1. Frequent use of spankings by mother	−.68
	2. Regular use of physical punishment	−.67
	3. Mild penalties	.57
	4. Frequent use of spankings by father	−.51

*The factor loadings reflect the item correlations with the end of the factor as it is described; thus, nonacceptance of child correlates .79 with the *hostility* end of the factor.

lating work which attempted to correct the fact that "we have rarely attempted to systematically relate individual test data to environmental data in ways that are designed to increase our understanding of the [developmental] interactive process between the individual and the environment (p. 491)." Although Wolf makes a beginning at meeting the foregoing criticism, his initial attempts fall short of providing a conceptual framework which, in principle, may account for the dynamics involved in relating environmental and organismic dimensions within a developmental context.

The essence of Wolf's procedure consists of breaking down global environmental descriptive terms, such as socioeconomic status, into more meaningful ongoing environmental processes that affect both academic achievement and general intelligence—the two particular organismic variables of concern to him. The environmental process variables thought to be related to academic achievement include: the climate created for achievement motivation, the opportunities provided for verbal development, the nature and amount of assistance provided in overcoming academic difficulties, the activity level of the significant individuals in the environment, the level of intellectuality in the environment, and the kinds of work habits expected of the individual. The environmental process variables thought to be of significance to the development of general intelligence include: stimulation provided for intellectual growth, opportunities provided for, and emphasis on, verbal development, and the provision for general types of learning in a variety of situations. Environmental ratings for both academic achievement and general intelligence were found to correlate with their respective organismic variable counterpart at much higher levels than did a gross environmental measure such as socioeconomic status. The importance of Wolf's work is that it has opened the way for relating environmental differences variables to individual differences variables.

Cross-Cultural Commonalities and Differences in Traits

The search for cross-cultural commonalities and differences in traits based on factor-analytic techniques have mainly focused on the abilities domain. Cross-cultural comparisons in terms of ability factors are concerned with the general question of the invariance of factors (e.g., see Buss and Royce, 1975a). To the extent that similar factors are identified cross culturally, one may infer invariant dimensions of individual differences, which in turn should enhance the importance of considering factors as useful theoretical constructs. Although most studies concerned with cross-cultural comparisons in the abilities domain base their conclusions about the invariance of the obtained factors on subjective criteria, an increasing number of investigators have attempted to arrive at some quantitative indice of factor similarity. Representatives of the first strategy include Vernon, Irvine, and MacArthur. Vernon (1965, 1969) has carried out an extensive testing program in England, the West Indies, Africa, and the Canadian north, where he has given Western-type ability tests, based on the assumption that it is legitimate to make such comparisons to the extent developing cultures are striving towards Western technology.

Although Vernon's findings concerning ability factors are complex and not subject to easy summary, it can be said that, in general, based on a subjective evaluation of factor pattern loadings, the same factors appear cross culturally, although significant differences were noted. A similar finding was reported by Irvine (1969), who has reviewed the results of several factor analyses on African people. In the African samples reviewed by Irvine, a common educational system (Western) was seen as imposing a similar factor structure. MacArthur (1968), working like Irvine within the framework of British hierarchical models of abilities, concluded that higher-order ability factors are more similar than lower-order factors cross culturally. MacArthur's samples included Canadian Indians, Eskimos, and whites.

A more potent procedure in this area is to attempt some sort of quantitative index for the factor similarity across cultures. To the extent that factor invariance is demonstrated across cultures, quantitative comparisons are logically justifiable. If this is not the case, it makes no sense to compare cultures on factors or tests that have not been demonstrated to tap common sources of individual differences. Thus Vernon would seem to be in error to the extent that he has made quantitative comparisons across cultures using the tests as the dependent variables, when in fact it is not conclusive that the various tests are tapping the same factor. A more rational procedure would seem to be, first, to determine the degree of factor similarity across cultures based on available factor-matching procedures, and then, for those factors in which invariance has been demonstrated cross culturally, make quantitative comparisons on the factors. One wonders why Vernon made use of factor analytic techniques when ultimately he makes cross-cultural comparisons on the original test variables. This strategy defeats the purpose of factor analysis, that is, arriving at more *basic* dimensions of individual differences.

A criticism similar to that made regarding Vernon's work has been made by Irvine (1969) with respect to the work of Lesser, Fifer, and Clark (1965) and Stoddsky and Lesser (1967). These two studies

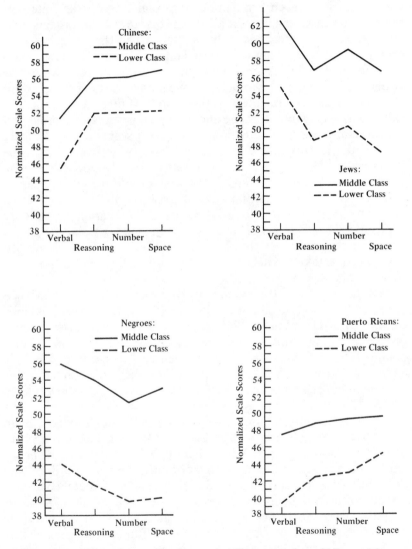

Figure 7.4 Patterns of normalized mental ability scores for middle- and lower-class Chinese, Jewish, Negroe, and Puerto Rican children (from Lesser, Fifer, & Clark, 1965).

reported different ability test profiles for different ethnic groups (Chinese, Jewish, black, and Puerto Rican—see Figure 7.4). Although the profile patterns for each ethnic group was similar across socioeconomic levels, there were mean differences within ethnic groups associated with socioeconomic class. As Irvine correctly points out, however, it is necessary to demonstrate that the tests are intercorrelated in a similar manner for all groups before one may assume that the tests measure the same abilities. Only when the latter has been demonstrated is it permissible to make group comparisons in terms of mean-level performance. This criticism again comes down to one of demonstrating the invariance of one's constructs. To the extent that test variables are intercorrelated in a similar manner across cultures, one may infer that the underlying constructs are similar and are therefore directly comparable. Because it seems highly unlikely that all the factors of the typical test battery will turn out to be structurally invariant across two given cultures as determined by some index of factor similarity, the best procedure to adopt is to make cross-cultural quantitative comparisons only on those factors that have been demonstrated to be structurally invariant. This more appropriate strategy has yet to be adopted, since those investigators who have sought to seek some quantitative index of factor similarity have failed to take the next logical step and make quantitative comparisons across cultures.

With respect to the attempt to demonstrate factor invariance across cultures, Vandenberg's (1959, 1967b) work on the cross-cultural study of Thurstone's (1938) primary mental abilities was probably the earliest attempt. In one study (Vandenberg, 1959), the factors obtained from Chinese students attending American universities were compared with Thurstone's (1938) factors obtained from American college students. Five factors were found to show a high degree of similarity, that is, congruence indices ranged from .93 to .91, where a congruence indice (which may be thought of as similar to a correlation coefficient—but not always) has a maximum value of 1. In a follow-up study, Vandenberg (1967b) compared the original Chinese group to a new sample of South American college students in terms of ability factors. Seven factors were matched across groups, with congruence indices ranging between .95 and .78. More recently, Vandenberg (1973) has calculated congruence indices on ability factors obtained from Canadian and Filipino sixth and eighth graders—data that was originally reported by Flores and Evans (1972). Vandenberg's analysis indicated that at least four factors were highly similar (congruence indices ranging between .95 and

.79). As part of a large on-going team project in Hawaii assessing the genetic and environmental aspects involved in ability performance, a preliminary report (De Fries, et al., 1974) reveals a highly similar ability structure across Americans of Japanese ancestry and Americans of European ancestry. Coefficients of congruence for the four factors examined ranged from .96 to .99.

Brief mention should be made of an important model for explaining cross-cultural differences in certain ability dimensions—assuming that such dimensions are, in fact, invariant across cultures. Berry (1971) has proposed a model for relating individual development to the physical environment or ecological demands (see Figure 7.5). The model states that ecological variables may have direct or indirect (as mediated by culture, socialization, nutrition and disease, gene pool) effects on individual development in various domains. Similarly, the individual can modify the physical environment—thereby emphasizing the reciprocal relationship between ecology and the individual. Of particular interest is Berry's analysis of cultural differences in certain spatial and perceptual skills. Thus with respect to cultures that vary in terms of their ecology and means of subsistence, Berry (1971) argued that:

> . . . hunting peoples are expected to possess good visual discrimination and spatial skill, and their cultures are expected to be supportive of the development of these skills through the presence of a high number of "geometrical spatial" concepts, a highly developed and generally shared arts and crafts production, and socialization practices whose content emphasizes independence and self reliance, and whose techniques are supportive and encouraging of separate development. Implicit in this argument is the expectation that as hunting diminishes in importance

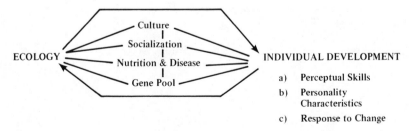

Figure 7.5 Model relating individual development to ecological and other variables (from Berry, 1971).

across samples ranked in terms of this ecology dimension, the discrimination and spatial skills will diminish, as will each of the three cultural aids (p. 328).

In this way, Berry explained differential skills developed in such cultures as the Canadian Eskimo, Australian Aborigine, Sierra Leone Temme, New Guinea Indigene, etc.

FURTHER READING:

Ferguson, G. A. On learning and human ability. *Canadian Journal of Psychology.* *8:* 95–112 (1954).

Ferguson, G. A. On transfer and the abilities of man. *Canadian Journal of Psychology.* *10:* 121–131 (1956).

Fleishman, E. A. On the relation between abilities, learning, and human performance. *American Psychologist. 27:* 1017–1032 (1972).

Gagné, R. M. (Ed.). *Learning and individual differences.* Columbus, Ohio: Merrill, 1967.

Vernon, P. E. *Intelligence and cultural environment.* Methuen, London, 1969.

Chapter 8

EDUCATIONAL PRACTICE, MASTERY LEARNING, AND INDIVIDUAL DIFFERENCES

Overview of Mastery Learning

Whereas in the previous chapter we considered, in part, the relationship between learning and individual differences in abilities, in the present chapter we take a more focused critical look at the role individual differences play in educational practice. Of particular interest here is the theory and technology of mastery learning, as espoused most recently by Bloom (1971, 1973, 1974), implied earlier by Carroll (1963), and elaborated and reviewed by Block (1971, 1974). Bloom's theory of mastery learning is based on the belief/assumption that, given the right circumstances, the majority of individuals are able to master to a certain criterion a specified learning task in an educational setting. Traditional educational practice assumes that there will be large variability on the learning criterion variable, and according to Bloom, such as assumption permits educators to abdicate what he believes their major responsibility—to provide the necessary instructional means to ensure that the majority of students learn to mastery. Bloom believes that the prevalent assumption, that there must be large variability in learning performance, is maintained and reinforced by the actual practice of educators. Thus the traditional approach to instruction involves the following sequence: large variability on input variables (abilities, interests, aptitudes, motivation, work habits, etc.) → uniform "treatment" effect (identical time for and kind of instruction) → large variability maintained on output variable (learning-performance criterion variable).

In other words, large initial individual differences in, say, aptitudes, are reflected in the learning performance variable to the extent that there are no differential "treatments" (instruction).

Whereas traditional approaches to instruction assume that there must be large differences on the criterion variable, according to the philosophy of mastery learning, instruction may be considered unsuccessful to the extent that there are large individual differences in the learning-performance outcome. The latter state of affairs implies that, traditionally, only a small proportion of students achieve criterion. Mastery learning is committed to the goal of having the majority of students (80% is the frequent proportion mentioned) perform at a level that, under traditional procedures, only about 20% of the students achieve. Mastery learning for the majority of students is achieved by providing sufficient *time* during which additional and/or differential instruction on the learning task occurs.

Time is a central concept in the theory of mastery learning, in which the belief that the majority of individuals can achieve high levels on a learning criterion variable becomes operationalized through a strategy of providing sufficient time as needed for all individuals. What Bloom has done is to translate some of Carroll's (1963) ideas on a model of school learning into a new philosophy and technology of educational instruction and learning. According to the Carroll model, rather than viewing aptitudes as predicting the final level on the criterion variable under conditions of constant instructional time, it may be of value to conceptualize aptitudes as predicting the time necessary to reach a given level of performance on a criterion variable under conditions of ideal instruction. In other words, individual differences in aptitudes become transformed conceptually into individual differences in the time required for learning, the implication being that given sufficient time, most individuals should be able to reach criterion. This slight shift in the conceptualization of aptitudes within an educational context permits the possibility of taking steps to ensure that all, or the majority rather than a minority of students, achieve mastery learning. Under conditions of both uniform time and instruction individual differences in aptitudes for learning are directly translated into a normal probability curve on the criterion achievement variable, but this is not the case in mastery learning. Rather than keeping time and kind of instruction constant and, of necessity, allowing criterion performance to vary, in mastery learning both time and kind of instruction are permitted to vary across individuals, and achievement is held constant.

TIME

		vary	constant
CRITERION	vary	MAXIMIZE POTENTIAL	TRADITIONAL INSTRUCTION
	constant	MASTERY LEARNING (early)	MASTERY LEARNING (later)

Figure 8.1   The four instructional approaches generated by either varying or holding constant the two variables, time or instruction and criterion performance.

A useful way of contrasting Bloom's theory of mastery learning and traditional instructional approaches is to consider them within the context of the two variables, time and criterion performance, where each of these variables is held constant or permitted to vary. Figure 8.1 illustrates the four possibilities. Traditional instruction holds time constant and permits the criterion variable to vary, whereas mastery learning, at the initial stages, holds the value on the criterion variable constant across individuals and permits time for instruction to vary. At more advanced stages in a mastery-learning program, Bloom claims that the individual differences in time required for instruction to reach criterion level diminishes and approaches a vanishing point. In Bloom's own words, "individual differences in achievement, time, or learning rate are largely a function of the preparatory or prior instructional approaches and that under ideal conditions individual differences in school learning approach a vanishing point" (Bloom, 1973, p. 57). The later, more advanced stages of mastery learning fall into that cell in Figure 8.1 in which both time and the criterion variable are constant. According to Bloom, this would seem to be the ideal educational situation for which we should be striving. Discussion of the remaining cell, labeled Maximize potential, is deferred to the end of this chapter, where it is argued that an educational setting in which time, kind of instruction, and the criterion variable are permitted to vary provides the best possible situation for attaining educational goals.

Bloom on Individual Differences

Consider for the moment Bloom's acceptance of Carroll's reconceptualization of individual differences in aptitudes as predicting, under ideal instruction, the time necessary to reach a common or constant (across individuals) criterion level. It would seem that the Carroll model has merely substituted for individual differences in the criterion variable individual differences in the learning rate or time necessary to reach criterion level. In other words, it makes no difference if one holds either instructional time or criterion level constant with respect to the existence of individual differences, because they will simply be defined in terms of that which is permitted to vary. Of course, one could argue that by reconceptualizing individual differences in aptitudes in terms of time necessary to reach mastery on the learning criterion variable, the way is now open to implement educational strategies that lead to a greater proportion of individuals achieving mastery, and such an educational goal is clearly desirable. In other words, one can accommodate individual differences in aptitudes for learning by adjusting the time and nature of instruction. In this way, large variability or individual differences on such organismic input variables as aptitudes and abilities need not necessarily be reflected in large individual differences on the learning criterion variable, but, rather, may be reflected in the time and nature of instruction necessary to reach a given mastery level on the criterion variable. However, variability in the latter is thought to approach zero as mastery learning progresses, and so Bloom is claiming more than that he is simply accommodating individual differences in the instructional process. He is claiming to eliminate individual differences in learning rate, instructional time, or school achievement as mastery-learning programs unfold.

It should be clearly stated at this point that Bloom does acknowledge the existence of large individual differences in such traits as abilities, aptitudes, and motivation, and has even written a whole book (Bloom, 1964) on the stability and chance of individual differences dimensions across time. Recently Bloom has stated that although aptitudes may be highly predictive of learning outcomes under traditional instructional methods, such a relationship evaporates under mastery-learning strategies. The point to be made here, however, is that Bloom could not, and probably would not, deny the existence of large individual differences as measured by a variety of traits (e.g., abilities, aptitudes, interests, motivation) even *after* conditions of mastery learning. For example, after all individuals in an introductory statistics course have achieved mastery under conditions of mastery learning, there would still be large variability on numerous traits. What Bloom has said with respect to vanishing individual differences under conditions of mastery learning is that *individual differences in school achievement for a particular learning task* is thought to approach a vanishing point. Thus it is important to appreciate the precise nature of Bloom's claim for vanishing individual differences before undertaking a critique.

Implicit in Bloom's theory of mastery learning is a deep commitment to an extreme environmentalist position, and, contrary to the last point made, looming in the background is the more general implication that present individual differences in aptitude and ability traits would largely vanish if the environment were adequately controlled. With respect to individual differences in school achievement, if one can manipulate the environment to a sufficient degree (providing the necessary time and kind of instruction), then, according to Bloom, individual differences in school achievement, time on instruction, and/or learning rate eventually approach a vanishing point. This belief that one can create, maintain, or, in short, control behavior with such precision within a controlled environment would seem to be a naive belief requiring reexamination. "In the opinion of this writer, much of what has been termed individual variation may be *explained* in terms of environmental variation" (Bloom, 1964, p. 9, emphasis added). Even if one accepts the controversial position that most of the variance in school achievement, abilities, aptitudes, and personality are due to environmental variation, this does not mean that such variation in organismic variables has been "explained" in any rigorous sense of that word. To really explain the variation of traits in terms of variation in the environment necessitates an elaborate psychological theory of person-environment interaction and the nature of that process. Unless one can explain (rather than simply "account for") the environment-related variation in human traits in the more rigorous sense hinted at here, the precise control of behavior with the aim of eliminating individual differences in traits is an impossibility.

There are several more cogent arguments one can muster against the notion that individual differences can and do approach a vanishing point under conditions of mastery learning. Some of these arguments are based on technical considerations, others on conceptual analyses, and still others on educational philosophy. Let us now present more fully the case against vanishing individual differences during mastery learning.

Technical Considerations

One can note a few technical points that, when considered, can make Bloom's notion of vanishing individual differences "vanish." First, Bloom may achieve the results he does largely because his samples are highly selected and there is little variability with respect to learning aptitudes as compared to the general population; that is, Bloom's samples are drawn from a restricted range along the normal curve. Bloom's samples are typically not representative of the population of students that he wishes to generalize across, because not all levels of socioeconomic level, learning aptitudes, abilities, and the like are represented *within* a given classroom. To the extent that streaming occurs and a given classroom represents a relatively homogenous group with respect to variables relevant to school achievement, there is a much greater possibility to reduce individual differences in school achievement. What if Bloom's samples were more representative of the population of students, that is, highly heterogeneous on variables strongly related to school achievement? Would he then be able to obtain the great reduction in variability on school achievement, time of instruction, and/or learning rate typically reported for highly homogeneous samples? Probably not.

Another factor that may be operating to artificially yield the kind of results Bloom has reported is that the ceiling on the school achievement test may be too low. If one "chops" an achievement test at too low a level, of course individuals will cluster at the high end, thereby yielding a negatively skewed distribution rather than a normal one. Providing the opportunity for more superior achievement could do much to eliminate the clustering of individuals around a given criterion level. Constructing school achievement tests that are much more open ended at least provides the opportunity for superior students to set themselves apart from the majority of students.

A final technical consideration which may also spuriously contribute to Bloom's empirical results revolves around the issue of the sensitivity of the criterion instrument. Consider the following situation. In Figure 8.2a we have the hypothetical normal distribution on a criterion variable under traditional instruction. In Figure 8.2b we have the distribution predicted after mastery learning, that is, the majority of individuals falling in, say, the stanine category 9. In such a distribution there is only one value along the criterion variable into which a given individual may fall. However, if one were to make much *finer* discriminations along the criterion variable, one would probably get a normal probability curve within the original reduced

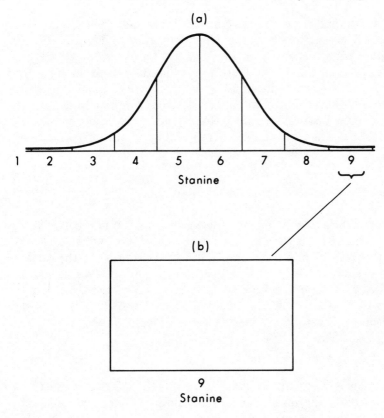

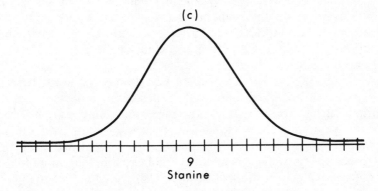

Figure 8.2 The distribution on the criterion variable under *(a)* traditional instruction, *(b)* mastery learning, and *(c)* mastery learning with a more sensitive criterion measure.

band width or score range after mastery learning. Figure 8.2c illustrates this possibility. Although it is true that in Figure 8.2c the absolute variance is much smaller than in Figure 8.2a, in comparing Figures 8.2b and 8.2c, there are individual differences in the latter but not in the former, in spite of identical ranges on the criterion variable. Thus one may eliminate or reduce individual differences by using a blunt instrument that is simply not capable of making the finer discriminations required for yielding a normal probability curve.

Surface Trait–Source Trait Distinction

According to trait theory, there are a limited number of basic unitary source traits that combine in varying ways to yield a variety of surface traits. Thus, for example, the source traits from the various domains such as the abilities, temperament, and motives determine a surface trait such as school achievement. Reproducing for convenience the basic factor equation, or what Cattell (1957) calls the specification equation, one expresses this idea as follows:

$$z_{xi} = b_{x1}F_{1i} + b_{x2}F_{2i} + \ldots + b_{xk}F_{ki} \qquad (8.1)$$

where z_{xi} is a score on variable x for individual i, the bs are the k factor loadings for variable x and are unique for that variable, and the Fs are the k factor scores for individual i and unique for that individual. Thus, for example, performance on some surface trait such as school achievement is specified by weighting a certain set of factors or traits in which the higher the weights or factors loadings, the more important individual differences in factor scores become in determining individual differences in the surface trait (e.g., Cattell and Butcher, 1968).

Although the model expressed in Equation 8.1 is not immune to criticism, it has worked quite well for predicting a person's score on various surface traits from a knowledge of the factor loadings for that surface trait and the person's factor scores on the source traits. A basic property of the model in Equation 8.1 is that it is additive and compensatory. What this implies is that two different individuals with different values on the set of source trait factor scores involved on the right side of Equation 8.1 could theoretically get *identical* scores on the surface trait on the left side of Equation 8.1. This follows because if one is low on a given trait, he can make up for this deficiency by a high score in another trait with respect to a given surface trait score. This digression on the basic factor equation is necessary because it serves to make the very important point that one could theoretically have several different individuals with identical or very similar scores on a surface trait yet be very different in terms of the more basic underlying source traits that determine or account for the observed behavior. In terms of the Bloom model, many individuals may yield little or no variability on school achievement, yet the "reasons" why they all score around the same value may be quite different. That is to say, each individual may have a different combination or pattern of levels on the source traits (a unique profile) which, when "plugged" into the model as expressed by Equation 8.1, will all yield identical or at least very similar surface trait scores. Now, has there been a reduction of individual differences, assuming that as a result of mastery learning both time on instruction and criterion level (surface trait) are relatively constant across individuals? If by the term individual differences we are referring to variability in the more basic and fundamental source traits, clearly such differences may be large, even after mastery learning has been implemented and been successful. Some would argue that we should restrict the term individual differences to refer to variability in such unitary source variables. According to the latter, reasonable view, there are large, pervasive individual differences in the source traits that determine or account for identical or at least similar performance scores in the surface trait. In such a situation, do individual differences in school achievement approach a vanishing point? The answer is not necessarily, nor even probably, because of the individual differences in the underlying source traits for school achievement. Individuals vary greatly in terms of *why* they are performing at a given criterion level. Descriptively, individuals may perform identically, yet the deeper and more penetrating theoretical question is the following: how do individuals differ in the way they achieve roughly the same level in school achievement? Sameness at the descriptive level of a surface trait does not imply sameness at the explanatory or causal level of the source traits. In a fundamental sense (i.e., primary source traits), individuals vary greatly after mastery learning, and it is probably misleading for Bloom to say that individual differences in school achievement approaches a vanishing point under conditions of mastery learning.

The Category Mistake

Probably the most serious criticism of Bloom's notion of vanishing individual differences revolves around the idea that it is a category mistake to make psychometric inferences from educative "treatments." What this involves is keeping clear the two basic uses tests may serve—tapping how individuals differ in trait level to plan differential placement, counseling, training, and the like, and evaluating the effectiveness of a "treatment" condition such as educational instruction. Carver (1974) has recently called these two dimensions of tests *psychometric* and *edumetric,* respectively, although there is earlier literature on this distinction (for reviews see Cronbach, 1971b; Glaser and Nitko, 1971). The purpose in the construction and use of psychometric tests is to measure stable individual differences along certain trait dimensions that may be useful in predicting other kinds of behavior. Such tests are *norm referenced;* that is, they are designed to measure an individual with respect to or compared with other persons in the standardization group. Variability between persons is assumed, and a good test is one that adequately discriminates between individuals thought to vary in the underlying trait. An edumetric test, on the other hand, does not attempt to make comparative or across individual discriminations, rather, it evaluates an individual vis-à-vis an absolute standard. Such tests are *criterion referenced* insofar as they are constructed on the basis of being able to measure absolute performance on some clearly defined criterion. The typical achievement test is an edumetric test in which a person is assigned a score on the basis of how well he mastered the content the test sampled. Measuring gain or growth of individuals is the aim of an edumetric test rather than making comparisons across individuals.

As argued by Carver (1974), the purpose, item selection, validity, reliability, and score interpretation all differ for psychometric tests as opposed to edumetric tests, although there are those who have disagreed with some of Carver's points (e.g., Cronbach, 1975b; Gladstone, 1975; Haladyna, 1975). However, it seems reasonably clear that psychometric and edumetric tests do serve radically different purposes, and to use a test for edumetric reasons and then argue on the basis of one's results that the psychometric properties of the group have changed, is to commit a category mistake. "If one wishes to select, place, or group students on the basis of test scores, the test is psychometric; if one wishes to ascertain student performance with respect to passing a standard, the test is edumetric" (Haladyna, 1975, p. 604). Bloom is clearly using tests for edumetric purposes in his mastery-learning programs. The purpose of his tests are to evaluate the gain or growth as a result of the educational "treatments." It is sheer folly to argue on the basis of achieving one's educational goal, as evaluated by edumetric tests, that there is reason to believe that individual differences in school achievement have vanished.

A major point here is that one could conceivably design a psychometric test in school achievement for the same subject matter that had been learned to mastery as evaluated by an edumetric test. In other words, the individual differences are there if one is willing and able to design and use a test that can maximize the discrimination between individuals. The purpose of such a test would be quite different from an edumetric test. It would not, of course, make sense to comment on or make inferences about the success or lack of success of one's educational program on the basis of a test whose purpose was to compare individuals to other individuals rather than assess absolute performance on a given content criterion variable. The distinction between norm-referenced and criterion-referenced tests and the differing inferences each affords has been well expressed by Nitko (1970):

> In most circumstances one *or* the other kind of information [norm-referenced versus criterion-referenced] is of primary concern. The test constructor can choose to maximize either criterion-referenced information or norm-referenced information, but seldom can he maximize both. Since norm-referenced scores derive most of their meaning from distributions in which we can distinguish one individual from another, judicious selection of test items with the help of statistical analysis will maximize this distinction. Such statistical selection of items for criterion-referenced tests makes little sense, however. The classes or domains of tasks which define a behavior are determined, insofar as is possible, before the test is constructed and then representative samples are drawn for inclusion on any test. To screen out some items for inclusion on a particular test because they possess desirable statistical characteristics will change the definitions of the behavioral categories . . . The kind of information desired when criterion-reference tests are used is the behaviors an individual does or does not possess and whether or not the test

yields meaningful normative-standard scores is often of
secondary importance (Nitko, 1970, pp. 7–8).

Another aspect of the category mistake which Bloom makes
involves the meaning of individual differences. Individual differences
are defined by the variability in test scores if the purpose of the test
is to sort out people along an underlying trait to make differential
placements, predictions, and so forth. *Critical* in the idea of individual differences is the notion of applying the *same* treatment to a
number of individuals, the idea being that each individual receives
the same stimulus input so that any variability in response must be
due to what is inside the organism. This is what is meant by individual differences. It is a snapshot in time—freezing the differences
between individuals along certain organismic variables for certain
purposes.

When one introduces a program of education aimed at having
all individuals achieve criterion, one focuses on intraindividual
change rather than interindividual differences. Individuals are
given *differential* treatments (varying time and kind of instruction)
in the former situation so that they all achieve a given absolute
level on a criterion variable. The goals and purposes of this instructional program, which is focused on intraindividual change, are orthogonal to the aims and goals of arriving at a statement about
individual differences. These two issues are conceptually separate
and cannot "speak" to each other. One cannot buttress the results
of edumetric tests on the basis of psychometric considerations and
vice versa.

Educational Philosophy and Mastery Learning

Implicit in Bloom's notion of vanishing individual differences is
an egalitarian philosophy of education which states that all individuals should be educated to the same level of difficulty. As defined by
Bloom, the attempts to eliminate individual differences in school
achievement is, on closer inspection, an impoverished view of educational practice. Bloom's mastery learning techniques work best on
convergent thinking material in which there are specific answers
required for test items. Thus mathematics is the most common subject matter selected on which to implement a mastery learning program. Such training programs are probably not the ultimate goal of
education. Later transfer and especially divergent or creative think-

ing are completely ignored in mastery learning (e.g., see Cronbach, 1971a). The success of one's education program ultimately is judged on the kinds of behavior that mastery learning is not equipped to foster.

A more critical argument can be made in attempting to break down an educational philosophy that takes as its goal identical performance of all individuals on the criterion variables. Reference to Figure 8.1 indicates that there is one cell yet to be discussed—the Maximize Potential cell in which both time for instruction and criterion performance are permitted to vary. This situation would probably be the ideal—permitting all individuals to maximize their unique potential by providing the necessary time for and kind of instruction required to develop their educable potentiality. This situation would be a definite improvement over traditional instructional practice, because individual differences are recognized and accommodated by providing differential instruction. In effect, an educational program that permits time, kind of instruction, and criterion performance to vary has as its goal shifting upward the entire normal distribution of criterion scores obtained under traditional instruction. In such a situation, individuals of superior ability would be sufficiently challenged to go beyond the levels that the majority of individuals are expected to attain. The main advantage of the Maximize Potential philosophy over mastery learning is that the former would ensure that each individual is sufficiently challenged to develop fully his skills and abilities. Sufficient time and instruction is provided for all students as needed or, one would hope, demanded in the pursuit of knowledge. The fast learners would go on to spend time on more advanced topics rather than wait around for everyone to achieve a uniform mastery level.

The Theoretical Bankruptcy of Mastery Learning

It has been noted above that Bloom acknowledges the existence of individual differences ("That 'individual differences' between learners exist is indisputable," Bloom, 1971, p. 49), but that he believes they need not be reflected in school achievement ("What is disputable is that these variations must play a role in student learning and must be reflected in our learning standards and achievement criteria," Bloom, 1971, p. 49). As also argued, Bloom's notion that mastery learning entails vanishing individual differences is thought to be erroneous. In closing, it would be valuable to consider briefly Bloom's adoption of Carroll's idea that, under ideal instruction, aptitudes should predict the time necessary for reaching mastery learning—where individual differences in aptitudes thus become translated into the time necessary to reach criterion.

Time as a variable is thought by Bloom to hold much promise within educational research:

> For the educational researcher, there are many attractive features in the use of time as a variable. Time can be measured with as much precision as the researcher desires. The measures of time have many properties that are almost impossible to secure in our conventional measures of academic achievement: equality of units, an absolute zero, and clear and unambiguous comparisons of individuals (Bloom, 1974, p. 684).

Unfortunately, any advantages of using time as a major variable in psychological research become dwarfed when the disadvantages are considered. As developmental psychologists are realizing (e.g., Wohlwill, 1970a), time as a variable (in this case expressed as age) is really quite uninteresting—serving to explain little *psychologically*. Rather than being conceived as an independent variable, developmentalists are now looking at time as a dependent variable, that is, useful for simply describing rather than explaining age-related change. What the developmentalists are beginning to appreciate about the limitations and/or role of the time variable in getting at psychological explanations should transfer over to the field of learning and individual differences. That is to say, stating that individual differences in aptitude for learning should be conceived in terms of the time required to reach mastery learning tends to shut off looking at such individual differences in learning in terms of the underlying processes and "mechanisms" that explain the differential behavior. For Bloom, any kind of individual differences in aptitudes for learning are reduced to *one* common variable—individual differences in the time required to reach mastery! Such an extreme reductionistic approach to individual differences in learning aptitudes dismisses in one fell swoop a growing literature on trying to get at a greater *understanding* of individual differences in a learning situation (for reviews, see Cronbach, 1957, 1975a; Gagné, 1967; Glaser, 1970; Glaser and Resnick, 1972). In defining a vast domain of individual differences in terms of time, one forfeits any possibility of penetrating to a deeper theoretical level for purposes of explaining such differences and, ultimately, tailoring the person-educational environment fit.

FURTHER READING:

Block, J. H. (Ed.). *Mastery learning: Theory and practice.* New York: Holt, Rinehart and Winston, 1971.

Block, J. H. (Ed.). *Schools, society, and mastery learning.* New York: Holt, Rinehart and Winston, 1974.

Bloom, B. S. Time and learning. *American Psychologist,* 1974, *29,* 682–688.

Glaser, R., and Nitko, A. J. Measurements in learning and instruction. In R. L. Thorndike (Ed.), *Educational measurement.* Washington, D.C.: American Council on Education, 1971.

Chapter 9

HEREDITARY BASIS OF
INDIVIDUAL DIFFERENCES

The major "schools" of personality theory have traditionally been strongly environmentalist in their explanation of individual differences. This is fairly obvious in the case of the behavioristic tradition. Watson, one of the early behaviorists who is sometimes referred to as the father of behaviorism, stated:

> Give me a dozen healthy infants, well-formed, and my own specified world to bring them up in and I'll guarantee to take any one at random and train him to be any kind of specialist I might select—regardless of his talents, penchants, tendencies, abilities, vocations, and race of his ancestors (Watson, 1930, p. 104).

Behaviorism, closely tied to vigorous definitions of the environment through basic conditioning and learning paradigms, might be expected to decry the effect of genetic influences on behavior. One can argue that the Freudian-psychoanalytic tradition in personality is also highly environmentalist. Freud claimed that the source of all psychological energy is the id, where the id is biological by definition. Nevertheless, there would be no personality development, no social character, no values or derived motivations, if this energy were not diverted (displaced) by the *environment* to be invested into more suitable "objects" than the instinctive goal objects such as food and sex.

Darwin preceded Watson and Freud, and his evolutionary theory was generally accepted by scientists, including behavioral scientists. It may impress modern researchers as paradoxical that evolutionary thinking would be readily accepted by early behavior scientists as applicable to physical characteristics but not to psychological characteristics (Galton was an exception here—see Chapter 1). Thus we should examine some of the possible reasons behind this paradoxical situation. First of all, there is the influence of the cultural ethos which opposed the European aristocratic traditions and argued that a person's position in life is not a birthright but a product of his experiences. This kind of view was closely associated with liberal thinkers such as John Stewart Mill. The environmentalist tradition was also able to offset a fatalistic (and sometimes punitive) approach to mental illness. After all, if mental illness were construed to be a product of genetic-physiological influences, institutionalization could be defended on the grounds that science, at this time, had no control over these factors. A second contributor to the dominance of the environmentalist ethos was undoubtedly the lack of adequate methodology for research into genetics at the turn of the century. Genetics at the time was a relatively new science. A third contributor was probably the underdeveloped state of physiological research in psychology. As psychologists have done more and more research searching for physiological determinants of behavior, it becomes increasingly reasonable to expect that genetic influences underlie physiological processes and from there contribute to behavior. Thus behavior-genetics did not become an established field of psychology until the 1960s.

Behavior-Genetic Levels of Analysis

Our general goal in taking the behavior-genetic approach to individual differences is to analyze individual differences or the *variance* (σ^2) in overt behavior *(phenotypic differences)* into the proportionate contributions of genetic variance sources, environmental variance sources, and the variance due to an interaction between the two, where this is feasible. This yields the following equation:

$$\sigma_P^2 = \sigma_G^2 + \sigma_E^2 + \sigma_{GE}^2 \tag{9.1}$$

where the subscripts *P*, *G*, and *E* refer to phenotype, genetic, and environment, respectively.

Further comment on Equation 9.1 is in order. Although it does make conceptual sense to partition the observed total variance of a measure into additive genetic and environmental components, it by no means follows that one can do the same thing for individual scores. In fact, it is *not* meaningful to ask how much of a particular individual score is due to heredity and how much to environment. Both of these influences are 100% important or required in terms of causing a particular behavior to occur, since one cannot have a behavior occurring without either a biological organism to emit it or an environment in which it is to occur. It does make sense, however, to ask how much of the variability among persons (not absolute performance scores but deviations around the group mean) on a certain variable such as an ability is due to heredity and how much to environment. It is extremely important to separate these two types of questions, because they still are often confused in talking about the hereditary basis for behavior. Thus the goal is to develop research designs that can enable us to estimate the relative magnitude of these components. In this way we can determine whether the components σ_G^2, σ_E^2, σ_{GE}^2 are statistically significant and estimate the magnitude of their contribution to individual differences in the context of a particular environment and a particular gene pool sampled.

Equation 9.1 represents a statistical breakdown of individual differences. Eventually we would like to be able to analyze the genetic and environmental terms into more refined components, but in most cases this represents a much more advanced state of research which will require many more years to complete. From genetic theory, for example, we know that genes are located on chromosomes found in the nuclei of cells. In the body cells, chromosomes occur in pairs—as do the genes located on them. In human body cells there are 23 pairs of chromosomes. In the formation of *gametes* (sperms and eggs), this number must be reduced by half; otherwise we would double the number of chromosomes with each succeeding generation. The reduction division in the formation of gametes is referred to as *meiosis*. During meiosis, there is also a process whereby corresponding regions of the paired chromosomes exchange genetic material. In this way new combinations of genes are produced in the gametes, leading to genetic diversity. That is to say, the next generation will share genetic material with the parental generation, but it will also have a unique arrangement of genes.

As we try to become more explicit about the nature of genetic contributors, we pass from the chromosome level of analysis to genes located on the chromosomes, and from there to the study of biochemical genetics. With regard to the latter, John D. Watson and

Francis Crick have found that a complex molecule referred to as DNA (deoxyribonucleic acid) forms the genetic material at a biochemical level of analysis. DNA exerts its influence on the organism by giving the code (from its exact chemical arrangement) for the production of amino acids which are then combined into more complex enzymes and proteins of the body.

We have, then, four levels of analysis that might be of interest to behavior genetics: the statistical level, the chromosome level, the gene level, and the biochemical level. The first of these is of most use to the field of individual differences, because it is very difficult to study the other three levels of analysis in higher organisms such as man. One particular difficulty in behavior genetics is that the complex behaviors we study are typically determined by complex genetic systems, that is, by polygenes rather than by single genes or chromosomes with major identifiable effects on behavior. An individual gene in a polygenic system (such as that related to intelligence) might have a small quantitative effect on increasing or decreasing intelligence (phenotype), but its effect on phenotype would not be qualitatively recognizable, as would gene effects on a phenotype such as eye color. We can, however, provide some examples of fairly dramatic effects that single genes or chromosomes do have on behavior.

Chromosome Effects: One of the more interesting chromosome effects is found in connection with the sex chromosomes. In man, the twenty-third pair of chromosomes is referred to as the *X-Y* pair. One of these chromosomes *(X)* carries a full allotment of genetic information. The shorter chromosome *(Y)* carries very little information. Sex of the individual is determined by whether the individual inherits two *X* chromosomes or an *X* and a *Y* chromosome. The *XX* arrangement produces a female; the *XY* arrangement produces a male. In some cases, a male will be born with an extra *X* chromosome *(XXY)* or *Y* chromosome *(XYY)* because of a failure in normal meiosis. The latter condition seems to be related to violent-aggressive and antisocial behavior. As support for this contention, the frequency of the *XYY* condition in the general population is only 1/300, but roughly 1/30 in prison populations.

Major Gene Effects: A single major gene pair has been found to be responsible for the condition of phenylketonuria (PKU) associated with severe mental retardation. The gene responsible for this condition is recessive to the matching dominant gene for normal behavior. Thus if one chromosome bears the recessive gene while the other chromosome bears the dominant gene, the individual will be normal, though he will be a carrier for the pathological state. If, however, an individual receives both recessive genes, the phenylketonuric condition will appear. In the normal biochemical reactions of the body, phenylalanine is broken down into tyrosine by the enzyme phenylalanine hydroxylase. This enzyme is lacking in the phenylketonuric condition, with the result that there is an accumulation of phenylalanine, which leads to chemical damage to the central nervous system and mental retardation. Because of the development of chemical tests to diagnose this condition in infancy, it can now be substantially remedied by providing the afflicted infant with a diet low in phenylalanine. This is an important principle, for it illustrates that genetically based abnormalities can be modified or corrected by environmental intervention strategies. Genetic determination of a behavioral trait does not necessarily imply immutability.

Weak and Strong Statistical Analyses

Present indications are that differences in ability, temperament, and motivation traits are determined by polygenes. Thus the most relevant level of analysis for research is at the statistical level. Here we have to separate the research designs into those that provide relatively convincing evidence of genetic influences in and of themselves (strong designs), and those that are convincing by virtue of sheer weight of evidence from a number of studies (weak designs). The difference between these designs relates primarily to the degree of confounding extraneous variables that may mask the true genetic effects.

Weak Designs: (1) *Twin studies* provides us with two major research designs: the study of identical or monozygous twins *(MZ)* versus fraternal or dizygous twins *(DZ)* in which each set of twins is reared together, and the study of *MZ* twins reared apart versus *MZ* twins reared together. The first design is only moderately convincing and is examined here, but the second can provide very strong evidence for the predominance of genetic or environmental effects (depending on the data), and will be considered later. The study of *MZ* versus *DZ* twins is based on the premise that *MZ* twin differences are a result of environmental *(E)* differences only (because *MZ* twins are genetically identical), whereas *DZ* twin differences are a result of both genetic *(G)* and environmental *(E)* differences. Thus we can use this information in conducting a twin study and analyze the data by some appropriate statistical variation based on the following model:

$$\frac{\sigma^2_{DZ} - \sigma^2_{MZ}}{\sigma^2_{DZ}} = \frac{(\sigma^2_G + \sigma^2_E) - \sigma^2_E}{\sigma^2_G + \sigma^2_E} = \frac{\sigma^2_G}{\sigma^2_G + \sigma^2_E} \qquad (9.2)$$

which states that the observed variance in *DZ* twins minus the observed variance in *MZ* twins divided by the observed variance in *DZ* twins is equal to the genetic variance over the total (genetic plus environmental) variance. The final ratio is referred to as a *heritability index,* and it expresses the genetic contribution to the observed variance of individual differences, as a proportion of the total phenotypic individual differences or variance.

Criticism of this model should be noted. One serious deficiency of studying *MZ* versus *DZ* twins is that these researches typically deal only with the *within* family variance rather than including the *between* family variance. Thus this design ignores important variance components (the between-family variance for both genetic and environmental sources) that are required for a more complete estimate of heritability. Also, the environmentalist may point out that heritability may be spuriously high, because identical twins tend to be treated more alike by other people than are fraternal twins and thus the environmental component may not be comparable. Another point to note is that identical twins often model themselves after one another, which again will reduce σ^2_{MZ}. On the other hand, there are influences that tend to reduce heritability spuriously, that is, indicate a greater role for environmental contributors. One of these influences is that *DZ* twins may also model themselves after one another and be treated alike by other persons because they are mistaken for *MZ* twins (often from birth). This reduces σ^2_{DZ} and therefore reduces heritability. Another source that may spuriously reduce heritability concerns prenatal competition, which is greater for *MZ* twins. Thus some characteristics, such as birth weight, tend to be more discrepant for *MZ* than for *DZ* twins. Finally, it should be noted that older twins tend to adopt complementary roles rather than simply model themselves after one another. This will tend to inflate the σ^2_{MZ}, thereby reducing heritability. In summary, all these influences cannot be sufficiently controlled for by the model expressed in Equation 9.2, and research in this general area has increasingly looked for other, more adequate, designs.

(2) *Pedigree studies* are representative of some of the earliest and

least successful attempts at demonstrating the heritability of behavioral traits. Around the turn of the century, researchers were able to show that there was a tendency for criminal behavior as well as high or low intelligence, to "run in families." But because the environment of parents and their offspring (and other relatives) are more closely aligned than in the general population (as well as their genetic material), this kind of study completely confounds heredity and environment. Such studies are mainly useful at the gene level of analysis rather than the statistical. For example, when a major gene is manifested clearly in the population, it can be traced through the family with known probabilities of appearing in each individual.

Strong Designs: (1) *Identical twins reared together versus reared apart.* Occasionally, identical twins are separated shortly after birth and placed in different adoptive homes. These situations are rare, but when they have occurred, they provide excellent data. If genetic influences predominate, the correlation between twins reared apart should be close to unity. If, on the other hand, there are no genetic influences, the correlation should be no greater than in the general population, that is, effectively zero. This conclusion is based on two premises: *(a)* that the environment in the prenatal and early infancy period prior to separation has not had a strong effect in producing correlated scores, and *(b)* that the separated twins are not placed in highly similar environments, which might yield a high correlation. However, even if both of these assumptions are violated, it does not seem reasonable that the environments of different families would be matched more closely than the environments for ordinary siblings. Thus if siblings generally correlate 0.5, for example, and *MZ* twins reared apart correlate 0.8, it would seem reasonable to conclude that heredity is playing a strong role in accounting for individual differences variance.

(2) *Foster-child studies* are based on comparing the correlations of the child with both the biological parent and the adopting or foster parent. If the former is greater, there is evidence for genetic effects. This is based on two assumptions: *(a)* again, that the prenatal and early infancy period is not of major importance as a contributor to environmentally induced correlations between the biological parent and the child; and that *(b)* the child is not placed in an adopting home in which the parents closely match the behavior of the biological parents. If such a study is conducted and the assumptions are not seriously violated, the results supply evidence for genetic effects, and the environmentalist opposition to this conclusion is relatively weak. For example, if the environmentalists argue that the second assump-

tion is violated, the result would have to be high correlations between the child and *both* the biological and foster parents. To the extent the observed discrepancy between the two correlations are found, the environmentalist position is weakened.

(3) *Holding the environment constant* designs can be used (theoretically at least) to study sex differences, race differences, or social-class differences. Thus if the environment is matched as closely as possible for, say, children from two races, any differences between the two groups can only be due to genetic influences. The great difficulty in this design is that in practice it is virtually impossible to assure this environmental matching. We do not really know all the conditions that should be matched, and even if we did, different deeply entrenched social expectations and roles would be placed on the child because of other obvious racial or sex attributes.

(4) *Holding heredity constant studies,* unlike studies of human beings, are carried out in animal studies in which heredity is systematically controlled. For example, if mice or rats are intensively inbred (by brother-sister matings) for a number of generations, the result will be to fix all genetic loci. That is to say, all gene pairs become homozygous (as opposed to heterozygous). The reason for this becomes apparant in the following simplified example:

Generation	Genotypes at a Given Locus		
G_1	AA	Aa,aA	aa
G_2	AA	AA,Aa,aA,aa	aa

In this example, we are making use of self-fertilization, the most intense type of inbreeding. It is clear that the proportion of homozygotes *(AA* or *aa)* is increasing with each generation (in the first generation, 1/2 of the individuals are homozygous, whereas in the second generation, the proportion is 2/3). The same *trend* will be followed in less extreme forms of inbreeding: parent-child, brother-sister, first cousins, second cousins, and so forth. Inbreeding resulting in complete homozygosity (after sufficient generations) will yield pure strains of animals, that is, homozygous at all loci. In this situation, all animals (within a pure strain) will be as genetically identical as are *MZ* twins. Thus if laboratory environments are matched between different strains, any differences must be due to heredity. Often we find that the production of homozygosity in strains brings out deleterious genes. Such genes are usually recessive

and therefore not manifested in the general population of their heterozygous states, but do become apparent in their homozygous state
(e.g., *aa*). The loss of vigor brought about by an increase in
homozygosity is called *inbreeding depression,* and is often corrected
when strains are cross bred, resulting in an increase in heterozygosity
(referred to as hybrid vigor).

(5) *Inbreeding depression* is a condition that can often be taken
advantage of in studying human-behavior genetics. The incest taboo
is almost universal, but a mild degree of inbreeding is some societies
(such as first-cousin marriages) may be considered to be normal.
Thus if we can assume that environmental conditions are equal for
children of cousin versus noncousin marriages, inbreeding depression should be evidence for genetic effects.

Multiple Abstract Variance Analysis (MAVA).

One of the more important developments concerning research designs aimed at unravelling genetic and environmental
variance sources centers around Cattell's (1960) multiple abstract
variance analysis (MAVA). Although the statistical level required
for following the technical niceties of this model are quite demanding, the basic logic is quite straightforward. Cattell begins
by setting out the major sources that produce individual differences or variances. These are:

1. σ^2_{we} = the variance within families due to environment
2. σ^2_{wg} = the variance within families due to genetic factors
3. σ^2_{be} = the variance between families due to environment
4. σ^2_{bg} = the variance between families due to genetic factors

It can be seen that Cattell provides for between-family variance
sources in addition to within-family sources, and this procedure has
a distinct advantage to those designs that consider only the latter
(e.g., comparing *MZ* and *DZ* pairs of twins each reared together).
Another advantage of the MAVA method is that it is able to consider
covariance terms in addition to the variance components. By covariance it is meant the effect due to the possibility that the environment
and heredity are often correlated. For example, children who tend
to be endowed with genes that provide for relatively high levels of
intelligence also tend to be reared in relatively enriched environments. Thus family heredity and environment are not independent
in this example (i.e., they are correlated), and one must add the

effects of this correlation (the covariance term) to the genetic and environmental variance components. An example of a within-covariance term would be that situation in which there is a positive correlation between genetic and environmental influences within the family. Such a situation would arise when a genetically superior child, with regard to intelligence, is actively encouraged and stimulated by the parents, whereas the other children who have a lesser advantage, genetically speaking, are not given such challenging intellectual problems. In a similar manner, it is possible to conceive of additional covariance terms, and Figure 9.1 sets out the six logical possibilities. In the more simple MAVA method, there are 10 abstract variance components, that is, the four main sources and the six possible covariance terms. In passing, it can be noted that extensions of this basic model include setting out the various interactional terms.

Confining our attention to the 10 basic abstract variance components, the next step is to set out the appropriate components contributing to the observed variance for various sample groups. For example, consider the following equation:

$$\sigma_{st}^2 = \sigma_{wg}^2 + \sigma_{we}^2 + 2r_{wg \cdot we}\sigma_{wg}\sigma_{we} \tag{9.3}$$

This equation states that the observed variance for sibs (brothers and sisters) reared together is equal to the within-family genetic variance

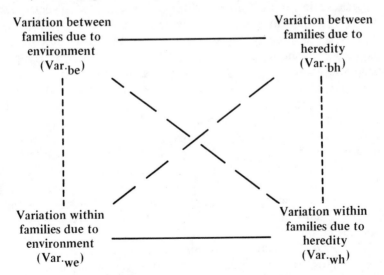

Figure 9.1 The six possible correlations between heredity and environment for between and within families (from Butcher, 1968).

plus the within-family environmental variance plus a covariance term for these sources. In a similar manner, it is possible to construct equations for sibs reared apart, unrelated children reared together, fraternal twins reared together, identical twins reared apart, and so forth. Once a sufficient number of such equations are formed, it is possible to solve for the unknown hypothetical variances (hence abstract variance analysis) on the right side of the equations.

Although the MAVA method is a superior model for probing the complexities surrounding the relative contributions of heredity and environment to individual differences, there are some drawbacks that should be noted. On the theoretical side, there are typically more unknown abstract variances to solve for than independent equations, thus making the ultimate solution indeterminate. Some of the possible covariance terms, however, may be assumed to be zero, enabling a solution to be found. On the practical side, it has been estimated that a full 5000 subjects would be required to carry out a complete study using this method. We may anticipate that as data banks become more and more a part of researchers' resources, the MAVA method will come into much greater use than has been the case thus far.

Common Misconceptions in Nature-Nurture Findings

Because nature-nurture controversies have existed in society for many generations (longer than we have had adequate research designs to resolve some of the issues), it is not unnatural that stereotyped responses should accompany this topic. More specifically, preconceptions about the role of heredity and environment in producing individual differences have been directly related to aristocratic-elitist versus equalitarian philosophies, to racism and prejudice, to equalitarian social roles for men and women, and to the desirability of promoting social mobility. The result is that misconceptions are frequent and difficult to modify. Furthermore, the scientific responsibility to evaluate results carefully and rationally is very great—in fact, greater than has been realized to date. Scientists have too often allowed their preconceptions and political-social philosophies to bias their assessments of research results. The following are some of the important common misconceptions.

Either-Or Thinking. This misconception has been more amenable to change than the others. Scientists as well as laymen used to ask whether a certain behavior was determined by heredity *or* environment. We now realize that *both* heredity and environment are 100% required or necessary for determining or causing behavior, because behavior cannot occur divorced from an organism or an environment. In terms of producing individual differences around a group mean (or variance), both heredity and environment are again involved, although now it is possible to apportion the importance of these two sources in relative terms (heritability). It cannot be stressed too strongly, however, that such a partition of relative components refers to a population rather than an individual, and it is possible only when speaking of individual differences variance rather than the causes of behavior.

Unchangeability of Genetically Determined Individual Differences. We often continue to draw incorrect implications from the evidence for genetic contributors as if we still accepted either-or thinking. Thus even if behavior in a certain environment is 100% heritable in a given population, it may still be modifiable by appropriate environmental manipulations. However, the environmental manipulation must be outside the range of experiences of individuals in the population from which the 100% heritability was obtained. A case in point involves PKU (described earlier). In this situation, if we consider a population of those with PKU, individual differences will be due 100% to genetic factors. Environmental manipulation need not always be chemical (i.e., dietary) in nature. It is conceivable, for example, that we could alter intelligence considerably by introducing educational experiences outside the range of our present concepts of education. Schaie's data on intergeneration improvements in both *Gf* and *Gc* tend to support this. Heritability does not provide a rationalization for fatalism.

Relativeness of Heritability. It is important to stress that the heritability ratios reported for any trait should be understood as applying *only* to a certain specified population. The defining characteristics of this population must include a statement about the degree of environmental variation sampled, as well as the range of genetic structures sampled. The latter is necessary, because by increasing the range of environments to be included, the heritability will decrease, whereas the reverse would occur if one were to increase the range of genetic structures sampled. Thus it is important to recognize that heritability is always a *relative* concept, intimately tied to the population under study.

Heritability and Mean Differences. A very serious error that has been made in the past concerns heritability and the inferences permitted regarding differences in population means (e.g., in the abilities domain). What is typically done is to infer that if a certain trait is highly heritable and there are population mean absolute differences in this trait, such absolute differences must be due to genetic differences between the gene pools of the two populations. However, one cannot make any inferences regarding absolute mean population differences being due to genetic factors on the basis of heritability. Even if the heritability of a trait is 100%, absolute population differences may be due to environmental factors. This point is obvious if one recalls the exact meaning of heritability. That is, it refers only to individual differences or variance *within* a given population, and within-population heritability estimates provide no basis for making between-population heritability estimates. This potential error of inference has obscured research involving the reasons why blacks consistently scored lower than whites on intelligence measures, and is further considered in Chapter 10.

Genetic Limits.   There is an old expression that "genetics set the limit while environment determines the degree of expression of behavior." Although this statement is no longer consistent with behavior-genetic thinking, it is still expressed, even by geneticists. For example, this type of thinking finds support in pointing out that, because man does not have wings (the genetic limit), he cannot fly. This, however, is a confusion of the terms genetic-limits (intraspecies) and species-limits (interspecies). Species are certainly limited— man does not have the appendages to fly and mice do not have the cerebral capacity for higher mathematics. But this limit is set by the total biological makeup of the species. Within a species, genes and enviornment *jointly* determine behavior variability. Thus in one type of environment a certain genetic structure will be advantageous, whereas in a slightly different environment a different genetic structure will have the edge. This observation makes it clear that it makes as much sense to talk about environmental limits as genetic limits. Another danger in the traditional focus on the genetic limit is that it *implies* that heritability is somehow more important than environment in determining behavior, which, of course, is completely false.

Heredity versus Learning.   Although geneticists may paradoxically misuse the term genetic limit, psychologists frequently set genetics in opposition to learning. In fact, *an individual behavioral deviation or difference can be learned as well as be genetically determined.* "Learned" can be set in opposition to the term "instinctive," but not "genetic," although even in the former opposition there are subtleties to be considered (e.g., Hebb, 1953). An example illustrating that learning and genetic influences are not to be pitted against each other involves the numerous studies demonstrating the genetic basis for individual differences in conditionability or learning in animals. Following this logic, it is quite conceivable that individual differences in values, interests, attitudes, and even conscience or superego may be heritable (i.e., individual differences determined by genetic factors), although they are obviously learned as well. Instinctive behavior, on the other hand, implies that learning (at least beyond minimal experiental contacts) is not required for the development of a complex behavioral pattern, although such complex behavior patterns may depend on more simple kinds of learning.

Empirical Findings: Mental Abilities

The fact that different levels of general intelligence "runs in families" has been long observed. This observation was noted at the turn of the century by Sir Francis Galton, for example, in his book *Hereditary Genius*. A more recent and impressive statement of genetic contributors is provided by Erlenmeyer-Kimling and Jarvick (1963), who summarized the available studies at the time in this area (see Figure 9.2). These observed relationships are close to those expected on genetic grounds for all classes of familial relationships. Of course, this *overall* pattern can also be said to support an environmentalist position, because genetic propinquity of individuals tends to parallel their environmental-familial propinquity. Thus we must look at specific aspects of the relationships observed in order to more fully understand the nature-nurture issue for intelligence. First of all, there is some support for the environmentalist position in several types of relationships. Unrelated children reared together and foster-parent–child scores correlate +.2, although the genetic relationship is, of course, zero. Note, however, that selective placement of children by social workers could explain this correlation. In other words, it could be that children to be placed who come from high socioeconomic levels are channelled to similar adoptive environments. Such unrelated adoptive children and their adoptive parents may have superior genes, thus providing for greater-than-chance positive correlations. Siblings reared apart should correlate +.5 (on genetic grounds), but in fact they correlate +.4, thus supporting the effects environment may have (although sampling and measurement error could just as easily account for this difference). Further in this regard, *MZ* twins reared together correlate +.9 whereas apart they correlate +.8, although the genetic relationship is the same.

MZ Twins Reared Apart

The most impressive evidence for genetic effects in the Erlen-meyer-Kimling and Jarvik study is to be found in the four studies reported that deal with *MZ* twins who were reared apart. Here the expected genetic correlation is 1.0 and the expected environmentalist correlation is 0.0. Jensen (1970) has closely examined these four studies and reported that there is no strong evidence for related environments in the placing of the twins in their separate homes. Thus the high correlation that have been found here must be explained on genetic grounds.

MZ Twins versus DZ Twins

The data reported showing *MZ* correlations versus *DZ* correlations also supports the genetic position if we assume that the criticisms of the method itself (discussed earlier) do not bias results in favor of one position over the other. In this case, both *DZ* and *MZ* results are close to the expected correlations on genetic grounds.

Foster-Child Studies

It is well established that as a child becomes older, his intelligence correlates increasingly with the intelligence of his (biological) parents. But is this relationship primarily due to heredity or environ-

Category		0.10 0.30 0.50 0.70 0.90 0.00 0.20 0.40 0.60 0.80	Groups Included
Unrelated persons	Reared apart		4
	Reared together		5
Fosterparent - child			3
Parent - child			12
Siblings	Reared apart		2
	Reared together		35
Twins — Two - eggs	Opposite sex		9
	Like sex		11
Twins — One - egg	Reared apart		4
	Reared together		14

Figure 9.2 Summary of the literature reporting correlations between IQs of individuals with different degrees of genetic relationship (from Erlenmeyer-Kimling and Jarvik, 1963).

ment? Honzik (1957) has analyzed data from a study by Skodak and Skeels (1949) that deals with this question by correlating the intelligence of the developing (adopted) child between the ages of 2 and 15 with both adopting parents and biological parents. As can be seen from Figure 9.3, the correlation with foster-parent intelligence, as assessed by educational level, is no higher than would be expected from the Erlenmeyer-Kimling and Jarvik data, whereas the correlation with biological parents increases with age to approximately .4. Of course we must recognize the statistical distinction between the correlation of scores and the average absolute scores, because Skodak and Skeels (1949) had found a substantial increase in the average intelligence of the children placed in adopting homes. Thus even if the absolute scores of foster children increase beyond the level of their biological parents, if there are still higher correlations with the biological parents as opposed to the foster parents, this is evidence for a genetic effect in producing individual differences. Skodak and Skeels reported that the IQ of adopted children was 106, whereas the IQ of their biological mothers, from inferior socioeconomic backgrounds, was only 85.7. This suggests a threshold concept in the development of intelligence, such that a certain level of stimulation is required to permit intellectual growth, and that above this level individual differences may be more related to genetic factors.

More about Multiple Abstract Variance Analysis (MAVA)

Empirical findings regarding the heritability of temperament traits using the MAVA indicate that the variances of Cattell's factor *A* (sizothymia) and factor *H* (Parmia) are determined much more by genetic influences compared with other traits. In addition, in the abilities domain, close to four-fifths of the variance of fluid intelligence is genetically determined, whereas for crystallized intelligence the figure is only two-thirds to three-quarters (Cattell, 1971). In more general terms, the findings indicate greater variance associated with the within-family environment as opposed to the between-family environment, thus favoring a "psychological" as opposed to a "sociological" view of the importance of environment. Finally, it can be mentioned that deviations due to heredity correlate negatively with deviations due to the environment, especially for those between families as opposed to those within families. This may suggest that society in general exerts pressure on genetically deviant individuals to con-

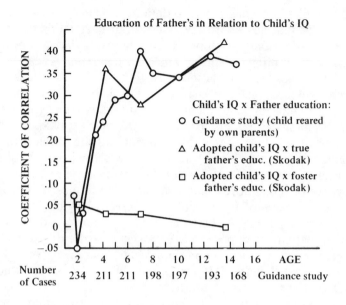

Education of Father's in Relation to Child's IQ

Child's IQ x Father education:

○ Guidance study (child reared
   by own parents)

△ Adopted child's IQ x true
   father's educ. (Skodak)

□ Adopted child's IQ x foster
   father's educ. (Skodak)

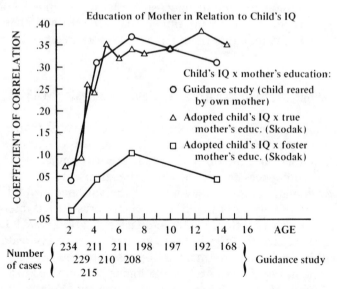

Education of Mother in Relation to Child's IQ

Child's IQ x mother's education:

○ Guidance study (child reared
   by own mother)

△ Adopted child's IQ x true
   mother's educ. (Skodak)

□ Adopted child's IQ x foster
   mother's educ. (Skodak)

Figure 9.3 Correlations between child's IQ and education of biological and foster parents (from Honzik, 1957).

form to some sort of social mean, that is, in a direction opposite to the deviations produced by genetic factors.

Inbreeding Depression

The incest taboo is an almost universal phenomenon. Only in rare cases has incest been practiced on a regular basis. For example, the royal families of the Incas and Egyptians believed that this practice was justified and necessary to maintain purity of their line, which was thought to descend from the gods. In most cases, however, it appears that inbreeding has detrimental effects. Schull and Neel (1965), for example, have demonstrated the detrimental effects of first-cousin marriages in Japan. In this instance, such marriages have traditionally been socially sanctioned. Thus we would not expect the offspring of such marriages to be socially disadvantaged, because they would not have been adversely treated. Yet these children score lower in all 11 subscales of the WISC, with scores ranging from 4 to 12% below the nonconsanguineous mean. Cohen et al. (1963) have found a similar inbreeding depression in an Israeli study involving matched groups from first-cousin and nonconsanguineous marriages.

There are a few studies of instances in which abortion has not been practiced when pregnancy resulted from incest; instead, the children have been adopted. Observed intelligence is found to be strongly depressed in these cases, with a relatively high rate of retardation. Thus Lindzey (1967) found that almost half of the children from father-daughter and brother-sister matings could not be adopted because of retardation. The parents of these children were matched with nonrelated parents of similar intellectual, physical and socioeconomic characteristics. The latter groups produced children with an incidence of mental retardation similar to that of the general population, permitting the inference that the children resulting from incestual relations were retarded because of the unique blood (read genetic) relationship between their parents.

Animal Studies

Numerous animal studies have been conducted to demonstrate genetic effects in animal behaviors such as maze learning or conditioning. For example, Tryon (1942) selected and rated rats at the two extremes of the distribution for maze-learning ability to produce offspring for succeeding generations of similar notings. By mating only the brightest with the brightest and the dullest with the dullest in each generation, he was able to demonstrate increasing separation in maze-learning ability of the two groups and produced the maze-bright and maze-dull strains of rats. Other studies have demonstrated conditioning and learning differences between inbred strains of rats or mice.

Primary Mental Abilities

It is possible to examine different traits in the abilities domain and to make more precise statements regarding the heritability of intelligence. Vandenberg (1969) has summarized twin studies on primary mental abilities and has shown that there is considerable variation in heritability, depending on the type of ability dealt with. In going from ability factors with high heritability to those with lower heritabilities, the rank order is as follows: word fluency, verbal ability, spelling and grammar, spatial visualization, number ability, reasoning, memory, and, finally, clerical speed and accuracy. These results are somewhat unexpected in terms of the theory of fluid and crystallized intelligence. In particular, the verbal factor appears as highly heritable (though it is a Gc factor), whereas the reasoning factor (Gf) is often found to be not significant in heritability. One consideration that must be brought to bear of course, is that a characteristic can be highly biological though not highly heritable. For example, gross body weight may have low heritability in some animal studies (Falconer, 1960, pp. 167–168). This might also apply to the reasoning factor. Moreover, the verbal factor may be less dependent on social-cultural influences than would be assumed on common-sense grounds. The interpretation here would be that in a given culture all individuals have ample opportunity to practice and over-learn verbal skills. Any remaining variability on this factor could then be due to genetic factors. It should also be noted that the heritabilities reviewed by Vandenberg are all based on only within-family variance components. If the between-family variance were also considered, this could alter the heritability for the various factors.

Empirical Findings: Personality

An indication of the variety of personality inventories that have been used in nature-nurture studies (almost totally studies of twins) is provided in various reviews by Vandenberg (e.g., Vandenberg, 1967a). These measures range from temperament through needs, attitudes, and interests. None of these areas has been studied as intensively as intelligence, however, making it difficult to make any definite statement about heritabilities for specific traits. When sufficient replications of studies have accumulated, such statements will be possible. It is also important to approach this area of study with different research designs to increase confidence in the results. To date, alternate methods such as foster-child studies have not been employed to any significant degree. However, the following points are worth making. First of all, there is sufficient evidence of hereditability in dimensions of interests and attitudes to encourage further research. These areas have traditionally been thought of primarily as domains of the sociologist or social psychologists. The genetic contribution in these areas, however, is quite compatible with Fruedian theory or Cattell's dynamic lattice. That is, the "energy" for interests and attitudes ultimately comes from a biological source according to these models, thereby making individual differences influenced by genetic factors. Figure 9.4 represents the heritabilities of scales from the Stern activities index from a study by Vandenberg (1969). These scales are derived from Murray's theory of needs, but appear to cover a wide range from biological needs (e.g., aggression, affiliation) to interests (e.g., science, humanities). When the scales are factored to give higher-order constructs, the latter yield interpretations that seem to reflect more *basic* needs such as self-assertion, orderliness, and sensuousness. We might predict then that the scales (essentially at the level of first-order factors) would have heritabilities reflecting both biological and social-cultural sources of individual differences, but that the higher-order dimensions (essentially second-order factors) would have generally higher heritabilities. This is exactly what is found in Figure 9.4. The scale yields a bimodal distribution of heritabilities, and the higher-order constructs yield a distribution that accentuates high heritabilities for these constructs.

There are also enough data on the heritability of temperament (again from twin studies) such that we can estimate heritabilities for neuroticism-anxiety and extraversion-exvia. Poley (1975) has plotted a frequency distribution of heritabilities based on five studies of twins for scales related to these two constructs. Again the distribution of heritabilities is bimodal (Figures 9.5 and 9.6), but the results tend to favor the 30–39% category. Because of the property of the statistic calculated (heritability from twin studies), however, we may have to limit these conclusions to within-family heritability. Generally, the limitations of twin studies discussed earlier apply here as well. Thus the reader must be

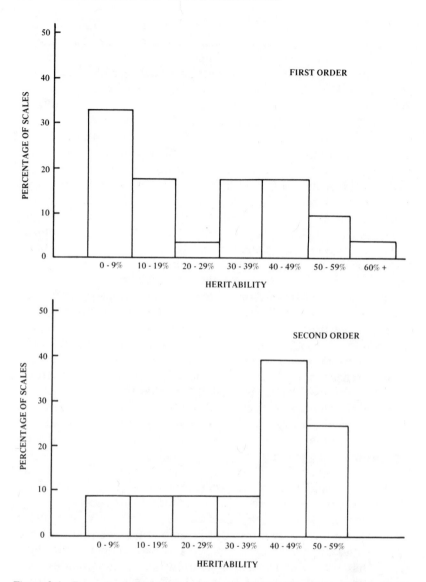

Figure 9.4 Percentage of scales from Stern's activities list with a given heritability at the level of first-order and second-order factors (data from Vandenberg, 1969).

cautioned against directly translating these values into a proportionate genetic contribution.

Future research on the heritability of personality traits must

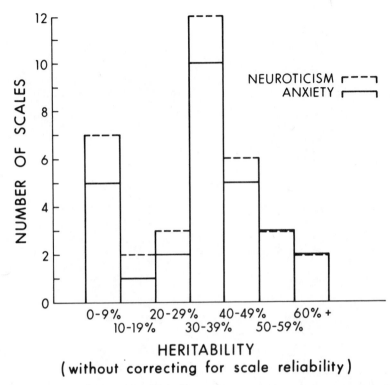

Figure 9.5 Percentage of scales measuring neuroticism-anxiety with a given heritability (from Poley, 1975).

take into consideration the interaction between the biological and genetic bases of traits and the environmental influences that act on these traits, particularly from parental and peer relations. In this way we can hope to understand more fully the reason for individual differences in traits, rather than relying on nature-nurture ratios alone. It is, of course, very difficult to design studies that allow us to separate genetic and environmental influences developmentally.

The trait psychologist tends to subscribe to the view that many important dimensions of personality and abilities appear very early in life (in the preschool years) without specific shaping by the environment. These traits are then acted on by the environment. This philosophy is reflected in the Thomas-Chess-Birch (1968) study described earlier. This study was conducted in the context of clinical work and was very much concerned with the interaction between early-appearing dimensions of temperament and environmental in-

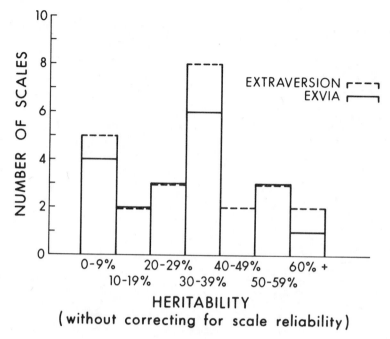

Figure 9.6   Percentage of scales measuring extraversion-exvia with a given heritability (from Poley, 1975).

fluences that could lead to psychopathology. In the course of the study, 42 children developed various behavioral problems. Two major clinical categories in the study consisted of "difficult children" among the cases of active disorders (10 out of 34 cases of active disorders) and "passive-symptoms" (8 out of the total of 42 clinical cases). In reference to the difficult child the authors point out:

> These children were variously characterized by their mothers, the interviewers, and all other members of the reserach team in terms of a series of pejorative labels, ranging from the expression "difficult children" by the more sedate and formal of our colleagues to "mother killers" by the more graphic and less inhibited (p. 75).

As they point out, their symptoms correspond largely to factor *A*. These children are typically irregular in their functions, negative and intense in mood, tend to be uncooperative and withdrawn in the face of new problems, and are slow to adapt. Specific complaints about their behavior may be related to such problems as difficulties at bedtime, noncooperation in new endeavors such as school, and aggressiveness toward siblings and peers. The frustrations parents experience as a result of this earns the label "mother killer." Although most of these children tend to develop behavioral problems, the authors point out: "These children are not truly nonadaptive, they are slowly adaptive. Once they have made their adjustment, their responsiveness to a situation may often be indistinguishable from that of children who had adapted quickly" (p. 77).

Furthermore, the temperament trait may eventually come to have positive attributes. In considering those who did not develop behavioral problems:

> The children in this latter group were able to adopt, albeit slowly, to successive demands for normal socialization as they grew older, and learned to behave in ways that were consonant with those of their families, their schools, and their peer groups. Once they had learned the rule, so to speak, they functioned well and consistently. The fact that they also functioned energetically because of their tendancies to exhibit high intensity levels often became an asset in their positive interactions with the environment (pp. 78–79).

Of course, these children place great demands on parents. One source of difficulty seemed to be caused by the environmentalist tradition, which places the onus for the child's difficulties on the parent—particularly the mother. The result is parental guilt and anxiety. In addition, the child tends to compound his problems by evoking resentment and hostility in the parents. In those cases in which the child was able to make a successful adjustment, parental attitudes were of utmost importance. Consistency in directing the child's activities and in the use of discipline, combined with control over inclinations to resentment toward the child, seem to be most significant. This proved to be very difficult to carry out, and cooperation between parents was often required.

Cases involving "passive symptoms" were related to factor B. Here we have temperament manifestations of low activity, strong withdrawal reaction, and negative mood. From Table 6.3 we have seen that these differences are most apparent for later years in the study. This is consistent with an interpretation of factor B as involving introversion, with the social aspect of introversion becoming more apparent in ages 4 and 5 and leading to problems for the child. In fact, the passive child is described as follows:

> The children included in the passive group were largely non-participators. They stood on the sidelines watching, taking no part in the activity. Where the nonparticipation was simply that and no more, it was considered to be passive rather than active. To be included in the passive group, it was essential that the youngster show neither evidence of anxiety nor defenses against anxiety. Thus, the nonparticipator who stood aside crying was considered to have active symptoms (Thomas, Chess, and Birch, 1968, p. 34).

The problems of the passive child seem to be related to the parents' and teachers' expectations that the child cannot meet. Because of his slowness and withdrawal he may appear to be dull or obstinate. Once again, it is not the temperament itself that creates the problem, rather, it is the interaction between temperament and environment. Moreover, this aspect of temperament may also have its positive attributes if properly channeled. For example, from Table 6.3 we can see that a high degree of persistence may be associated with this overt passivity, possibly related to the high cortical excitation which Eysenck would predict to be related to introversion.

The significance of the Thomas-Chess-Birch report is of both a theoretical and a practical nature. On the theoretical side, there is the contribution to the study of behavior genetics, particularly the issue of genetic-environmental interactions. The authors have expressed the environmentalist opposition to their work when it was begun:

> A number of factors were responsible for the neglect of temperament as an area of investigation. Important among these was the general disrepute of earlier constitutional views that had ascribed heredity and constitution as cause for complex personality structure and elaborate psychopathological syndromes. It was our respected experience in the early and mid-1950's to find most of our colleagues reproaching us for returning to an outdated and discredited constitutionalist position when we expressed the idea that individual organismic behavioral differences important for development might exist in young children (pp. 5–6).

On the more applied side, this study helps to alleviate the burden of guilt placed on the parents of a "problem child" by the strict environmentalist approach. By taking a biological framework, however, it does not relieve the parent of responsibility for the healthy development of the child, for it points out the positive aspects of the types of temperament that create problems, and, in addition, how parents can help in bringing out these positive features rather than neurotic symptom development. In terms of the latter, a more explicit development of the Eysenckian framework by reanalysis of data would probably be helpful. We have seen from the data presented that there is good evidence for two major dimensions of temperament and two classes of symptoms related to these which cover almost half of the cases studied. A more explicit attempt to employ the Eysenckian framework would likely encompass most of the cases. Thus difficult children (highly emotional or high N children according to Eysenck) are described as having symptoms related to excessive fears and phobias on the one hand (neurotic-introverted symptoms) and lying and stealing on the other hand (neurotic-extraverted symptoms). This distinction is important in at least two ways: *(a)* the classification of temperament and symptoms is simplified by the Eysenck framework, and although some information is lost, most information would be retained; *(b)* the introversion-extraversion distinction in the case of high-N children predicts the specific nature of symptoms as well as the remedies that should be used. Thus according to Gray's view of N and E, the parent needs to accentuate the use of rewards in the socialization of the high-N, high-I child, and needs to exert more control in the case of the high-N, high-E child.

Postscript on Behavior Genetics

Behavior genetics as a separate field of study is a relatively recent phenomenon—most people placing its beginning around 1960 with publication of Fuller and Thompson's *Behavior Genetics* (1960). As noted at the beginning of this chapter, behavior genetics was born and nurtured within an atmosphere of extreme environmentalism—a legacy of behaviorism. The aim of those initially working to give shape to the science of behavior genetics was quite simple—to demonstrate the inadequacy of strict environmentalism in explaining behavior and individual differences in behavior. As noted by Vale (1973), behavior genetics has proved its point after some 15 years of research. Genes do make a difference in behavior. But where does the field go from here?

If behavior genetics is to make a contribution to psychology in the future, it is necessary to go beyond "merely" demonstrating the importance of genes for behavior. To the extent that we ultimately wish to *understand* behavior, behavior geneticists must sit back and reevaluate their present methods and goals. As one behavior geneticist notes:

> Behavior genetics, whatever its intention, has often been simply an extension of quantitative genetics and has suffered the model-directed weakness of a fundamentally limited approach. Classical genetic techniques do not provide information about mechanisms of behavior, but about the transmission of genes. Good behavioral phenotypes are rare, and, without the assumption of trait equivalence, a genetics of behaviors is not practicable. Further, even if a genetics of behaviors were practicable, in all probability it would not provide any new essential information about the mode of transmission of genes (Vale, 1973, p. 880).

Vale is arguing here for redirecting the field of behavior genetics so that it can contribute (more) to the understanding of behavior. After criticizing the field of behavior genetics for focusing on traditional questions of genetics per se (but substituting psychological characteristics rather than morphological or physiological), Vale offers some suggestions for research strategies that employ genotypes in the analysis of behavior. Some of these suggestions include charting out the gene-behavior pathways and explicating the variables underlying genotype X treatment designs. Behavior genetics must move beyond its initial demonstration of the genetics of behavior and the focus on genetic transmission to an explication of the role of genotypes in behavior.

FURTHER READING:

Cancro, J. (Ed.). *Intelligence: Its nature, genetics and development.* Urbana: University of Illinois Press, 1971.

Ehrman, L., Omenn, G. S., and Caspari, E. W. *Genetics, environment, and behavior: Implications for educational policy.* New York: Academic, 1972.

Fuller, J. L., & Thompson, W. R. *Behavior genetics.* New York: Wiley, 1960.
Hirsch, J. Behavior genetics and individuality understood. *Science,* 1963, *142,* 1436–42.
Hirsch, J. (Ed.). *Behavior-genetic analysis.* New York: McGraw-Hill, 1967.

Chapter 10

RACE, SEX, AND SOCIAL-CLASS DIFFERENCES

Issues related to race, sex, and social-class differences are in a fundamental way tied to the nature-nurture problem. That is to say, the question asked tends to be "to what extent are race (or sex or class) differences in intelligence (or personality, motivation, etc.) due to heredity, and to what extent are they due to environment?" For race and sex differences in particular, it is difficult, if not impossible, to design a study to give a direct answer to the question. That is, we cannot standardize the environment for different races or sexes, because belonging to a particular race or sex itself alters the environment by changing the expectancies of other persons. In other words, we cannot readily identify groups of blacks raised as whites, or whites raised as blacks; nor can we identify boys raised as girls or girls raised as boys. Research conducted to date has only approximated the ideal kind of research design, consequently, the conclusions are of a highly controversial nature. It is true that the work of behavior genetics has demonstrated the importance of genetic contributors to individual differences within a population. However, we cannot automatically generalize from this observation to conclude that genetic factors are important in between-group or population comparisons involving race, sex, or social-class. What behavior genetics has done in this area of study is to establish that it is reasonable to ask these kinds of questions, although unequivocal answers may be a long time in coming. The scientific "respectability" of such questions has only recently emerged because of a long-lasting setback following the fascist distortions of genetic theory in the 1930s. We have more to say concerning the political and idealogical aspects of searching for group differences in psychological characteristics in the later sections of this chapter.

Race Differences

The most controversial aspect of race differences at present relates to IQ differences. This issue is still far from being resolved in spite of what one would be led to believe by the views of a few extremists on both sides of the nature-nurture issue. Although the possibility of genetics as a contributor to race has long been a taboo topic to many researchers, there are no a-priori reasons to rule out the genetic hypothesis. Genetically separated groups, whether separated by geographical or social barriers, will develop different gene pools, that is, different gene frequencies. These differences in gene frequencies should be reflected in behavior if the findings of behavior genetics are valid, and *may* (but not necessarily) be reflected in differences in intelligence. Jensen (1969) has probably stirred up more controversy than any other recent writer on this topic. Based on his review of available research, Jensen points to three important arguments that suggest genetic influences in black-white differences:

(1) The well-established difference (11 to 15 IQ points in favor of whites) tends to be less for verbal types of tests than culture-fair tests. If social environment were depressing the IQ of blacks, one might expect it to be manifested more in verbal tests. In opposition to this argument one can note that there may well be environmental differences accounting for differential scores on culture-fair tests. Even more to the point, one may question the logic of the concept of culture-fair tests of IQ, because such tests are constructed and validated in terms of North American white society.

(2) When "equally" disadvantaged minorities such as Indians or Mexicans are compared with blacks, the latter obtain lower IQ scores. In opposition to this point, we note that no study would be able to match these groups on all relevant socioeconomic variables, because not all these variables would be known to the investigator. That is to say, the matching procedure itself can be questioned when it is applied to intelligence. Race differences in variables such as nutrition or early childhood stimulation may be important and can easily be overlooked by gross socioeconomic matching procedures.

(3) When the social-class levels of blacks and whites are "matched," blacks obtain lower IQ scores and higher rates of mental retardation. We can direct the same criticisms applied above to these

data. Moreover, social-class matching is very dubious when applied to blacks and whites because the entire educational system has traditionally differed for blacks and whites. To consider a black lawyer to be matched with a white lawyer in terms of socioeconomic status is missing the basic point of the environmentalist position.

There are also some important arguments that point to environmental influences in race differences.

(1) In particular, blacks tested by blacks have been found to score higher than blacks tested by whites (Katz, Roberts, and Robinson, 1965; Moore and Retish, 1974). This finding has been explained in terms of establishing better rapport when both are of the same race. In this way test anxiety, which is certainly detrimental to performance, is reduced. The role of anxiety also suggests the possibility that personality differences in general may help to explain some of the race differences in intelligence by their effect on mental ability.

(2) Careful matching of black-white sociocultural variables in some studies has actually yielded identical IQs (Mercer, 1971). It would appear from the Mercer study that total matching to a white environment is crucial here, including such variables as parental attitudes toward education, home ownership, and nuclear family units.

Because of extreme difficulty of designing sound studies that adequately control the differential environment in comparing blacks and whites on IQ tests, those researchers favoring a genetic interpretation of the existing mean differences in IQ have sought support in indirect evidence. Thus a substantial portion of Jensen's (1969) original essay was devoted to reviewing the evidence for the heritability of IQ in white populations. Observing that within-group heritability estimates reported in the literature average around .80, Jensen rightly cautions that one cannot infer anything on this basis concerning between-group heritability. That is to say, although within-group heritabilities may be high and may even be unity, any between-group differences in *mean* IQ may still be due to environmental differences. The logic of the concept of heritability simply does not permit direct inferences from within-group individual differences to between-group mean differences. Block and Dworkin's (1974) example in this regard serves to drive the point home:

> Imagine that we take two handfuls of seed from a genetically heterogeneous sack. We carefully prepare two homogeneous nutrient solutions. One is normal; the other lacks essential nutrients and trace elements. We grow the two

handfuls in the two homogeneous nutrient solutions with homogeneous lighting, temperature, humidity, etc. Since each lot has perfectly uniform environmental conditions, the heritability of height in each lot will be 1.0. But there will be a large difference in the average height of the two lots, a difference ascribable entirely to the environmental difference in nutrients (p. 43).

More recently, Jensen (1973) has modified his original, cautious attitude and has argued that high within-group heritabilities in IQs *do* suggest that between-group differences in mean IQ are largely due to genetic factors. Thus he has stated:

Formerly, the heritability of a trait *within* populations cannot tell us the heritability of the difference *between* population means. High heritability *within* populations, however, adds to the *plausability* of the hypothesis that genetic factors are involved in the difference between populations. High *within*-group heritability *cannot* prove *between*-group heritability, but it does increase the *a priori* liklihood of finding genetic components in the average difference between groups (pp. 355–356, original emphasis).

In this passage we see that Jensen still recognizes the logical impossibility of making direct inferences from within-group heritabilities to between-group heritabilities. This does not prevent him, however, from arguing for the possibility of such inferences based on more indirect evidence. Thus Jensen devotes an entire chapter developing the theme that it makes good sense to go inductively from within-group heritability to between-group heritability.

Making inductive rather than deductive inferences from within-group heritabilities to between-group heritabilities is also characteristic of a recent study by Scarr-Salapapk (1971), who studied both race and socioeconomic differences. Although this study was concerned more with socioeconomic than race differences per se, it is advantageous to consider it here because it throws some light on the problem of going from within-group heritabilities to between-group heritabilities—a strategy favored by Jensen in interpreting race differences in IQ. The major finding in the Scarr-Salapapk study was that the individual differences variance in high socioeconomic children (for both blacks and whites separately) was explained mainly by genetic factors, whereas the individual differences variance in disadvantageous socioeconomic groups (for both blacks and whites separately) was explained by mainly environmental differences. In other words, the within-group heritability differed depending on socioeconomic status rather than race. Following Jensen's thesis that one may go inductively from within-group heritabilities to between-group heritabilities, these finding lend some support to the argument that *environmental* factors are responsible for the lower mean and lower heritability of I.Q. in lower socioeconomic groups. Crucial in this interpretation, however, is the assumption that the same environmental factors affect the development of I.Q. the same way across socioeconomic groups. To the extent that this assumption is incorrect, that is, that different environmental factors operate in different ways in the development of IQ in different groups, no unambiguous conclusions can be made about the origin of socioeconomic differences in mean IQs. In effect, the assumption that the same environmental factors are operating in the same way in the development of IQs across different groups reduces to the positions that there is no interaction between genotype and phenotype. Few, if any, behavior geneticists are willing to assume no genotype-phenotype interactions, which brings us to the concept *norm of reaction* and its consequences for undermining interpretations of group differences in mean IQs based on differential within-group heritability.

Because the norm of reaction concept is so important in under-cutting any argument based on the interpretation (environmental *or* genetic) of group mean differences in IQ, a closer look at this concept will prove instructive. The norm of reaction may be defined as that function which maps environment and genotype into the phenotype. Figure 10.1 represents two genotypes as a function of an environmental variable and the phenotypic value. The heritability of the phenotypic variable P depends on the environmental range sampled as well as the portion of individuals having either genotype g_1 or genotype g_2. Assuming equal representation for the two genotypes in the population under consideration, those persons who have low values on the environmental dimension will have a lower heritability when compared to those individuals who are high on the environmental-variable scale, where it is assumed there is a moderate degree of environmental variation for both groups. Thus in this example, the differential heritabilities parallell those found by Scarr-Salapapk, although the mean values for the groups would be reversed. Because of the differential interaction between genotype and the environment, different norms of reaction could just as well have yielded reversed differences in means between the two groups. Thus it is equally possible that the group with the low heritability could have a lower phenotypic mean than the group with the high heritability, or vice versa. In other words, the concept of norm of reaction and, by implication, environment-genotype interaction, precludes making inferences from different within-group heritabilities to interpreting mean group differences in IQs.

Equally damaging as the above arguments against Jensen's thesis that race differences in IQs are largely due to genetic factors is the growing dissatisfaction with the basic concept of heritability itself in this of research. Thus Block and Dworkin (1974) have argued persuasively that the concept of heritability has little if any value when applied to human populations. Because of the interactive nature of genes and environment, small differences in genes may produce large environmental effects. This may come about, for example, when a child, who has an advantageous genotype for intelligence, magnifies that advantage by creating an environment that reinforces his initial advantage. Traditional models of heritability would count such environmental differences as genetically based. After reviewing additional indirect genetic effects which are difficult to distinguish from environmental effects, Block and Dworkin (1974) conclude that "no one knows *how* to separate the variance due to indirect genetic effects from the variants due to direct genetic effects, at least within

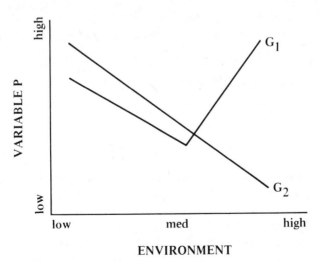

Figure 10.1 Two genotypes as a function of an environmental variable and the phenotype value.

the constraints on human experimentation" (p. 51). Because of this and other violations of the underlying assumptions of the concept of heritability, it has been argued that this concept provides little, if any, useful information for purposes of altering environments in a favorable way. Thus it is often assumed that if heritability is high for a trait such as IQ, there is relatively little that can be done to improve the mean score. This line of reasoning confuses heritability with immutability. Thus a high heritability in no way implies that environmental changes will not alter the overall means. In light of the questionable value of estimating heritability in human populations, one cannot help agreeing with Hirsch (1970), who has concluded that "the plain facts are that in the study of man a heritability estimate turns out to be a piece of 'knowledge' that is both deceptive and trivial" (p. 98).

Since Jensen bases much of his argument on the high heritability within white populations, these comments on the dubious value of heritability serves to call into question the usefulness of his tack. Another line of evidence that is damaging to Jensen's overall strategy may be found in Kamin (1974). In this book, Kamin questions whether the often-reported value of heritability of around .80 is sufficiently justified. Meticulously reviewing the classical studies in the literature which supposedly support the interpretation of a high heritability for IQ, Kamin concludes that thus far there is no evidence to justify the conclusion that IQ is in any way heritable. Kamin has devoted separate chapters in evaluating the original twin studies, kinship studies, and studies of adopted children bearing on the issue of heritability and IQ. The major researchers in the field are found to be plagued by inappropriate statistical analyses, faulty sampling techniques, and outright gross discussions of raw data. Although several investigators are faulted on the grounds of slipshod work, Sir Cyril Burt is particularly taken to task for irresponsible scientific writing. Burt's work is well known to those in the field, and from England he has written greatly, spreading the doctrine that differences in intelligence are largely due to innate factors. In a careful review of Burt's work, Kamin convincingly demonstrates the inadequacy of Burt's data and questionable "adjustment" of raw scores. One never knows what tests Burt used or how he obtained his samples—making replication of his finding an impossible undertaking. Errors in calculation and reporting are so rampant in Burt's work that Kamin considered it practically, if not totally, worthless in shedding light on the interpretation of IQ differences.

The extent to which typographical errors in data reporting,

mistaken interpretations of original data, and outright gross distortions of findings make their way into the accepted body of scientific fact are treated in a separate chapter by Kamin. Here we learn the dangers of consulting secondary sources in this area rather than the original researches. Jensen, Herrnstein, and others are shown to be blameworthy for propagating earlier errors of data reporting by reproducing figures and tables from secondary sources that contain intentional and unintentional errors generally favoring the genetic camp. If the reader has been able to remain skeptical of Kamin's argument thus far, this chapter leaves no room for sympathizing for his opponents. One cannot help concluding that the existing evidence for a genetic interpretation of IQ differences is highly suspect. That is *not* to say, of course, that there is no significant genetic component in determining individual differences in IQ. Rather, thus far, this hypothesis cannot be supported based on present findings. The message of Kamin's book may be interpreted as "don't bother trying to estimate the heritability of I.Q. since the methodological problems are at present insurmountable."

In conclusion, we can say that the mean IQ difference between blacks and whites has yet to be adequately explained. Indirect evidence for the genetic hypothesis is at best inconclusive. Certain environmental conditions are definitely conductive to lower IQ scores in blacks, but the degree to which they exert an influence is not known. It is worth noting, however, that even given a 15-point IQ difference between races, most of the IQ distributions overlap; in other words, differences between groups is much smaller than differences within groups. Thus only 23% of white scores exceed Negro scores. We can now ask whether there are not more important issues to be resolved in this area. For example, Sitkei and Meyers (1969) have found that profiles of mental abilities depend very much on race as well as social class (Figure 10.2). It then becomes important to consider the implications of findings such as this for educational programs that best utilize the strengths of each group. Such a policy would not oppose the general aim of upgrading the intellectual level of all groups. To the extent that equal overall general intelligence is achieved, one may still find that the patterns of specific abilities differ across groups, and such findings would be of considerable interest to differential psychology.

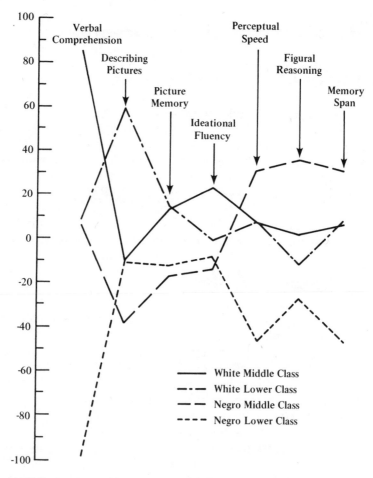

Figure 10.2 Profiles of middle- and lower-class Negro and white 4 year olds on seven abilities (from Sitkei and Meyers, 1969).

Sex Differences

A great deal of research has established sex differences on a number of psychological traits. Tests of general intelligence are usually constructed in such a way so as to eliminate any sex differences —thus preventing any conclusions to be drawn regarding sex differences in this respect. However, there are well established sex differences in several different mental abilities. Males sometimes surpass females in verbal comprehension, although female scores are usually higher in verbal fluency. Reasoning tests tend to favor males, as do

spatial tests, the latter being reflected in superior mechanical aptitudes in males. Females are generally superior in memory abilities.
Sweeney (1953) has offered the hypothesis that male superiority in
spatial-reasoning abilities is due to the process of "restructuring" in
problem solving. That is, males are able to discard a given system of
organizing information and to try out new systems until a solution
is reached. Related to the findings of sex differences in spatial abilities
is the observation that females perform less well than males do on
measures of field independence. To the extent that field independence
taps some aspect of independence as measured by temperament tests,
this finding is not surprising. However, there are difficulties in accepting the general idea of sex differences in field independence. Of
particular importance is the difficulty of obtaining the supposed sex
differences in college populations. It could be argued here that there
is a selection process operating such that females in college are higher
on field independence than their noncollege age-cohorts. Another
difficulty is the idea that field independent measures are strongly
correlated with tests of spatial ability. To the extent that sex typing
provides males with more opportunity to engage in spatial tasks, the
implication is that sex differences in field independence may be elimi-
nated by giving females more training and experience on spatial
tasks. This conclusion is based on an environmental interpretation
of sex differences as opposed to a biological one—a topic we now
consider in greater detail.

Broverman, Klaiber, Kobayashi, and Vogel (1968) have used a
similiar argument as Sweeny's (1953) and have added some physiological speculations in what has become a highly controversial theory
of sex differences in abilities. The authors begin their analysis by
listing some of the major differences in abilities between males and
females. They consider females to be superior in "simple, overlearned repetitive behavior measured in terms of speed, accuracy, or
frequency of occurrence and which require minimal central media-
tion." On the other hand, male superiority is described as "complex
behaviors requiring problem solving, delay, a reversal of usual habits." Parallels are noted for sex differences in animals. For example,
female rats develop conditioned avoidance responses more rapidly
and are more active in open-field and activity-wheel situations. Male
rats typically excell in more complex learning situations such as
mazes.

Turning, then, to a physiological-pharmocological level of analysis, Broverman et. al. note the well-established difference in the
production of sex hormones, androgen and estrogen, with the former

characteristic of males and the latter characteristic of females. They then refer to animal studies that link androgen and estrogen to an activation-inhibition balance of the nervous system. This balance is identified with adrenergic (activating) and cholinergic (inhibiting) neurotransmitters. The net result of this relationship is that females are physiologically more "activated" than males, and this in turn is linked to sex differences in behavioral activation.

Of course, this argument requires a generalization from animal data to human data. Parlee (1972) has criticized the theory on these grounds, suggesting that although animal studies may in many cases be relevant to human behavior, this does not apply here. She states: "Without in any way casting doubt on the relevance of animal research to human psychology, it seems fair to say that an argument that depends on an analogy between spontaneous motor activity in rats and reading speed in humans leaves much to be desired" (p. 182). Another important criticism offered by Parlee is that the initial psychological concepts of simple overlearned perceptual-motor tasks and more complex perceptual-restructuring tasks may not be very reliable as descriptions of the major cognitive sex differences. That is, they ignore some varieties of sex differences, and the concepts themselves are hypotheses that have yet to be adequately established.

In considering sex differences in personality, the following are usually reported: higher scores on factor A (affectothymia) and factor I (premsia) in females and higher scores on E (dominance) and H (venturesomeness) in males. In terms of Eysenck factors, males score higher on E, females score higher on N. Jackson (1967) reports major sex differences in dominance (males higher) and harmavoidance and nurturance (females higher).

Aside from cataloguing sex differences in personality, we also require some explanation for them. Once again, the explanation is more controversial than is the description of sex differences. Three major sources of evidence are used to help resolve the issue. (1) Sex differences that appear very early in childhood are usually taken as support for biological determinants. (2) Similarly, sex differences that are replicated across a variety of cultures offer support for biological determinants. (3) An ideal "research design" to deal with the issue would entail raising biological males as females (or biological females as males). To some extent this design has been made possible by cases of males who have genital-anatomical defects at birth. In some of these instances, infant biological males have been surgically transformed into females and raised as females. Empirical evidence can be found in conjunction with these different designs.

Sex differences in personality and motivation in early childhood are commonly reported as consistent with the trait differences outlined earlier. That is, boys are typically more active and aggressive. Girls are typically more nurturant and emotional. Attributing these differences at least in part to biological influences is further supported by the fact that they appear with considerable frequency in cross-cultural studies as well as within a single society.

The issue of sexual reassignment at birth requires some special attention, because it offers an ideal situation for assessing the relative influence of biological and social factors. That is, if a biological male is anatomically reassigned as a female at birth, raised as a female, and develops female patterns of behavior, this would seem to provide strong support for the environmentalist position. It is on the basis of such evidence that Money (1972) concludes that sex differences are almost completely culturally determined. However, there is one very important confounding in this type of evidence that needs to be considered. In conjunction with anatomical reassignment, sex hormones are usually administered to the child. The hormones themselves may be very important as biological influences in the development of behavioral sex differences.

Biologically oriented psychologists have tended to interpret sex differences in behavior in the context of their adaptive significance in the evolution of the species. For example, Bruell (1969) has stated that if within a species we encounter anatomical, physiological, or behavioral differences between the sexes, we have prima facie evidence for the workings of evolutionary forces; sexual dimorphism is always a product of natural selection. Gray and Buffery (1971) have described the possible basis for evolutionary pressures in shaping major sex differences in cognitive and emotional behavior in mammals. Thus they consider the male superiority in spatial ability observed in a variety of mammalian species to be a result of the greater male involvement in territorial claims. Superior linguistic abilities in human females, on the other hand, are considered to be a result of the closer relationship between the growing infant and the mother and the greater need, therefore, for females to have the ability to socialize the next generation. This approach to sex differences can also be generalized for emotional behavior. For example, the sex difference in aggressiveness, which is reported in a variety of species of mammals, is considered to be a result of the greater involvement of males in establishing dominance hierarchies. A case for sex differences in fearfulness, on the other hand, is more complex. Although primate females tend to be more fearful than males, rodent males tend to be more fearful than females. Thus a cross-species generalization is more difficult to formulate. Gray and Buffery deal with this problem by pointing out that, although in primates the dominance hierarchy tends to combine both sexes, in rodents the dominance hierarchy is almost exclusively a male interaction. The authors suggest that to function successfully within a dominance hierarchy, male rodents need the capacity both for dominance behavior and withdrawal submissiveness (i.e., fearfulness). A strong relationship in turn exists between most of these sex differences and the basic division of roles between males and females in reproductive behavior. That is, females tend to be more responsible for the raising of the next generation of species, and males, in turn, are freer to relate directly to other mature members of the species.

In regard to environmental interpretation of the development of different sex roles, which embody sex differences in abilities, temperament, and motives, Mussen (1969) has reviewed three general theoretical approaches that stress the importance of social processes. *Social-learning theory* enjoys a wide following within psychology, stressing traditional and experimental learning concepts within a social context. The essence of this position revolves around the idea that sex-appropriate behavior in the child is shaped by parents and others through the delivery or withdrawal of reinforcement, the latter often being social in nature. Thus girls are rewarded for being passive and dependent, and boys are encouraged to be aggressive and independent. The basic sex roles established in the young child are thought to occur in a variety of different situations—a phenomenon known as stimulus generalization. Thus the early female disposition to behave in a passive and dependent manner leads to lower levels of achievement in later life as compared to the aggressive and independent patterns of boys. The latter statement needs to be qualified somewhat in that girls outperform boys in grade school—where their tendencies to conform to authority figures and obey put them at an advantage. Somewhere in the teens, however, sex differences in academic achievement become reversed, when later scholastic achievement is more dependent on the kinds of dispositions males have been socialized to exhibit.

An important development within social-learning theory for explaining the development of sex roles involves the role of imitation —also called observational learning, vicarious learning, or modeling (Bandura and Walters, 1963). In this view, sex role behavior may be learned by imitating the behavior of appropriate sex models, where there is no necessity to reinforce the behavior initially. Once imitative behavior occurs, of course, it may be strengthened by the operation of appropriate combinations of reinforcement and punishment. A second general theoretical approach to explaining the development of "appropriate" behavior involves a similar view as imitative learning, and is known as *identification.* Social learning theorists tend to regard identification as simply imitative learning, although there have been those who have used the concept of identification without reference to social-learning theory. Thus, for example, defensive identification is a notion developed by Freud, in which the boy identifies with the father to avoid fear of his father, whereas the girl identifies with the mother out of fear of the loss of the mother's love.

A third theory accounting for different sex role behavior is Kohlberg's (1966) *cognitive-developmental* theory of sex typing. Influenced by both the recent attention Piagetian theory is receiving as well as the recent stress on motives such as curiousity, mastery, exploration, and competence, it is Kohlberg's view that cognitive activity (the active selection and organization of perception and knowledge) is most significant in acquiring sex-role behavior. Thus the child attains sex-role behavior by sex labeling perceived sex differences that exist in sex-role stereotypes. The early sex labeling of the child is thought to lead to such processes as identification rather than vice-versa; in other words, it is the child who (cognitively) initiates the process of sex labeling. In this way, sex roles are cognitively established early in development and lead to accompanying sex-typed values and attitudes. Thus a boy, for example, develops competence motivation, and masculine roles mainly by arriving at the cognitive distinction that he "belongs" with those who exhibit this behavior (he is physically a boy—a cognitive act).

Social Class Differences

That society is hierarchically structured in terms of socioeconomic classes (i.e., differential power, wealth, education, opportunity) is apparent to the most casual observer of society. Different social classes afford differential experiences to the developing child—largely based upon different socialization patterns. Although a comprehensive review of the different socialization practices would take us too far afield from the major topic of this book, the reader should appreciate that any observed socioeconomic differences in traits must ultimately consider differential socialization and developmental processes. The last statement holds even if there are significant socioeconomic differences in gene frequencies.

Of the social class differences in psychological traits, those related to mental abilities are the best established. There is a strong positive correlation between IQ and social class when the entire range of the latter are considered. Moreover, these differences appear early in life in the offspring of a particular social class and persist through maturity. More interesting is the question of profile differences in primary mental abilities between social class. Dockrell (1966) has considered this question for lower- and middle-class children in two English schools (see Figure 10.3).

Once again, in this area we cannot automatically generalize from the heritability of intelligence itself to proposing that there is a genetic basis for social class differences. However, if intelligence in the general population does in fact have a substantial heritable component (as some would lead us to believe) and if intelligence is related to occupational and career success (as it undoubtedly is), social mobility should be taking place in terms of gene frequencies affecting mental ability. That is to say, the upper social classes should be gaining genes favoring high intelligence at the expense of the lower social classes. Put in other terms, social mobility should be reduced to some degree with each generation as these gene frequencies become fixed within each social class.

Incorporating some of the above ideas on social class differences in IQ is the work of Jensen and Herrnstein—whose views we now examine. It has already been mentioned in Chapter 7 that the attempt to identify intelligence as learning ability has not stood up to empirical test. An exception to this general conclusion is revealed in Jensen's (1969) research on a two-level theory of mental abilities. In Jensen's view there are two fundamental genotypes of ability, where by genotype Jensen refers to the physiological substraight of intelligence regardless of whether it is genetically or experiencially conditioned. Level-I ability is called *associative learning ability* and refers to the capacity to receive, store, and later retrieve material with a high degree of accuracy. This basic learning ability does not involve any high-level mental operations such as elaboration, transformation, or manipulation of the in-coming information in order to arrive at the appropriate output by the organism. Reception and reproduction of the input with a degree of accuracy is all that is required for high performance on this trait, and Jensen likens it to the performance of a tape recorder. In contrast to level I, level-II ability or *conceptual learning and problem solving,* is characterized by such

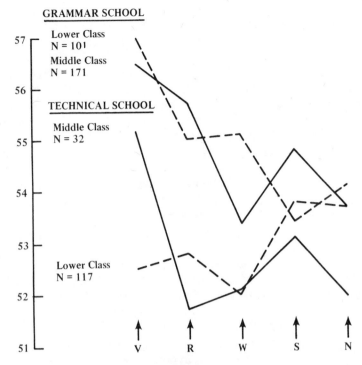

GRAMMAR SCHOOL

Lower Class
N = 101

Middle Class
N = 171

TECHNICAL SCHOOL

Middle Class
N = 32

Lower Class
N = 117

V   R   W   S   N

Figure 10.3 Profiles of lower- and middle-class children in two English schools on five mental abilities (from Dockrell, 1966).

higher-level mental operations as transformation and manipulation of the in-coming information prior to making the appropriate response. Jensen gives the following as examples of level-II ability: symantic generalization, concept formation, encoding and decoding of stimuli in terms of past experience, relating new learning to old learning, and transfer in terms of concepts and principles. This concept of ability bears striking resemblance to Spearman's *G*, that is, general intelligence. In fact, most standard intelligence tests would probably measure level-II ability.

In Jensen's view, individual differences in level-I and level-II abilities are largely seen as having a genetic basis. This idea goes back to Jensen's arguments about the high heritability of intelligence. Because we have concerned ourselves with the heritability of intelligence elsewhere, this aspect of Jensen's theory is subject to criticisms noted previously, and further considered shortly. However, Jensen does consider an interesting idea about the interrelationship of both level-I and level-II abilities that does not require acceptance of his genetic interpretation of individual differences in such traits. According to Jensen, there is a hierarchical dependence of level-II ability on level-I ability. In other words, a high score on level-II ability depends on a high level of performance on level-I ability, but not vice versa. This hypothesized relationship makes good intuitive sense to the extent that higher level cognitive tools are dependent on basic or more elementary cognitive operations. Because a high score on level-I ability is seen as a necessary but not a sufficient condition for a high score on level-II ability, it is possible to have a person who scores high on level I but not necessarily high on level II, although a person who scores high on level II must necessarily score high on level I. This kind of functional dependence of level II on level I implies a twisted-pair correlational relationship between each of these two ability types, (e.g., see Figure 3.11 substituting level I and level II for IQ and creativity, respectively).

Most relevant in the present context is that Jensen postulates that level-I ability is equally distributed across all socioeconomic status groups. That is to say, there is no correlation between level-I ability and social class. Level-II ability, however, is thought to be distributed differentially as a function of social class, resulting in a positive correlation between level II and social class. Figure 10.4 illustrates Jensen's view on the hypothetical distribution of level-I and level-II ability in lower- and middle-class populations. Jensen explains the differential distribution of level-II ability in terms of assuming a largely genetic determination of individual differences in both of these abilities. Thus those individuals from high socioeconomic status groups who are low on either level-I or level-II abilities tend to gravitate to lower socioeconomic status levels. Moving from high socioeconomic status to low socioeconomic-status implies that they *may* carry good genes for *either* level I *or* level II. Gravitating from lower to higher socioeconomic status groups, however, implies that good genes for *both* level I and level II are brought into this population gene pool.

Differential correlations between level-I and level-II abilities have been found by Jensen. Thus level I correlates very high with level II among middle-class children, whereas in lower socioeconomic status groups the correlation is considerably lower. This differential correlation between the two abilities is descriptively explained in terms of hypothesized scatter diagrams which are based to some extent on some data that Jensen has collected. Figure 10.5 illustrates the correlation scatter diagrams for the relationship be-

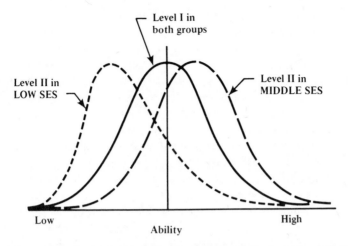

Figure 10.4   Hypothetical distributions of level-I (solid line) and level-II (dashed line) abilities in middle-class and culturally disadvantaged populations (from Jensen, 1969).

tween level-I and level-II learning abilities for both low and middle socioeconomic status groups. Thus in this Figure 10.5 we can see the basis for the previously mentioned twisted pair phenomenon.

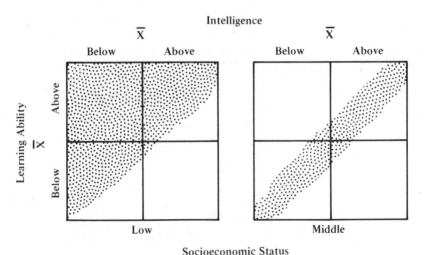

Figure 10.5   Schematic illustration of the essential form of the correlation scatter diagram for the relationship between associative learning ability and IQ in low socioeconomic status and upper-middle socioeconomic status groups (from Jensen, 1969).

The developmental range of both level-I and level-II abilities are thought to differ according to Jensen, and these differences are illustrated in Figure 10.6. In this figure, we also see that there are assumed to be no differences in the development of level-I abilities across socioeconomic status groups. In general, level-I abilities are seen as developing at an accelerated rate and having a general developmental function that is not differentiated according to social class. Level-II ability, in contrast, is thought to develop more slowly than level-I ability, first obtaining prominence around the ages of 4 to 6. Unique about level-II ability is the socioeconomic status differences in developmental function, in which lower socioeconomic groups have a lower developmental curve.

Based on differences in level-I and level-II abilities, Jensen advocates that the educational system should gear itself toward differential educational opportunities dependent on different patterns of abilities. Implicit in this view is that those individuals who are low in level II but high in level I should receive instruction that is largely based on associative rather than cognitive learning. As pointed out by some of Jensen's critics, this strategy will only serve to maintain existent intellectual deficiencies in lower socioeconomic status groups. The challenge for the educational psychologist is to devise

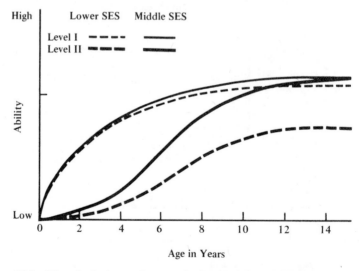

Figure 10.6 Hypothetical growth curves for level-I and level-II abilities in middle-socioeconomic-status and low socioeconomic-status-populations (from Jensen, 1969).

techniques whereby the higher cognitive tools may be achieved by disadvantageous groups.

A recent and highly controversial interpretation of the existing IQ differences found between different social classes has been offered by Herrnstein (1971, 1973) and incorporates some of the ideas of Jensen. Herrnstein advances the thesis that our society is, and will become more so, a *meritocracy;* that is, social standing will be largely based on inherited individual differences in IQ. The argument is based on four premises:

1. If differences in mental abilities are inherited, and
2. If success requires those abilities, and
3. If earning and prestige depends on success,
4. Then social standing (which reflects earnings and prestige) will be based to some extent on inherited differences among people (Herrnstein, 1973, pp. 197–198).

This syllogism requires the acceptance of the assumption that differences in mental abilities are largely inherited. Indeed, Herrnstein adopts a similar position as Jensen, accepting the evidence indicating that the heritability of IQ is around .80. We have already noted that the heritability of IQ is yet to be demonstrated by adequate empirical research. Further, the criticism that it is highly questionable whether heritability estimates can be applied to human populations makes Herrnstein's thesis suspect, or at least lacking in sufficient evidence. To the extent that our society carries out its egalitarian goals of providing uniform and equal environments for all individuals, it is Herrnstein's belief that such a policy will result in an even larger proportion of the variation in IQ being determined by genetic factors. In this way, social policies aimed at eliminating environmental differences will ultimately produce a caste system based on inborn ability.

In addition to the criticism of heritability ratios that undermine Herrnstein's syllogism, his ideas have also been subject to attack on the basis of extra-scientific arguments. Thus Chomsky (1972) faults Herrnstein's argument on the grounds that it reflects capitalistic ideology. Chomsky points out that Herrnstein assumes that people will labor only for gain rather than for intrinsic satisfaction or socially beneficial work without large material reward. Implicit in Herrnstein's argument is that people must be driven to work by the promise of such rewards as power and wealth. Chomsky argues for an alternative view in which there are other motivating factors determining one's vocation. Intrinsic satisfaction and socially useful works are two such variables Chomsky considers important in attracting individuals with high IQ's–variables that are not correlated with the existent status hierarchy of materially rewarded vocations.

Chomsky's critique of Herrnstein's thesis may be seen as an onslaught on capitalistic ideological thinking. Implicit in Chomsky's view is the idea that Herrnstein's thesis is a mere reflection of capitalistic ideology which will serve to justify and preserve the status quo. Thus Chomsky draws attention to the fact that a more just society is possible by disavowing the assumption that people are motivated for only material gain and power, thereby upsetting the attraction of high-IQ people to materially rewarding careers.

Politics, IQ Testing, and Group Differences

That science is influenced by politics and politics is influenced by science is amply demonstrated when reviewing the history of IQ testing in North America. Kamin's (1974) book traces a sad chapter in the history of IQ testing in the United States. In these pages we learn of the intimate relation between science and politics and, further, that one's politics determines to a significant degree one's interpretation of scientific data. The issue involves restrictive immigration in the early part of the century and, more specifically, the scientific justification for passing overt discriminatory immigration laws against southeastern European people. Using the best available IQ tests at the time, psychologists found that recent immigrants, especially those whose first language was not English, scored significantly lower than native-born Americans. Such a finding should not surprise anyone in light of the obvious culture-bound nature of these tests. In spite of the more reasonable interpretation of the findings, however, the race and ethnic differences measured by *American* IQ tests were interpreted as reflecting exclusively innate differences in IQs. If America was not to degenerate into a racially inferior country, the argument went, steps had to be taken to prevent the inflow of genetically inferior people.

The passing of discriminatory immigration quotas during the 1920s was largely justified on the basis of the "scientific" findings of psychologists. The exclusive genetic interpretation of IQ differences occurred at a time when there was no field of quantitative genetics. Kamin's careful documentation of the gross misuse of IQ data at the time must certainly make us pause and reflect on the dangers of basing social policy on inconclusive scientific evidence. For those who believe that American society was founded largely on and nurtured by egalitarian principles, Kamin's documentation will surely come as a shock.

In another recent review of the controversy over the interpretation of IQ scores, Cronbach (1975c) documents the influence of the mood of society in bringing to light or suppressing particular scientific views. Thus one gets a feeling of déjà vu when reading about the IQ controversy during the early part of the twentieth century. The heriditarian interpretation of individual differences in IQ was prominent during the 1920s and 1930s but gradually subsided and was replaced by a strong environmental interpretation of intelligence. During the 1950s and 1960s the emphasis was on improving the educational system in the United States to provide world leadership in science and technology, thereby maintaining a position of power within the international community.

The recent flare-up of the IQ controversy, according to Cronbach, is largely attributable to the popular media. In Cronbach's view, both Jensen and Herrnstein carefully documented and qualified their original arguments on the subject of IQ interpretation, and there was little that was of a controversial nature with respect to race differences in IQs. However, their tentative conclusions and cautionary statements became distorted in the hands of the popular media. Being quoted out of context, which served to misrepresent their original cautious approach, had the effect of giving the issue widespread publicity and much heated debate. In Cronbach's view, journalists wield great power in determining what information becomes public and when. Thus subtle and technical scientific controversies should probably be confined to the pages of scientific periodicals and books rather than running the risk of being grossly misinterpreted and distorted for easy consumption by the lay public.

There have been many who have called for a moratorium on all research aimed at exploring the genetic basis for individual differences in I.Q. This view has been criticized on the grounds that the basic principle of academic freedom must be preserved, that is, a scientist should be free to pursue truth wherever it might lead. Both of these concerns, however, may be reconciled, and Block and Dworkin (1974) have offered a useful solution:

> Given the very substantial and immediate harms that are likely to occur as a result of pursuing research on the genetic basis for I.Q. differences, and given that the benefits are minor, what is a reasonable moral decision for individual scientists to make with respect to such investi-

gation? It is clear that, at the very least, investigators have a responsibility to do their utmost to make it less likely that their findings will be misunderstood and misinterpreted. Neither Herrnstein nor Jensen met this responsibility adequately (pp. 90–91).

Cronbach (1975c) voices a similar view as that outlined above. Rather than legislating against the carrying out of further research on the genetic basis for individual differences in IQs, Block and Dworkin (1974) propose the following:

> We are not saying that further research in the heritability of individual differences in I.Q. should stop. We are not saying that investigations that have race as one of the variables—e.g. of phenotypic differences or even of genotypic differences of *some* characteristics—should not be pursued. We are not even saying that at all times or at all places investigation of racial genotypic differences in I.Q. scores should stop. What we are saying is that at this time, in this country, in this political climate, individual scientists should voluntarily refrain from the investigation of genotypic race differences in performance on I.Q. tests (p. 98).

At a time when various minority groups are striving for equal rights and opportunities, the views of Jensen and Herrnstein may be misused to justify retarding social progress. Indeed, the recent distorted publicity given to the views of Jensen and Herrnstein may be interpreted as a backlash against further social progress in eliminating discrimination and unequal opportunity for minority groups. It would be difficult not to concur with the views of Block and Dworkin.

With respect to sex differences in psychological attributes, it is important to note that female *differences* do not imply female inferiority. To the extent that females have historically not enjoyed the same advantages as males in participating in society, political action should certainly be taken to eliminate discriminatory practices. At the time of the writing of this book (1975), the United Nations has declared this year as International Women's Year as part of a worldwide campaign for increasing the opportunities afforded to women. This step toward encouraging the removing of sex-role stereotypes that hinder the development of female potentiality is a welcome development in our society. The findings of sex differences from the study of an individual differences approach should serve as an impetus to remove those differences that put females at a distinct disadvantage in our society. Education, socialization, attitude change, and so forth will all be important in reducing nonsex-related sex differences such that in future descriptions of sex differences, the findings will, one would hope, be quite different from what they are at present.

FURTHER READING:

Block, N.J., and Dworkin, G. IQ, heritability and inequality, Part 2. *Philosophy and Public Affairs,* 1974, *4,* 40–90.

Dobzhansky, T. *Genetic diversity and human equality.* New York: Basic Books, 1973.

Furby, L. Implications of within-group heritabilities for sources of between-group differences: IQ and racial differences. *Developmental Psychology,* 1973, *9,* 28–37.

Kamin, L.F. *The science and politics of I.Q.* New Jersey: Lawrence Erlbaum, 1974.

Maccoby, E.E., and Jacklin, C.N. *The psychology of sex differences.* Stanford: Stanford University Press, 1974.

Chapter 11

TRAIT PSYCHOLOGY AND
PERSONALITY THEORY

What is the relationship of trait psychology to other psychological approaches in the study of personality? Is trait psychology a separate and distinct theoretical approach? At first glance it would seem that the study of psychological traits could be subsumed under other major schools of theories of personality, such as the psychoanalytic, behavioristic, or self-actualization approaches. That is to say, traits could be employed as theoretical constructs in testing various aspects of these theories. Only in the case of Skinnerian behaviorism would the latter possibility be in direct opposition to the basic approach of trait theory. Skinner's brand of behaviorism assumes that the unit of measurement is the discrete response and provides virtually no role for traits, or relatively broad patterns of responses, in its underlying assumptions. However, as seen in Chapter 7, there have been vigorous attempts to integrate traditional experimental learning concepts and principles into the study of growth and change of traits. We have also seen from Cattell's work with motivational component factors that it is possible to identify traits which are related to major psychoanalytic concepts. The emphasis of self-actualization theory on the growth of human *needs* makes this theory also compatible with the study of traits, for needs can be identified as traits.

Primarily because of factor analysis, however, the trait approach has come to acquire a relatively autonomous status which makes it distinct from other major approaches to the study of personality. Traits are no longer merely subsumed under personality theories (e.g., as dependent variables) as if they were of secondary importance to these theories. Trait research has led to a set of underlying assumptions about human behavior as well as some notions of its own, which, taken as a constellation, justifies thinking of modern trait psychology, based on the theory and methodology of factor analysis, as a school or theory of personality in its own right. This development has occurred partly through the application of mathematical innovations to the traditional problems of trait psychology. Nineteenth century faculty psychology and subsequent developments such as McDougall's work on human "instincts" had in common the goal of identifying the salient traits that were to form the basis of their theories. The dangers of creating endless and unweildly lists of "important" traits needed to be avoided if parsimony was to be achieved. Criteria for the inclusion of one trait construct over another were required, and factor-analytic-related concepts such as representative sampling of a domain, simple structure, and factor invariance served to resurrect early faculty psychology to scientific respectability. It was now possible to avoid the previously justifiable criticism that one set of traits identified by a given theorist might be considered to be quite arbitrary as a scheme for classifying behavior. Factor analysis and related mathematical developments were eventually able to deal with this obstacle and further the progress of trait psychology. That is, through these methods it became possible to assign objective mathematical criteria for the extraction of a trait.

The modern focus on the trait as defined mathematically and as the unit on which an understanding of behavior may be built is, then, of comparatively recent origin. Nevertheless, it has led to a certain view of behavior in general that tends to give this area of psychology a status as a separate personality theory. Some of the more important assumptions and characteristics of trait psychology are as follows:

(1) The covariation of responses that define a given trait may be considered as caused by any of a number of influences—from genetic contributors through to classical conditioning. Thus trait psychology has an inherently eclectic nature that allows us to bring in the relevant findings of other areas of psychology. It provides a highly useful overall description of the individual in terms of temperament, ability, and motivational dimensions, without placing any strong limitations on the ultimate explanatory constructs that can be used to account for behavior.

(2) In working with traits in the clinical-applied areas, they can be employed either as dependent variables or as important mediators or independent variables to be taken into consideration in accounting for differential behavioral findings. Traits as dependent variables are important for personality assessment. Traits as independent varia-

bles become important when one is interested in the role of disposi-
tional constructs vis-à-vis specific socially important behavior. As an
example of the latter, Poley (1974) has hypothesized that individuals
will be differentially predisposed to alcohol abuse depending on their
personality characteristics prior to their introduction to alcohol. In
particular, it appears that a trait pattern of extraversion predisposes
individuals to alcohol abuse, particularly where it is related to high
levels of activity, impulsivity, and aggression.

(3) There is usually a suggestion in the writings of trait psychologists that the trait is a fundamental unit in the psychological
development of the individual, and this thinking can be carried to the
point of connoting that the trait is, if not irreducible, at least resistant
to meaningful further reductionistic analysis. Thus traits are thought
to emerge relatively spontaneously early in the life of the individual
and to provide functioning in terms of mental abilities, motivation,
and temperament. There is also empirical support for this position.
Put in other terms, this represents recognition of the importance of
maturation as a force in the unfolding of the organized complexity
of behavior, although, of course, the effects of the environment in
moderating the growth and development of traits is not denied.
Neither psychoanalytic psychology nor behaviorism sees maturation
per se as an important force. Psychoanalysis assumes that the energy
of the id must be displaced by frustration from the environment to
shape the ego and superego. Until this shaping of instinctive energy
takes place, there is little in the way of human (socialized) qualities
in the young child. Similarly, behaviorism believes that behavior
must be shaped by the environmental contingencies of reward and
punishment. Until these processes (conditioning and learning) take
place, we have only rudimentary forms of behavior. An emphasis on
the importance of maturation tends to view behavior as unfolding in
an environmental climate rather than as being constantly shaped and
rechanneled by this environment. This characteristic gives trait psychology an important property in common with self-actualization or
growth-oriented views of personality. Unlike the latter, however,
trait researchers have not actively attempted to study possible
qualitative changes of traits through *stages* of development. However, there is nothing in trait psychology that necessarily contradicts
stage theory.

(4) Related to this point, a number of personality theorists place
a great deal of emphasis on the first 5 or 6 years of life. The early-
experience hypothesis, in fact, has generated a considerable amount
of research in animal psychology. Among personality theories, psy-

choanalytic thinking has been most influential in emphasizing early experience, but even some behavioristic theorists (e.g., Dollard and Miller, 1950) have taken a similar stand. Trait psychology also emphasizes that the early years of life is a period in which a highly complex structure of personality emerges, though the importance of the environment in shaping this structure is not as highly stressed. The trait psychologists' position on early maturation is an important contrast to the view that early experience is of crucial importance in personality development. That is, given an environmentalist philosophy and the observation of the early complexity of behavior, one could only conclude that early environmental contacts are of the greatest importance in producing this complexity. Trait psychology, on the other hand, has not been as explicitly tied to learning theory and the importance of early experience, although it would not deny the importance of these processes if pressed on the matter.

(5) The specific importance of genetic determinants as a facet of biological influences receives more attention in trait theory than any other personality theory. This gives trait psychology a fundamentally interdisciplinary nature, drawing on the findings of genetics as well as physiology. Genetic influences are believed to underly individual differences in abilities, temperament, and motivation, and empirical work certainly supports this. The underlying philosophy of trait psychology, that is, that individuals differ along major psychological dimensions and that such differences are quantifiable, nicely accomodates the view that some proportion of these differences is attributable to genetic factors. Population genetics, with its accompanying statistical models, is quite compatible with the quantitative-statistical-measurement approach of trait psychology.

(6) Although the trait is conceptualized as a unit of analysis, trait psychology does not necessarily rule out either narrower or broader concepts for analysis of behavior. For example, we can endeavor to explain individual differences in traits by such theories as Gray's work on sensitivity to reward and punishment as determinants of neuroticism and extraversion. On the other hand, we can conduct higher-order factor analyses to extract very broad dimensions of individual differences that may account for lower-order dimensions.

(7) Trait psychology places more emphasis on psychometrics or psychological measurement than any other personality theory. This emphasis has led to a tendency to include a greater variety of behaviors in the field of study, since whatever aspects of the personality are quantifiable may in principle be studied from a trait perspective.

Guilford has defined personality as the study of all individual differences, including abilities, temperament and motivation, interests, values, and attitudes. This definition of personality appears to be gaining in acceptance. Its great advantage is that it avoids the narrower focus of some schools of personality on a specific facet of behavior such as temperament or motivation. This breadth of study, therefore, provides the potential for interrelating different facets of individual differences such as abilities and temperament, or abilities and motivation, and Cattell (1971) has recently attempted such integration. In addition, the research on cognitive styles is an important attempt to link up what has traditionally been considered independent aspects of the total personality system. In contrast to this emphasis on integration within the trait approach, psychoanalysis is primarily a system dealing with motivation, as is self-actualization theory. Behaviorism is also limited, although it is the emphasis on learning (to the exclusion of genetic, biological, and/or maturational explanations) that limits this approach rather than being confined to a single domain of personality.

(8) In terms of the larger implications of trait psychology, we can note that personality theories tend to imply a particular viewpoint concerning broader philosophical issues such as the inherent "goodness" of human nature or human freedom. Thus self-actualization theory sees man as inherently good, with built-in forces toward higher attainments and self-actualization. It is the environment (society) that has the power to distort this growth process. Psychoanalysis and behaviorism, on the other hand, tend to regard man's basic nature in a fairly pessimistic light, requiring considerable molding to attain a form that will be harmonious with his fellow man. Trait psychology takes a relatively neutral position on this issue. The traits that appear in early life may be considered either positive or negative, depending on our social values, although with respect to unipolar traits, there is little disagreement over which end of the dimension is most valued.

(9) A personality theory may have broad social implications, implications which may be translated into various notions of a utopian society and a philosophy of social control. Skinner (1953, 1971, 1974) has, for example, dealt with the programming of the environment to achieve "the good life," and the trait psychologist Cattell (1972) has added the possibility of programming man's biological evolution. To the extent that we are able to understand the complexity of individual differences and the sources that influence such differences, society will be in a position to help chart out the direction

human evolution should take. It is important in such an undertaking to remember that the survival and adaptability of any species depends on variation, and any utopian view of man's future must retain the critical idea that human variation is a highly valuable property. Of course, this emphasis on individual *differences* does not imply inequality in a moral or ethical sense. Each individual may be different, but all individuals should theoretically be subject to the same rights in a moral and legal sense. Differences do not necessarily imply inequality, although in our imperfect society the two are often correlated.

This description may be considered as a current characterization of trait psychology. It is important to note, however, that this characterization represents a set of connotations that have evolved from work in the field of trait psychology rather than a set of necessary defining characteristics for trait psychology. Thus it is entirely possible that certain trait psychologists would not subscribe to some of the views outlined. For example, some trait psychologists may be more prone to emphasize the explicit role of learning in shaping various traits rather than the forces of maturation. However, maturation tends to be relatively more emphasized in trait psychology than in other major personality theories.

Trait psychology also has some connotations at this stage of its development that are essentially negative for social policy on the one hand and for scientific progress in psychology on the other hand. The psychology that has evolved out of the psychometric and the correlational tradition has become associated with a conservative, social-political philosophy. It has been taken by many individuals not only as support for a relatively rigid social-class system but also as support for political ideologies that border on racism. For example, in the fields of guidance and individual assessment in the educational system, the tradition of trait psychology may be perceived as more of a threat to individuals than as a means of enhancing the development of their potential. This negative view of individual differences and psychometrics stems from a tendency for psychological test results to be used to pigeonhole and limit individuals as much as to bring out their potential. For example, let us take a classroom situation in which the teacher may have opinions on how various students would fair on a standard test of intelligence but initially has no strong beliefs in this regard. Once standard psychological tests are introduced into this situation, the teacher-student relationship may change drastically, and the change may not be for the better because of the various connotations the test results have come to acquire. Ideally, students with lower scores on intelligence tests should receive special instruction designed to bring out their potential, but, as often happens, it may be that they will be categorized as less amenable to instruction and may not receive the kind of instruction that is warranted.

Of course, the serious student of individual differences and trait psychology will recognize that the use of individual differences to limit the potential of individual groups or races stems from misconceptions of the nature of differential psychology. Part of the answer to this problem lies in terms of further education of persons who are responsible for the assessment and use of test results.

There is, however, a more fundamental issue which relates to improving the value of the study of individual differences in terms of contributing to a better society. This issue is related to the emphasis on prediction in the study of individual differences as opposed to explanation and understanding such differences, although several chapters in this book have attempted to come to grips with the latter. This dichotomy has been associated with what Cronbach (1957, 1975a) has called the two major disciplines in scientific psychology —referring to the correlational approach (including individual differences and trait psychology) and the experimental approach. As Cronbach points out, there is no necessary conflict between these two approaches in psychology. However, psychologists have been very slow in developing the necessary synthesis. In recent years, of course, various experiments have been conducted in which factors or traits have been used as dependent variables in experimental designs. However, this is a very limited solution to the problem at hand. It is only very recently that a true synthesis of correlational and experimental approaches has begun, and few results are as yet available, although an important paper illustrating this kind of synthesis has been written by Estes (1974). Estes deals with a synthesis of learning theory (which has evolved out of the experimental tradition and deals with the processes of learning) and the measurement of intelligence (which has evolved out of the psychometric, individual differences tradition). Estes points out "The urgent need now is not for better means of classifying people with respect to intellectual functioning and correlating these classifications with other variables, but for understanding what brings about specific kinds of competence and incompetence in intellectual activity" (pp. 748–749).

Estes reviews a number of studies that have dealt with individual differences in tested mental abilities, and he ties in variations in test results with the strategies used by individuals in processing the information at hand. For example, differential success with the digit span test can be related to variations in the tendency to group sets of numbers (chunking). It is significant that chunking is an important influence in determining differences in normal children and adults as well as the mentally deficient or brain-injured individuals. The suggestion from this kind of research is that if variations in test results represent samplings of behavior that are important indicators of performance in processing information in real-life situations, then we might be better advised to use the test situation as a means for discovering the strategies an individual is using to process information, because we might then be able to improve on his strategies. This is consistent with Estes' view that the primary purpose of intelligence testing may become ". . . not of predicting intellectual performance, but rather of indicating the guiding measures that can be taken to improve intellectual performance" (p. 749). It would seem that this approach could be applied in general to the study of individual differences and trait psychology, and one of the more positive directions this field of psychology may now take is in terms of "getting inside" the organism for purposes of understanding the constellation of behaviors that define a trait, establishing the processes taking place, and using our understanding of these processes to further the development of human potential.

BIBLIOGRAPHY

Adorno, T. W., Frenkel-Brunswik, E., Levinson, D. J., and Sanford, R.N. *The authoritarian personality,* New York: Harper & Row, 1950.

Albert, R. S. Toward a behavioral definition of genius, *American Psychology,* 1975, *30,* 140–151.

Allport, G. W. *Personality: A psychological interpretation.* New York: Holt, 1937.

Allport, G. W. and Odbert, H. W. Trait names, a psychological study. *Psychological Monographs,* 1936, *47,* No. 1.

Allport, G. W. and Verron, P. E. A test for personal values. *Journal of Abnormal and Social Psychology.* 1931, *26,* 231–248.

Anastasi, A. (Ed.), *Individual differences.* New York: Wiley, 1965.

Baltes, P. B. Longitudinal and cross sectional sequences in the study of age and generation effects. *Human Development,* 1968, *11,* 145–171.

Baltes, P. B. and Nesselroade, J. R. Cultural change and adolescent personality development: An application of longitudinal sequences. *Developmental Psychology,* 1972, *7,* 244–256.

Bandura, A., and Walters, R. H. *Social learning and personality development.* New York: Holt, Rinehart and Winston, 1963.

Barker, R. *Ecological psychology.* Stanford: Stanford University Press, 1968.

Bayley, N. Mental growth during the first three years. In R. G. Barker, J. S. Kounin, and H. F. Wright (Eds.), *Child behavior and development.* New York: McGraw-Hill, 1943.

Bayley, N. Consistency and variability in the growth of intelligence from birth to eighteen years. *Journal of Genetic Psychology,* 1949, *75,* 165–196.

Bayley, N. *Bayley's Scales of Infant Development.* New York: The Psychological Corporation, 1968.

Becker, G. Individual differences among students who meet research subject requirements early versus later in the term as a source of sampling bias. *Social Behavior and Personality,* 1973, *1,* 71–80.

Becker, W. C. The relationship of factors in parental ratings of self and each other to the behavior of kindergarten children as rated by mothers, fathers and teachers. *Journal of Consulting Psychology,* 1960, *24,* 507–527.

Becker, W. C., Peterson, D. R., Luria, Z., Schoemaker, D. J. and Hellmer, L. A. Relations of factors derived from partent-interview ratings to behavior problems of five-year-olds. *Child Development,* 1962, *33,* 509–535.

Bentler, P. M. Assessment of developmental factor change at the individual and group level. In J. R. Nesselroade and H. W. Reese (Eds.), *Life-span developmental psychology: Methodological issues.* New York: Academic, 1973.

Berlyne, D. E. Behavior theory as personality theory. In E. F. Borgatta and W. W. Lambert (Eds.), *Handbook of personality theory and research,* Chicago: Rand McNally, 1968.

Berry, J. W. Ecological and cultural factors in spatial perceptual development. *Canadian Journal of Behavioral Science,* 1971, *3,* 324–336.

Block, J. H. (Ed.) *Mastery learning: Theory and practice.* New York: Holt, Rinehart and Winston, 1971.

Block, J. H. (Ed.) *Schools, society, and mastery learning.* New York: Holt, Rinehart and Winston, 1974.

Block, N. J., & Dworkin, G. IQ, heritability and inequality, Part 2. *Philosophy & Public Affairs,* 1974, *4,* 40–90.

Bloom, B. S. *Stability and change in human characteristics.* New York: Wiley, 1964.

Bloom, B. S. Mastery learning. In J. H. Block (Ed.), *Mastery learning: Theory and practice.* New York: Holt, Rinehart and Winston, 1971.

Bloom, B. S. Recent developments in mastery learning. *Educational Psychologist,* 1973, *10,* 204–221.

Bloom, B. S. Time and learning, *American Psychologist,* 1974, *29,* 682–688.

Bolz, C. R. Types of personality. In R. M. Dreger (Ed.), *Multivariate personality research: Contributions to the understanding of personality in honor of Raymond B. Cattell.* Baton Rouge: Claitor, 1972.

Boring, E. G. *A history of experimental psychology.* New York: Appleton-Century-Crofts, 1950.

Bowers, K. S. Situationism in psychology: An analysis and a critique. *Psychological Review,* 1973, *80,* 307–336.

Broverman, D. M., Klaiber, E. S., Kobayashi, G., and Vogel, W. Roles of activation and inhibition in sex differences in cognitive abilities. *Psychological Review,* 1968, *75,* 23–50.

Bruell, J. H. Genetic and adaptive significance of emotional defecation in mice. In E. Tobach (Ed.), *Experimental approaches to the study of emotional behavior.* Annals of the New York Academy of Science, 1969, *159,* 825–830.

Burt, C. The structure of the mind: A review of the results of factor analysis. *British Journal of Educational Psychology,* 1949, *19,* 100–111, 176–199.

Burt, C. The differentiation of intellectual abilities. *British Journal of Educational Psychology,* 1954, *24,* 76–90.

Burt, C. Critical notice: the psychology of creative ability. *British Journal of Educational Psychology,* 1962, *32,* 292–298. Also in P. E. Vernon (Ed.), *Creativity.* New York: Penguin Books, 1970.

Burt, C. Factorial studies of personality and their bearing on the work of the teacher. *British Journal of Educational Psychology,* 1965, *35,* 368–78.

Buss, A. R. A conceptual framework for learning effecting the development of ability factors. *Human Development,* 1973, *16,* 273–292. (a)

Buss, A. R. An extension of developmental models that separate ontogenetic changes and cohort differences. *Psychological Bulletin,* 1973, *80,* 466–479. (b)

Buss, A. R. Learning, transfer, and changes in ability factors: A multivariate model. *Psychological Bulletin,* 1973, *80,* 106–112. (c)

Buss, A. R. A general developmental model for interindividual differences, intraindividual differences, and intraindividual changes. *Developmental Psychology,* 1974, *10,* 70–78. (a)

Buss, A. R. Generational analysis: Description, explanation, and theory. *Journal of Social Issues,* 1974, *30*(2), 55–71. (b)

Buss, A. R. Multivariate model of quantitative, structural, and quantistructural ontogenetic change. *Developmental Psychology,* 1974, *10,* 190–203. (c)

Buss, A. R. An inferential strategy for determining factor invariance across different individuals and different variables. *Multivariate Behavioral Research,* 1975, *10,* 365–372. (a)

Buss, A. R. More on the Age X cohort developmental model: A reply to Labouvie. *Psychological Bulletin,* 1975, *82,* 170–173. (b)

Buss, A. R. Galton and the birth of differential psychology and engenics: Social, political, and economic factors. *Journal of the History of the Behavioral Sciences,* 1976, *12,* 47–58.

Buss, A. R., and Royce, J. R. Detecting cross-cultural commonalities and differences: Intergroup factor analysis. *Psychological Bulletin,* 1975, *82,* 128–136. (a)

Buss, A. R., & Royce, J. R. Ontogenetic changes in cognitive structure from a multivariate perspective. *Developmental Psychology,* 1975, *11,* 87–101. (b)

Butcher, H. J. *Human intelligence: Its nature and assessment.* London: Methuen, 1968.

Campbell, D. T., and Fiske, D. W. Convergent and discriminant validation by the multitrait-multimethod matrix. *Psychological Bulletin,* 1959, *56,* 81–105.

Campbell, J. *The hero with a thousand faces.* Cleveland: World, 1956.

Cancro, J. (Ed.) *Intelligence: Its natures, genetics and development.* Urbana: University of Illinois Press, 1971.

Carroll, J. B. A model of school learning. *Teachers College Record,* 1963, *64,* 723–733.

Carver, R. P. Two dimensions of tests: Psychometric and edumetric. *American Psychologist,* 1974, *29,* 512–518.

Cattell, R. B. *Description and measurement of personality.* Yonders-on-Hudson, New York: World Book, 1946.

Cattell, R. B. The three basic factor-analytic research designs—Their interrelations and derivatives. *Psychological Bulletin,* 1952, *49,* 499–520.

Cattell, R. B. *Personality and motivation: Structure and measurement.* Yonkers-on-Hudson, New York: World Book, 1957.

Cattell, R. B. The multiple abstract variance analysis equations and solutions for nature-nurture research on continuous variables. *Psychological Review,* 1960, *67,* 353–372.

Cattell, R. B. The nature and measurement of anxiety. *Scientific American,* 1963, *208,* 96–104. (a)

Cattell, R. B. Personality, role, mood, and situation-perception: A varifying theory of modulators. *Psychological Review,* 1963, *70,* 1–18. (b)

Cattell, R. B. Theory of fluid and crystallized intelligence: A critical experiment. *Journal of Educational Psychology,* 1963, *54,* 1–22. (c)

Cattell, R. B. *The scientific analysis of personality.* London: Penguin Books Ltd., 1965.

Cattell, R. B. The data box: Its ordering of total resources in terms of possible relational systems. In R. B. Cattell (Ed.), *Handbook of multivariate experimental psychology.* Chicago: Rand McNally, 1966. (a)

Cattell, R. B. Guest editorial: Multivariate behavior research and the integrative change. *Multivariate Behavioral Research,* 1966, *1,* 4–23. (b)

Cattell, R. B. The esopodic and equipotent principles for comparing factor scores across different populations. *British Journal of Mathematical and Statistical Psychology,* 1970, *23,* 23–41. (a)

Cattell, R. B. Separating endogenous, exogenous, ecogenic, and epogenic component curves in developmental data. *Developmental Psychology,* 1970, *3,* 151–162. (b)

Cattell, R. B. *Abilities: Their structure, growth, and action.* Boston: Houghton Mifflin, 1971.

Cattell, R. B. *A new morality from science: Beyondism.* New York: Pergamon, 1972. (a)

Cattell, R. B. Real base true zero factor analysis. *Multivariate Behavioral Research Monographs,* 1972, No. 72–1. (b)

Cattell, R. B. *Personality and mood by questionnaire.* San Francisco: Jossey-Bass, 1973.

Cattell, R. B., and Butcher, H. J. *The prediction of achievement and creativity.* New York: Bobbs-Merrill, 1968.

Cattell, R. B., and Child, D. *Motivation and dynamic structure.* New York: Halsted Press, 1975.

Cattell, R. B., Coulter, M. A., and Tsujioka, B. The taxonometric recognition of types and functional emergents. In R. B. Cattell (Ed.), *Handbook of multivariate experimental psychology.* Chicago: Rand McNally, 1966.

Cattell, R. B., and Dickman, K. A dynamic model of physical influences demonstrating the necessity of oblique simple structure. *Psychological Bulletin,* 1962, *59,* 389–400.

Cattell, R. B., Eber, H. W., and Tatsuoka, M. *Handbook for the sixteen personality factor questionnaire.* Champaign, Illinois: Institute for Personality and Ability Testing, 1970.

Cattell, R. B., and Warburton, F. W. *Objective personality and motivation tests,* Chicago: University of Illinois Press, 1967.

Cave, R. L. A combined factor analysis of creativity and intelligence. *Multivariate Behavioral Research,* 1970, *5,* 177–191.

Chomsky, N. Psychology and ideology, *Cognition,* 1972, *1,* 11–46.

Coan, R. W. Facts, factors, and artifacts: The quest for psychological meaning. *Psychological Review,* 1964, *71,* 123–140.

Coan, R. W. Child personality and developmental psychology. In R. B. Cattell (Ed.), *Handbook of multivariate experimental psychology.* Chicago: Rand McNally, 1966.

Coan, R. W. The changing personality. In R. M. Dreger (Ed.), *Multivariate personality research: Contributions to the understanding of personality in honor of Raymond B. Cattell.* Baton Rouge, Louisiana: Claitor, 1972.

Cohen, J. The impact of multivariate research in clinical psychology. In R. B. Cattell (Ed.), *Handbook of multivariate experimental psychology.* Chicago: Rand McNally, 1966.

Cohen, T., Bloch, N., Flam, Y., Kadar, M., and Goldschmidt, E. School attainments in an immigrant village. In E. Goldschmidt (Ed.), *The genetics of migrant and isolate populations.* New York: Williams & Wilkins, 1963.

Corcoran, D. W. J. The relation between intraversion and salivation. *American Journal of Psychology,* 1964, *77,* 298–300.

Craik, K. H. The assessment of places. In P. McReynolds (Ed.), *Advances in psychological assessment,* Vol. II, Palo Alto: Science and Behavior Books, 1971.

Craik, K. H. An ecological perspective on environmental decisionmaking. *Human Ecology,* 1972, *i,* 69–80.

Cronbach, L. J. The two disciplines of scientific psychology. *American Psychologist,* 1957, *12,* 671–684.

Cronbach, L. J. Comments on "Mastery learning and its implications for curriculum development." In E. W. Eisner (Ed.), *Confronting curriculum reform,* Boston: Little, Brown, 1971. (a)

Cronbach, L. J. Test validation. In R. L. Thorndike (Ed.), *Educational measurement.* Washington, D. C.: American Council on Education, 1971. (b)

Cronbach, L. J. Beyond the two disciplines of scientific psychology. *American Psychologist,* 1975, *30,* 116–127. (a)

Cronbach, L. J. Dissent from Carver. *American Psychologist,* 1975, *30,* 602–603. (b)

Cronbach, L. J. Five decades of public controversy over mental testing. *American Psychologist,* 1975, *30,* 1–14. (c)

DeFries, J. C., Vandenberg, S. G., McClearn, G. E., Kuse, A. R., Wilson, J. R., Ashton, G. C., and Johnson, R. C. Near identity of cognitive structure in two ethnic groups. *Science,* 1974, *183,* 338–339.

Dellas, M., and Gaier, E. S. Identification of creativity: The individual. *Psychological Bulletin,* 1970, *73,* 55–73.

Dobzhansky, T. *Genetic diversity and human equality.* New York: Basic Books, 1973.

Dockrell, W. B. Secondary education, social class and development of abilities. *British Journal of Educational Psychology,* 1966, *36,* 7–14.

Dollard, J., and Miller, N. E. *Personality and psychotherapy.* New York: McGraw-Hill, 1950.

Dreger, R. M. (Ed.) *Multivariate personality research: Contributions to the understanding of personality in honor of Raymond B. Cattell.* Claitor Press, 1971.

DuBois, P. H. A test-dominated society: China, 1115 B.C.–1905 A.D. In A. Anastasi (Ed.), *Testing problems in perspective,* Washington, D. C.: American Council on Education, 1966.

Duffy, E., and Crissy, W. J. E. Evaluative Attitudes as related to vocational interests and academic achievement. *Journal of Abnormal and Social Psychology,* 1940, *35,* 226–245.

Dunham, J. L., Guilford, J. P., and Hoephner, P. Multivariate approaches to discovering the intellectual components of concept learning. *Psychological Review,* 1968, *75,* 206–221.

Eckhardt, W., and Alcock, N. Z. Ideology and personality in war/peace attitudes. *Journal of Social Psychology,* 1970, *81,* 105–116.

Edwards, A. J. *Individual mental testing; part I, history and theories.* San Francisco: Intext Educational Publishers, 1971.

Ehrman, L., Omenn, G. S., and Caspari, E. W. *Genetics, environment, and behavior: Implications for educational policy.* New York: Academic, 1972.

Ekehammar, B. Interactionism in personality from a historical perspective. *Pscho-logical Bulletin,* 1974, *81,* 1026–1048.

Endler, N. S. The case for person-situation interactions. *Canadian Psychological Review,* 1975, *16,* 12–21.

Engels, F. *The condition of the working class in England.* London: Panther, 1969.

Erlenmeyer-Kimling, L., and Jarvik, L. F. Genetics and intelligence: A review. *Science,* 1963, *142,* 1477–1479.

Estes, W. K. Learning theory and intelligence, *American Psychologist,* 1974, *29,* 740–749.

Eysenck, H. J. *Dimensions of personality.* London: Routledge and Kegan Paul, 1947.

Eysenck, H. J. *Psychology of politics.* London: Routledge and Kegan Paul, 1954.

Eysenck, H. J. *The dynamics of anxiety and hysteria.* London: Routledge and Kegan Paul, 1957.

Eysenck, H. J. (Ed.). *Experiments with drugs.* Oxford: Pergamon Press, 1963.

Eysenck, H. J. (Ed.). *Experiments in motivation.* Oxford: Pergamon Press, 1964.

Eysenck, H. J. *The biological basis of personality.* Springfield, Illinois: Thomas, 1967.

Eysenck, H. J. Causal theories of personality structure. In H. J. Eysenck, *The structure of human personality.* London: Methuen, 1970.

Eysenck, H. J., and Eysenck, S. B. G. *Personality structure and measurement.* London: Routledge and Kegan Paul, 1969.

Eysenck, H. J., and Rachman, S. *The causes and cures of neurosis.* London: Routledge and Kegan Paul, 1965.

Falconer, D. S. *Introduction to quantitative genetics.* New York: Ronald Press, 1960.

Ferguson, G. A. On learning and human ability. *Canadian Journal of Psychology,* 1954, *8,* 95–112.

Ferguson, G. A. On transfer and the abilities of man. *Canadian Journal of Psychology,* 1956, *10,* 121–131.

Ferguson, L. W., Humphreys, S. G., and Strong, F. W. A factorial analysis of interests and values. *Journal of Educational Psychology,* 1941, *32,* 197–204.

Flavell, J. H. Cognitive changes in adulthood. In L. R. Goulet and P. B. Baltes (Eds.)., *Life-span developmental psychology: Research and theory.* New York: Academic, 1970.

Fleishman, E. A. Individual differences in motor learning. In R. M. Gagne (Ed.), *Learning and individual differences.* Columbus, Ohio: Merrill, 1967.

Fleishman, E. A. On the relation between abilities, learning, and human performance. *American Psychologist,* 1972, *27,* 1017–1032.

Fleishman, E. A., and Hempel, W. E., Jr. The relation between abilities and improvement with practice in a visual discrimination reaction task. *Journal of Experimental Psychology,* 1955, *49,* 301–312.

Flores, M. B., and Evans, G. T. Some differences in cognitive abilities between Canadian and Filipino students. *Multivariate Behavioral Research,* 1972, *7,* 175–191.

Frederiksen, N. Toward a taxonomy of situations. *American Psychologist,* 1972, *27,* 114–125.

Fruchter, B. *Introduction to factor analysis.* Princeton: van Nostrand, 1954.

Fuller, J. L., and Thompson, W. R. *Behavior genetics.* New York: Wiley, 1960.

Furby, L. Implications of within-group heritabilities for sources of between-group differences: IQ and racial differences. *Developmental Psychology,* 1973, *9,* 28–37.

Gagné, R. M. *The conditions of learning.* New York: Holt, Rinehart, and Winston, 1965.

Gagné, R. M. (Ed.). *Learning and individual differences.* Columbus, Ohio: Merrill, 1967.

Gagné, R. M. Contributions of learning to human development. *Psychological Review,* 1968, *75,* 177–191. (a)

Gagné, R. M. Learning hierarchies. *Educational Psychologist,* 1968, *6,* 1, 3–6, 9. (b)

Galton, F. *Inquiries into human faculty and its development.* London: Dent, 1907 (first published in 1883).

Galton, F. *Hereditary genius.* Cleveland: World, 1962 (first published in 1869).

Garrett, H. E. Differentiable mental traits. *Psychological Record,* 1938, *2,* 259–298.

Garrett, H. E. A developmental theory of intelligence. *American Psychologist,* 1946, *1,* 372–378.

Gladstone, R. Where is fashion leading us? *American Psychologist,* 1975, *30,* 604–605.

Glaser, R. Individual differences in learning. In K. A. Neufeld (Ed.), *Individualized curriculum and instruction: Proceedings of the third invitational conference on elementary education.* Edmonton, Alberta: Department of Elementary Education, University of Alberta, 1970.

Glaser, R., and Nitko, A. J. Measurement in learning and instruction. In R. L. Thorndike (Ed.), *Educational measurement.* Washington, D.C.: American Council on Education, 1971.

Glaser, R., & Resnick, L. B. Instructional psychology. *Annual Review of Psychology,* 1972, *23,* 207–276.

Goldberg, L. R. Why measure that trait? An historical analysis of personality scales and inventories. Paper presented at the Western Psychological Association, April, 1970.

Gorsuch, R. L. *Factor analysis.* Toronto: Saunders, 1974.

Gray, J. A. Causal theories of personality and how to test them. In J. R. Royce (Ed.), *Multivariate analysis and psychological theory.* New York: Academic, 1973.

Gray, J. A., and Buffery, A. W. H. Sex differences in emotion and cognitive behavior in mammals including man: Adaptive and neural bases. *Acta Psychologica,* 1971, *35,* 89–111.

Guilford, J. P. Creativity. *American Psychologist,* 1950, *5,* 444–454.

Guilford, J. P. *Psychometric methods.* New York: McGraw-Hill, 1954.

Guilford, J. P. *Personality.* New York: McGraw-Hill, 1959 (a).

Guilford, J. P. The three faces of intellect. *American Psychologist,* 1959, *14,* 469–479. (b)

Guilford, J. P. *The nature of human intelligence.* New York: McGraw-Hill, 1967.

Guilford, J. P., and Zimmerman, W. S. Fourteen dimensions of temperament. *Psychological Monographs,* 1956, *70,* While No. 417.

Haladyna, T. M. On the psychometric-edumetric dimensions of tests. *American Psychologist,* 1975, *30,* 603–604.

Hayes, K. J. Genes, drives, and intellect. *Psychological Reports,* 1962, *10,* 299–342.

Hebb, D. O. *Organization of behavior.* New York: Wiley, 1949.

Hebb, D. O. Heredity and environment in mammalian behavior. *British Journal of Animal Behavior,* 1953, *1,* 43–47.

Herrnstein, R. J. I.Q. *The Atlantic Monthly,* 1971, September, 43–64.

Herrnstein, R. J. *I.Q. in the meritocracy.* Boston: Little, Brown, 1973.

Hirsch, J. Behavior genetics and individuality understood. *Science,* 1963, *142,* 1436–42.

Hirsch, J. (Ed.). *Behavior-genetic analysis.* New York: McGraw-Hill, 1967.

Honzik, M. P. Developmental studies of parent-child resemblance in intelligence. *Child Development,* 1957, *28,* 215–228.

Horn, J. L. Significance tests for use with r_p and related profile statistics. *Educational and Psychological Measurement,* 1961, *21,* 263–370.

Horn, J. L. Integration of structural and developmental concepts in the theory of fluid and crystallized intelligence. In R. B. Cattell (Ed.), *Handbook of multivariate experimental Psychology.* Chicago: Rand McNally, 1966 (a).

Horn, J. L. Motivation and dynamic calculus concepts from multivariate experiment. In R. B. Cattell (Ed.), *Handbook of multivariate experimental psychology.* Chicago: Rand McNally, 1966. (b)

Horn, J. L. Organization of abilities and the development of intelligence. *Psychological Review,* 1968, *75,* 242–259.

Horn, J. L. Organization of data on life-span development of human abilities. In L. R. Goulet & P. B. Baltes (Eds.), *Life-span developmental psychology.* New York: Academic, 1970.

Horn, J. L. Structure of intellect: Primary abilities. In R. M. Dreger (Ed.), *Multivariate personality research: Contributions to the understanding of personality in honor of Raymond B. Cattell.* Baton Rouge, Louisiana: Claitor, 1972.

Horn, J. L., & Cattell, R. B. Age differences in primary mental ability factors. *Journal of Gerontology,* 1966, *21,* 210–220.

Howarth, E. A source of independent verification: Convergencies and divergencies in the work of Cattell and Eysenck. In R. M. Dreger (Ed.), *Multivariate personality research: Contributions to the understanding of personality in honor of Raymond B. Cattell.* Baton Rouge, La.: Claitor, 1972.

Hundleby, J. D., and Connor, W. H. Interrelationships between personality inventories: The 16 P. F., the MMPI, and the MPI. *Journal of Consulting and Clinical Psychology,* 1968, *32,* 152–157.

Hunt, J. McV. *Intelligence and experience.* New York: Ronald, 1961.

Insel, P. M., and Moos, R. H. Psychological environments: Expanding the scope of human ecology. *American Psychologist,* 1974, *29,* 179–188.

Irvine, S. H. Factor analysis of African abilities and attainments: Constructs across cultures. *Psychological Bulletin,* 1969, *71,* 20–32. (b)

Jackson, D. N. *Personality research form manual.* Goshen, New York: Research Psychologists' Press, 1967.

Jarvik, L. F., Blum, S. E., and Varman, A. D. Genetic components and intellectual functioning during senescence: A 20-year study of aging twins. *Behavior Genetics,* 1972, *2,* 159–171.

Jenkins, J. J., and Paterson, D. G. *Studies in individual differences.* New York: Appleton-Century-Crofts, 1961.

Jensen, A. R. Varieties of individual differences in learning. In R. M. Gagne (Ed.), *Learning and individual differences.* Columbus, Ohio: C. E. Merrill, 1967.

Jensen, A. R. How much can we boost I.Q. and scholastic achievement? *Harvard Educational Review,* 1969, *39,* 1–123.

Jensen, A. R. IQs of identical twins reared apart. *Behavior Genetics,* 1970, *1,* 133–148.

Jensen, A. R. *Educability and group differences.* New York: Harper and Row, 1973.

Kagan, J., and Kogan, N. Individuality and cognitive performance. In P. H. Mussen (Ed.), *Carmichael's manual of child psychology,* New York: Wiley, 1970, Vol. I.

Kamin, L. J. *The science and politics of IQ.* Potomac, Maryland: Lawrence Erlbaum, 1974.

Katz, I., Roberts, S. O., and Robinson, J. M. Effects of difficulty, race of administrator, and instructions on negro digit-symbol performance. *Journal of Personality and Social Psychology,* 1965, *70,* 53–59.

Klein, G. S. *Perception, motives and personality.* New York: Knopf, 1970.

Kohlberg, L. A cognitive-developmental analysis of children's sex-role concepts and attitudes. In E. Maccoby (Ed.), *The development of sex differences.* Stanford, Calif.: Stanford University Press, 1966.

Kohlberg, L., and Kramer, R. Continuities and discontinuities in childhood and adult moral development. *Human Development,* 1969, *12,* 93–120.

Labouvie, E. W. An extension of developmental models: A reply to Buss. *Psychological Bulletin,* 1975, *82,* 165–169.

Lesser, G. S., Fifer, G., and Clark, D. H. Mental abilities of children from different social-class and cultural groups. *Child Development Monographs,* 1965, *30,* No. 4.

Lindzey, G. Some remarks concerning incest, the incest taboo, and psychoanalytic theory. *American Psychologist,* 1967, *22,* 1051–1059.

Lurie, W. A. A study of Spranger's value-types by the method of factor analysis. *Journal of Social Psychology,* 1937, *8,* 17–37.

Lykken, D. T. Multiple factor analysis and personality research. *Journal of Experimental Research in Personality,* 1971, *5,* 161–170.

MacArthur, R. Some differential abilities of Northern Canadian native youth. *International Journal of Psychology,* 1968, *3,* 43–51.

Maccoby, E. E., and Jacklin, C. N. *The psychology of sex differences.* Stanford: Stanford University Press, 1974.

Mefferd, R. B. Structuring physiological correlates of mental processes and states: The study of biological correlates and mental processes. In R. B. Cattell (Ed.), *Handbook of multivariate experimental psychology.* Chicago: Rand McNally, 1966.

Mercer, J. R. Institutionalized anglocentrism: Labelling mental retardates in the public schools. In P. Orleans & W. R. Ellis (Eds.), *Race, change and urban society,* Sage Publications, 1971.

Merrifield, P. R. An analysis of concepts from the point of view of the structure of intellect. In H. J. Klausmeier and C. W. Harris (Eds.), *Analysis of concept learning,* New York: Academic, 1966.

Mischel, W. *Personality and measurement.* New York: Wiley, 1968.

Mischel, W. Toward a cognitive social learning reconceptualization of personality. *Psychological Review,* 1973, *80,* 252–283.

Money, J. *Man & woman, boy & girl.* Johns Hopkins, 1972.

Moore, C. L., & Retish, P. M. Effect of the examiner's race on Black children's Wechsler preschool and primary scale of intelligence IQ. *Developmental Psychology,* 1974, *10,* 672–676.

Moos, R. H. Conceptualizations of human environments. *American Psychologist,* 1973, *28,* 652–665.

Mulaik, S. A. *The foundations of factor analysis.* New York: McGraw-Hill, 1972.

Mumford, L. *The condition of man.* London: Mercury Books, 1963.

Mussen, P. H. Early sex-role development. In D. A. Goslin (Ed.), *Handbook of socialization theory and research.* Chicago: Rand McNally, 1969.

Navran, L., and Posthuma, A. B. A factor analysis of the Strong Vocational Interest Blank for men using the method of principle factors. *Journal of Counselling Psychology,* 1970, *17,* 216–223.

Nesselroade, J. R. Application of multivariate strategies to problems of measuring and structuring long-term change. In L. R. Goulet and P. B. Baltes (Eds.), *Life-span developmental psychology: Research and theory,* New York: Academic, 1970.

Nesselroade, J. R., & Baltes, P. B. Adolescent personality development and historical change: 1970–1972. *Monographs of the Society in Child Development,* 1974, 39 (1, Serial No. 154).

Nicholls, J. G. Creativity in the person who will never produce anything original and useful: The concept of creativity as a normally distributed trait. *American Psychologist,* 1972, *27,* 717–727.

Nitko, A. J. Criterion-referenced testing in the context of instruction. Learning Research and Development Center, University of Pittsburgh, 1972.

Parlee, M. B. Comments on "roles of activation and inhibition in sex differences in cognitive abilities" by D. M. Broverman, E. L. Klaiber, Y. Kobayashi, and W. Vogel. *Psychological Review,* 1972, *79,* 180–184.

Pawlik, K. Concepts in human cognition and aptitudes. In R. B. Cattell (Ed.), *Handbook of multivariate experimental psychology,* Chicago: Rand McNally, 1966.

Peterson, D. R., and Cattell, R. B. Personality factors in nursery school children as derived from parent ratings. *Journal of Clinical Psychology,* 1958, *14,* 346–355.

Peterson, D. R., & Cattell, R. B. Personality factors in nursery school children as derived from teacher ratings. *Journal of Consulting Psychology,* 1959, *23,* 562.

Piaget, J. Piaget's theory. In P. H. Mussen (Ed.), *Carmichael's manual of child psychology.* New York: Wiley, 1970, Vol. I.

Poley, W. Personality predisposition, conditionability and alcohol consumption: A psychobiological approach. Paper presented at the Sixth Research Symposium of the Alberta Alcoholism and Drug Abuse Commission, Edmonton, Alberta, Canada, 1974.

Poley, W. Heritability ratios of major personality traits. Unpublished manuscript, University of Alberta, 1975.

Reinert, G. Comparative factor analytic studies of intelligence throughout the human life-span. In L. R. Goulet & P. B. Baltes (Eds.), *Life-span developmental psychology.* New York: Academic, 1970.

Rokeach, M. *Beliefs, attitudes, and values.* San Francisco: Jossey-Bass, 1968.

Rokeach, M. *The nature of human values.* New York: The Free Press, 1973.

Royce, J. R. The development of factor analysis. *Journal of General Psychology,* 1958, *58,* 139–164.

Royce, J. R. Factors as theoretical constructs. *American Psychologist,* 1963, *18,* 522–528.

Royce, J. R. The conceptual framework for a multi-factor theory of individuality. In J. R. Royce (Ed.), *Multivariate analysis and psychological theory.* London: Academic Press, 1973.

Scarr-Salapatek, S. Race, social class, and IQ. *Science,* 1971, *174,* 1285–1295.

Schaie, K. W. A general model for the study of developmental problems. *Psychological Bulletin,* 1965, *64,* 92–107.

Schaie, K. W. A reinterpretation of age related changes in cognitive structure and functioning. In L. R. Goulet & P. B. Baltes (Eds.), *Life-span developmental psychology.* New York: Academic Press, 1970.

Schaie, K. W. Methodological problems in descriptive research on adulthood and aging. In J. R. Nesselroade and H. W. Reese (Eds.), *Life-span developmental psychology: Methodological issues.* New York: Academic Press, 1973.

Schaie, W., and Strother, C. R. A cross-sectional study of age changes in cognitive behavior. *Psychological Bulletin,* 1968, *70,* 671–680. (a)

Schaie, W., and Strother, C. R. The effects of time and cohort differences on the interpretation of age changes in cognitive behavior. *Multivariate Behavioral Research,* 1968, *3,* 259–294. (b)

Schneirla, T. C. The concept of development in comparative psychology. In D. B. Harris (Ed.), *The concept of development.* Minneapolis: University of Minnesota Press, 1957.

Schull, W. J., and Neel, J. V. *The effects of inbreeding on Japanese children.* New York: Harper and Row, 1965.

Sciortino, R. Allport-Vernon-Lindzey study of values. 1. Factor structure for a combined sample of male and female college students. *Psychological Reports,* 1970, *27,* 955–958.

Sells, S. B. An interactionist looks at the environment. *American Psychologist,* 1963, *18,* 696–702.

Sitkei, E. G., and Meyers, C. E. Comparative structure of intellect in middle and lower-class four-year-olds of two ethnic groups. *Developmental Psychology,* 1969, *1,* 592–604.

Skinner, B. F. *Science and human behavior.* New York: Macmillan, 1953.

Skinner, B. F. *Beyond freedom and dignity.* New York: Knopf, 1971.

Skinner, B. F. *About behaviorism.* New York: Knopf, 1974.

Skodak, M., and Skeels, H. M. A final follow-up study of one hundred adopted children. *Journal of Genetic Psychology,* 1949, *75,* 85–125.

Spearman, C. General intelligence, objectively determined and measured. *American Journal of Psychology,* 1904, *15,* 201–293.

Spearman, C. E. *The abilities of man.* London: Macmillan, 1927.

Spranger, E. *Types of men* (trans. by P. J. W. Pigors). Halle: Niemeyer, 1928.

Stern, G. *People in context: Measuring person environment congruence in education and industry.* New York: Wiley, 1970.

Stinchcombe, A. S. Environment: The cumulation of events. A discussion of Jensen's paper "How much can we boost IQ and scholastic achievement?" *Harvard Educational Review,* 1969, *39,* 511–522.

Stodolsky, S. S., & Lesser, G. S. Learning patterns in the disadvantaged. *Harvard Educational Review,* 1967, *37,* 546–593.

Sweeney, E. J. Sex differences in problem solving. Stanford University, Technical Report No. 1, 1953.

Thomas, A., Chess, S., and Birch, H. G. *Temperament and behavior disorders in children.* New York: New York University Press, 1968.

Thompson, W. R. Traits, factors, and genes. *Eugenics Quarterly,* 1957, *4,* 8–16.

Thompson, W. R. Multivariate experiment in behavior genetics. In R. B. Cattell (Ed.), *Handbook of multivariate experimental psychology.* Chicago: Rand McNally, 1966.

Thurstone, L. L. *The vectors of mind.* Chicago: University of Chicago Press, 1935.

Thurstone, L. L. *Primary mental abilities.* The University of Chicago Press, 1938.

Thurstone, L. L. *Multiple-factor analysis.* Chicago: University of Chicago Press, 1947.

Thurstone, L. L. The differential growth of mental abilities. Chapel Hill, N.C. University of North Carolina, Psychometric Laboratory, 1955.

Thurstone, L. L., and Thurstone, T. C. Factorial studies of intelligence. *Psychometric Monographs,* 1941, No. 2.

Tryon, R. C. A theory of psychological components—an alternative to "mathematical factors". *Psychological Review,* 1935, *42,* 425–454.

Tryon, R. C. Individual Differences. In F. A. Moss (Ed.), *Comparative psychology.* Englewood Cliffs, N.J.: Prentice-Hall, 1942.

Tyler, L. E. *The psychology of human differences.* New York: Appleton-Century-Crofts, 1965.

Vale, J. R. Role of behavior genetics in psychology. *American Psychologist,* 1973, *28,* 871–882.

Vandenberg, S. G. The primary mental abilities of Chinese students: A comparative study of the stability of a factor structure. *Annals of the New York Academy of Science,* 1959, *79,* 257–304.

Vandenberg, S. G. Hereditary factors in normal personality traits (as measured by inventories). *Recent advances in biological psychiatry,* 1967, *9,* 65–104. (a)

Vandenberg, S. G. The primary mental abilities of South American students: A second comparative study of the generality of a cognitive factor structure. *Multivariate Behavioral Research,* 1967, *2,* 175–198. (b)

Vandenberg, S. G. Human behavior genetics: present status and suggestions for future research. *Merrill-Palmer Quarterly of Behavior and Development,* 1969, *15,* 121–154.

Vandenberg, S. G. Comparative studies of multiple factor ability measures. In J. R. Royce (Ed.), *Multivariate analysis and psychological theory.* London: Academic Press, 1973.

Vernon, P. E. *The structure of human abilities.* New York: Wiley, 1950.

Vernon, P. E. Creativity and intelligence. *Educational Research,* 1964, *6,* 163–169.

Vernon, P. E. Ability factors and environmental influences. *American Psychologist,* 1965, *20,* 723–733.

Vernon, P. E. *Intelligence and cultural environment.* London: Methuen, 1969.

Vernon, P. E. Multivariate appraches to the study of cognitive styles. In J. R. Royce (Ed.), *Multivariate analysis and psychological theory.* London: Academic Press, 1973.

Wallach, M. A., and Kogan, N. *Modes of thinking in young children: A study of the creativity-intelligence distinction.* New York: Holt, Rinehart & Winston, 1965.

Watson, J. B. *Behaviorism.* London: Kegan Paul, 1930.

Whiteman, M. Intelligence and learning. *Merrill-Palmer Quarterly,* 1964, *10,* 297–309.

Wiggens, J. S. *Personality and prediction: Principles of personality assessment.* Reading, Massachusetts: Addison-Wesley, 1973.

Williams, R. *The long revolution.* London: Chatto & Windas, 1961.

Wiseman, S. *Intelligence and ability.* Penguin Books, 1967.

Witkin, H. A., Dyk, R. B., Faterson, H. F., Goodenough, D. R., and Karp, S. A. *Psychological differentiation.* New York: Wiley, 1962.

Wohlwill, J. F. The age variable in psychological research. *Psychological Review.* 1970, 77, 49–64. (a)

Wohlwill, J. F. The emerging discipline of environmental psychology. *American Psychologist,* 1970, 25, 303–312. (b)

Wohlwill, J. F. *The study of behavioral development.* New York: Academic Press, 1973.

Wolf, R. The measurement of environments. In A. Anastasi (Ed.), *Testing problems in perspective.* Washington, D.C.: American Council on Education, 1966.

Woodruff, S. A., & Birren, J. E. Age changes and cohort differences in personality. *Developmental Psychology,* 1972, *6,* 252–259.

Wundt, W. *Frundzüge der physiologischen Psychologie,* 5th Ed. Vol. 3. Leipzig: W. Engelmann, 1903.

AUTHOR INDEX

SUBJECT INDEX

DATE DUE

5. 21. '81	
3. 08. '84	
12. 18. '87	
2. 18. '87	
MAY 1 5 1997	
FEB 0 2 1999	

BRODART, INC.   Cat. No. 23-221